Representations of Slavery

Representations of Slavery

Race and Ideology in Southern
Plantation Museums

Jennifer L. Eichstedt and Stephen Small

Smithsonian Books
Washington, DC

Published by Smithsonian Books
PO Box 37012, MRC 513
Washington, DC 20013
smithsonianbooks.com

Copy editor: Susan A. Warga
Designer: Brian Barth

This book may be purchased for educational, business, or sales promotional use. For information please write the Special Markets Department at the address or website above.

Eichstedt, Jennifer.
    Representations of slavery : race and ideology in southern plantation museums/ Jennifer Eichstedt and Stephen Small.
        p. cm.
    Includes bibliographical references and index.
    ISBN 1-58834-071-6 (alk. paper)- ISBN 1-58834-096-1 (pbk.: alk. paper)
            1. Southern States—Race relations. 2. Racism—Southern States.
3. Southern States—Cultural policy. 4. Slavery—Southern States—Historiography.
5. African Americans—Southern States—Historiography.
6. Plantation life—Southern States—Historiography.
7. Memory—Social aspects—Southern States. 8. Plantations—Southern States. 9. Historic sites—Southern States—Management.
10. Historical museums—Southern States—Management. I. Small, Stephen, 1963– II. Title.
F220.Al E37 2002
975.043'092—dc21   2001057730

British Library Cataloging-in-Publication Data available

Manufactured in the United States of America
30 29 28 27 26 25   3 4 5

Contents

Acknowledgments

From Jennifer L. Eichstedt

I would like to extend thanks to a number of people who have worked out these ideas with me and contributed to my writing process. At Mary Washington College, I thank Carol Corcoran, Judith Parker, Cedric Rucker, and Donald Rallis. At Humboldt State University, I am grateful to the other two members of our Junior Faculty Writing Group, Christina Accomando (English) and Mary Scoggins (anthropology), both of whom helped me tighten my thinking and writing in immeasurable ways. Also at Humboldt State, I'd like to acknowledge the presence and assistance of Marilyn Paik-Nicely, Betsy Watson, and two graduate students who worked in the field with me and transcribed notes, Sara Sutler-Cohen and Kitty Huffstutter. Kudos to members of my popular culture and race and ethnicity courses, who allowed me to work out ideas related to the project during class time. Thanks go to those faculty at Humboldt State who attended my colloquium talk on this research and gave valuable feedback, especially Judy Walton, Mary Scoggins, Christina Accomando, and Michael Eldridge, and to Maggie Gainer not only for setting up the colloquium but also for continually keeping an eye out for me and possible funding opportunities. Thanks also to Dolores McBroome, who allowed me to present this material in her museum studies course at Humboldt State; to Dean Karen Carlton, who supported my time off; and to Betsy Watson, who, as chair of the Sociology Department when I was hired, worked to protect my time so I could work on both my teaching and my research and publications. I would also like to thank members of the American Sociological Association, the Pacific Sociological Association, and the Popular Culture Association, all of whom attended presentations of papers on this topic and offered valuable feedback. Several individuals provided reviews of the manuscript that helped us tighten up the primary arguments; they include Joe Feagin and Jim Horton. I would also like to thank Raphael Allen at Duke University Press for the interesting and exciting talks regarding our work.

Financial support was provided through small grants from Mary Washington College and Humboldt State University Graduate Studies and Research, as well as through the Humboldt State University Foundation. A year of time provided by a National Endowment for the Humanities Fellowship for College Teachers was invaluable for completing research and providing a sustained amount of time for writing the manuscript. I thank Diana Guerrero, who was my dedicated writing partner while I was in Big Bear, California.

A huge thanks goes to Stephen Small, for his faith that I would be a good person to work with on this project, for his willingness to hash out ideas, and for his commitment to working it out when we had different visions of what we should be doing. Collaboration is both exhilarating and exhausting at times; thank you, Stephen, for being willing to go through both phases with me.

Last but not least, I would like to thank my family, both biological and chosen, for their interest and support in my work—even when it wasn't always clear what I was doing. My partner, Gina, put up with a great deal of traveling, the hated extension of my office into the rest of the house, and periods of great distraction as I lived in front of the computer; for this she deserves a homemade chocolate cake every single day. To everyone above, I would not have been able to complete my part of this without your continued support; by your presence I am truly blessed.

From Stephen Small

Many people helped me work on this project, and I hope I have remembered to include them all. Kito Robinson (then an undergraduate student at the University of California, Berkeley) served as a research assistant in Georgia in the early stages of the project. Antoinette Chevalier (then a graduate student at the University of California, Berkeley) completed tours and site visits in Louisiana and was a gracious host in New Orleans. Particular thanks to Colin Small, my brother, who tried to combine his vacation in Louisiana with the task of taking photographs at various sites throughout the state. Thanks also to my close friend and colleague David Minkus for his comments and insights on the many occasions that we discussed the project and related issues. Troy Duster continues to be a friend, confidant, and intellectual advisor, even from the other coast. Michael Omi has provided many helpful insights, and Howard Winant remains, unhesitatingly, a friend and colleague on all my projects. Thanks to David Theo Goldberg for many discussions regarding race, racism, and museums, and for offering personal support when I most needed it. Sincere appreciation to Patricia Penn Hilden for her enthusiastic support and encouragement. I'm deeply grateful to Percy Hintzen for his unfailing support as chair of the Department of African American Studies. Colleagues in the department have always provided encouragement and support, in particular Ula Taylor. I appreciate feedback and comments from those who attended talks given while the research and writing of this project was under way, including those given at the Center for African Studies and at the Institute for the Study of Social Change, both at the University of California, Berkeley; at a keynote presentation given at the 19th Century Interdisciplinary Studies Association Annual Conference at the University of Oregon, Eugene, in spring 2001; and on a paper presented jointly with Jennifer L. Eichstedt at the American Sociological Association's annual meeting in Anaheim, California, in August 2001.

I would also like to thank the Committee on Research at the University of California, Berkeley, for a research leave grant in 1997 that enabled me to complete the majority of the site visits in Georgia, and for a small grant in 1999 that enabled me to complete site visits in Louisiana. A Humanities Research Fellowship from the Townsend Center at the University of California, Berkeley, in 2001–2002 helped with the final aspects of writing, has made a crucial contribution to this book, and laid the foundation for further publications.

My heartfelt thanks go to Jennifer Eichstedt for the incalculable contributions that she has made to the research and writing of this book, for her tireless enthusiasm and focus, and for meeting deadlines. If it were not for her, the book would still be working its way through drafts. I also want to thank her for being a friend.

My appreciation goes to my daughters, Dionne and Nikishia, for staying in touch, visiting me, and keeping me laughing. My cousin, Yvonne, offered me a home, introduced me to the diasporic Jamaicans of greater Atlanta, and made sure I had Jamaican food whenever I needed it. I'm eternally grateful for her warmth, sincerity, and humanity during a period of immense personal stress. Thanks, also, to the penguins!

From both authors

Together, we would like to thank the people who assisted this process at Smithsonian Institution Press—Caroline Newman, Emily Sollie, Duke Johns, and copy editor extraordinaire Susan Warga. All deserve much gratitude for their support and suggestions for developing the book in even more powerful ways. We would also like to thank those reviewers who took the time and energy to provide us important feedback. To everyone who has assisted us, our deepest thanks.

Representations of Slavery

1 | Racialized Ideologies and Plantation Museums

This is a book on the plantation museum industry in the South. We started this work because we are interested in racialized practices and ideologies in the United States and curious about how these play out in the realm of culture. We formally began this project after each of us, separately and without awareness of what the other was doing, visited a few plantation museum sites; the absence of discussions of the system of slavery or those who had been enslaved was striking. We began to ask whether this was true of plantation museums everywhere, and if so, why. For us, as outsiders to southern culture, it seemed remarkable that slavery was so often absent at these museums. For insiders concerned about the public picture painted of the South and southerners, it doesn't come as much of a surprise. As others detail, many of these house museums were developed by white southern women who quite often are descendants of the white elite planter class of the preemancipation South (West 1999). Since slavery is generally, though not universally, recognized as a bad thing, it shouldn't be unexpected that white descendants of former slave owners don't discuss slavery. However, we were and are unsettled by the degree of "social forgetting," to use Irwin-Zarecka's phrase, at these sites. We believe that the United States and other countries move forward more effectively when they face and deal with the atrocities that have occurred. The lack of talk about an unresolved subject, in this case slavery, suggests its power and pain, and suggests that concerted social forgetting has become an organizing principle. "When even the minimal signs of memory work are missing, when graves are left invisible and

1

Photo opportunity at the Macon, Georgia,
Welcome Center. Visitors can put their heads in
the holes and imagine themselves as white residents
(owners) of a plantation.

unattended, for example, or stories remain untold, these are strong indications
indeed of a past confined to oblivion" (Irwin-Zarecka 1994: 13–14).

This study provides a systematic analysis of the strategic rhetorics that
are employed by plantation museums to manage, and in most cases confine to oblivion, the system of slavery and the presence of those enslaved.
We argue that these rhetorics are part of a racialized regime of representation that valorizes the white elite of the preemancipation South while generally erasing or minimizing the experiences of enslaved African Americans.

This is a topic that can be approached from numerous directions and
from different theoretical locations. That is, this book could be a study of
"whiteness," and indeed, a discussion of whiteness does wind throughout it.

However, it also could be a book about museums and how they operate. Again, while we do talk about what we perceive to be a very significant subsection of the museum industry, we are not writing this solely as a museum studies book. Our primary goal is to understand how plantation museums reflect, create, and contribute to racialized ways of understanding and organizing the world. We chose plantation museums because of our early experiences and because they seemed like an obvious place to look for racialized discourse—a discourse that might be expected to include some discussion of the system of enslavement. We also chose to study plantation museums because we are interested in how racialized ideologies and constructions operate in a cultural realm that is, at least on the surface, divorced from housing or employment markets. It is, of course, less obviously divorced from other cultural and ideological apparatuses, such as public schools or privately controlled mass media. Our argument is that racialization processes work in various locations, linked by shared and often overlapping ideologies and representations, to produce and reproduce racialized inequality and oppression.

We found through this work some fascinating constructions of southernness, whiteness, and slavery. These constructions, we believe, tell us a great deal about the present moment, as well as about the past that the plantation museums want to depict. Through this study we learned more about contemporary racialization, how it links with the past, and how it is represented materially and discursively. We have been able to detail how the social reproduction of racialized imagery and ideology is carried in a significant section of the heritage industry.

Our goal is to present a study of a specific section of the cultural terrain and to demonstrate the partial, and racialized, histories that are enacted. Specifically, we provide a richly detailed analysis of 122 former plantations that are now presented as tourist sites. Our primary focus is on plantation museums in Virginia (where we conducted research at fifty-four such museums), Georgia (twenty-nine), and Louisiana (thirty-nine). We have also conducted research at twenty major sites in five other states (Florida, South Carolina, Alabama, Mississippi, and Tennessee). In addition to sites that met our definition of a plantation museum, we extensively researched local, regional, and state history museums and tourism centers. While we do not explicitly discuss this second type of site, they have provided us with a much larger and deeper grounding in representational practices in the contemporary life of the three states under scrutiny.

The sites we have identified as plantation museums are overwhelmingly what we refer to as "white-centric." By this we mean that these sites normalize and valorize white ways of organizing the world, including the world of labor (and enslavement). Such a term also suggests that anything besides whiteness and white ways is superfluous and marginal. Finally, white-centric encoding works to sustain white dominance. In order to explore counternarratives of enslavement, we also analyzed twenty sites that are organized by, and often for, African Americans. We refer to these sites as "Black-centric." Our consideration of both white-centric and Black-centric sites allows us to examine a previously neglected area of popular culture and therefore shed a different light on contemporary understandings and representations of race and racism than is found in the extant literature on race in the United States. This work also makes a contribution to museum and cultural studies by demonstrating how the vast majority of institutions in this segment of the heritage industry construct narratives of U.S. history that valorize whiteness and mystify the experience of enslavement, both for the enslaved and for master-enslavers. We also demonstrate how these sites contribute to a very particular collective memory and, by extension, collective identification that legitimates contemporary inequalities.

Our primary arguments in this book are that most of the sites we have explored in depth tell a story of American history that centers around whites, males, and elites, and that these sites erase or minimize the presence, labor, and lives of enslaved Africans and African Americans. We argue that these sites work to construct and maintain public white (male-dominated) racial identities that both articulate with and bolster a sense of (white) pride in a partial history of freedom, democracy, and hard work. In this story, slavery and African Americans are presented as almost incidental to the growth of the South and, by extension, the United States.

Before we continue, let us add a note about language. You will notice that we use the terms *master-enslaver* and *enslaver* to talk about those who enslaved others. This is quite intentional. It is generally considered polite to talk about these famous men as planters, politicians, or "great leaders." We want to call attention to how the frame shifts if we also talk about them as enslavers. This emphasis, while in itself a partial distortion, complicates these other frames if applied consistently. And while these men were not politicians or great leaders every moment of every day, they were always enslavers. Their comfort and wealth were wrapped up with the fact that they enslaved other people, appropriating their labor and controlling their lives.

Such an approach, we believe, challenges commonly used language and frames of understanding that replicate systems of racism. It is also in line with suggestions by Michael Banton, Robert Miles, Stephen Small, bell hooks, Leon Higginbotham, and others within the field of race studies that we remove language that continues to mask systems of domination. We recognize that the term may be awkward for some, disturbing or irritating to others; however, we use it to unmask the ways that dominant language obscures the reality of enslaving human beings.

The other term that we use quite consciously is *enslaved* (instead of *slave*). We use it to counter a long tradition of erasing the basic humanity of enslaved people by naming them only in terms of a status that was imposed upon them. Using the term "enslaved people" emphasizes the point that *people* were enslaved and that who they were exceeded that status. Readers will note that throughout the book docents and a variety of other sources whom we quote employ the term *slave;* we have not, of course, changed the language in these cases. Through our use of different terminology we hope to call attention to the normal ways in which relations of domination are masked and the humanity of subordinated people's erased.

Social and Political Context

The South occupies a unique place in United States culture and history. It *is not* the only part of the country that used the labor of enslaved Africans and African Americans; however much the North likes to play it down, slavery was a vital part of its economy both before and after slavery was abolished there (Feagin 2000; Zinn 1999; Takaki 1990). The South, however, was the only section of the country willing to leave the Union in order to maintain its way of life, which was predicated on the ownership of other human beings. While that seems like an obvious point, and one that many white people of the "New South" seem interested in playing down, it does have a bearing on numerous facets of contemporary southern life. For instance, many white southerners' sense of personal and regional identity is connected with their feelings of pride in their families' Confederate past or with their belief that the North victimized the South. Museums and other cultural institutions help to shape that sense of identity and to communicate it to outsiders—that is, to visitors from the western and northern parts of the United States and tourists from outside the country. The work that museums large and small engage in is the building of identity, cultural memory, and community (Gable 1996; Azoulay 1994; Macdonald and Fyfe 1996). That is, museums work to tell us about people, places, and events that they think we should note. They speak of the desires and perceptions of curators, donors, and docents. They tell us not only about a region, place, or people but about the visions that those who developed them have about their world. Through museums we learn what a certain subset of a population (usually white and upper-class or upper-middle-class) deems important for us to know.

The plantation museum sites that we explore exist primarily, in their own understanding, to interpret the life of specific famous white people who lived on the plantations, to interpret the general time period in which the residents lived (with specific foci on wealth, architecture, and a sense of "historical romance"), and/or to interpret a site famous because of a particular event that happened at or near that location. These sites exist within the context of a booming heritage industry, whose success rests on its ability to connect visitors to the "glory" of United States history (Handler and Gable 1997; Lowenthal 1998). Prominent plantation heritage sites tell a particular type of story (white- and elite-centric) to a particular kind of tourist (white). The stories emphasize the hard work, civility, and ingenuity of plantation owners (who were almost invariably male) and provide a largely reverential characterization of gendered kinship relations in southern society, though there are variations across states. In Virginia, the primary story is that Virginia is the "birthplace of democracy"; also stressed are the gentility, civility, and hospitality of the plantation owners. Georgia's sites stress grandeur and hospitality as well, though such stories are regularly framed through references to the movie *Gone with the Wind* and to the romance and nostalgia that the movie evokes. A second related theme in Georgia is that of the Civil War and Georgia's role in that event. In Louisiana, wealth, grandeur, hospitality, and the tragedy of the Civil War are the primary tropes through which plantation tours are organized. During the antebellum era, Louisiana in general and the River Road (along the Mississippi) in particular were home to some of the richest men in the United States. There are also marked emphases in Louisiana on eighteenth-century life and on the cultural differences between Creoles of French origin and culture in the southern part of the state, Cajuns in the southwest, and the English in the parishes immediately below Mississippi. This concern to emphasize the cultural differences across the state, and in particular between the French Creoles and the rest of southern society, gives rise to a particular focus on eighteenth-century properties and lifestyles—rather than on the nineteenth century, which is more common elsewhere in the South—because this is the period in which these groups dominated. The historical differences in the practices of slavery between the states will be primarily discussed in chapter 2; however, where these differences are relevant they will be discussed throughout the book.

In summary, the story that plantation visitors are most likely to learn at white-centric sites is one of civility, grandeur, hard work, the development of democracy, and the tragedy of the Civil War. One is extremely unlikely to learn anything of real substance about the institution of slavery, the texture of enslaved people's lives, or the relationship between the enslavement of the majority of plantation residents and the master-enslaver's wealth. In plantation museum stories, visitors tend to receive information that individualizes and humanizes white people and presents them as multifaceted human agents with aspirations, emotions, experiences, responsibilities, and obligations. We are told of individuals' hopes, desires, successes, and failures, and provided with rich detail about their political, economic, and cultural contributions to the South, to the nation, and to "civilization" in general. In sharp contrast, enslaved African Americans are almost always depersonalized and dehumanized—we are rarely given their names or told of their hopes, aspirations, emotions, or experiences in any detail whatsoever, and we almost never hear anything about them as human agents struggling to secure their own destiny. The one common exception to this pattern is that we are often told enslaved people's names and given descriptions of their feelings when it is useful in the aggrandizement of elite white master-enslavers—for example, when they are described as "faithful servants" or "loyal slaves" of particular whites, or where whites did something deemed generous or magnanimous to the benefit of individual enslaved persons.

If what Richard Morris writes is true—that "memorials . . . endeavor to speak to present and future generations not only of how and why that past ought to be remembered, but also how and why the present and future ought to be shaped and lived" (1997: 41)—then the lack of incorporation of slavery or its minimization at these sites contributes to distortions in contemporary understandings of racialization, which suggest that whites (anywhere in the world) can create a livable world without engaging in a sustained conversation with people of color.

The fact that white southerners (and white Americans in general) create stories that emphasize the goodness of their ancestors is not surprising. As

David Wellman (1993) notes, the dilemma for white Americans is how to protect what they have (racial advantage) and simultaneously believe that the outcome is morally just and racially neutral. To do this in the context of ongoing racialized oppression and a history of brutal cruelty, horror, and exploitation requires that all individuals and institutions develop strategies for coping with racialized information and anxiety. One of the strategies that the South developed in the post–Civil War era was to construct the story of the "Lost Cause" and to push for a collective construction of the South as a victim of unjust northern aggression (Foster 1987). As we demonstrate, many of the sites we explore provide a preferred reading of material and symbolic resources that reinforces a white-centric vision of the South as victim; docents use the language of "the War of Northern Aggression" and tell myriad stories of the suffering when great wealth was lost by master-enslavers. Lest we seem to be stating that *only* the South is racialized and racist, we should note that we agree with Feagin (2000), Feagin and Vera (1995), Small (1994), Lipsitz (1998), Omi and Winant (1994), and others who argue that in the United States, economic and political institutions, ideological systems, and interpersonal relationships are all deeply impacted and shaped by racism. This means that most institutions are white-centric and more often than not work to maintain whites' racial advantage. Those institutions that are most successful in the current moment are those that maintain racialized boundaries through implicit means; that is, it is no longer as accepted for institutions and individuals to engage in behaviors that explicitly maintain racialized inequality. Because cultural institutions provide stories through which past and present statuses are explained, their reaffirmations of a racialized, racist order need to be carefully examined. Cultural production, while often seen by the public as a power-neutral site, is always about the embodiment and construction of meaning and power (Clifford 1988; Gray 1995; Fiske 1993; Hall 1980, 1997), and as this work demonstrates, racialization is a primary axis along which representations are constructed.

Conceptual Organization: Discursive Framework, Rhetorical Strategies, and Counternarratives

Throughout the book we will be defining our terms in detail and making clear the connections between the data and our conceptual organization. To set the groundwork, however, we have organized this section to provide a basis for understanding our arguments and terminology.

First, we have defined "plantation museums" as sites based on physical structures that were originally used as part of plantation complexes during the period of slavery and which now are organized to provide exhibits and tours of southern history, with an exclusive or extensive focus on the period of enslavement. This includes the so-called big house or mansion and any associated outbuildings (including cookhouses, coach houses, overseer's houses, barns, smokehouses, cribs for storing crops, "slave cabins," and garden structures such as wells, gazebos, or teahouses). We also included town or city homes that were owned by enslavers and regularly inhabited by them. These sites were often built in towns for the master-enslaver and his family as a retreat, either to escape the heat and disease of the countryside, as a place for leisure and culture, or as the basis for securing the education of the children, especially boys. As we discuss in the methodology section, we do not count among these sites museums that have only a partial focus on the period of enslavement (such as state, regional, or local history museums, cotton museums, and so on), though we do draw on these sites for our more general analysis.

Based on our fieldwork, we have developed the following frameworks for organizing and understanding the sites and patterns of representation. First, we suggest that there is a racialized regime of representation that is common to all of the white- and elite-centric sites. This regime both constructs and is constructed by a discursive framework of the South as genteel, beautiful, romantic, marked by honor and nobility, and filled with chaste white women and generally upstanding, brave white men. This discursive frame operates regardless of the extent to which these sites mention (or fail to mention) slavery and African Americans. The specifics of this framing, and extensive examples, are provided in chapter 3. We should note that while this discursive frame operates at all white-centric sites, its hegemony is disturbed at those sites that practice relative incorporation of the institution of slavery and those who were enslaved (the concept of relative incorporation and the sites that practice it are described in chapter 7).

Another aspect of all white-centric sites is that they activate and construct narratives of whiteness that generally valorize and normalize white, elite behaviors and mask the participation of these white individuals in the institution of slavery. This is in line with a presentation of plantation society as genteel and honorable. There are two main emphases in these narratives: whites as hospitable and generous, and whites as moral, democratic leaders. These narratives are generally made without explicit reference to the whiteness of those who are being discussed; rather, it is assumed and universalized. As we move through the chapters we explore the ways in which whites are presented and discussed in these sites in order to call attention to the powerful, though generally unmarked, framing of whiteness.

The organizing principles just outlined reference the primary organization of the white-centric sites. Through systematic analysis of richly textured data we have developed a typology of four primary representational/discursive strategies used to discuss slavery and African Americans (both enslaved and legally free) across these 122 sites. These four representational strategies we have called *symbolic annihilation and erasure* (elaborated in chapter 4), *trivialization and deflection* (covered in chapter 5), *segregation and marginalization of knowledge* (chapter 6), and *relative incorporation* (chapter 7). Each of these rhetorical or organizing strategies positions discussion of enslavement and enslaved people in different ways.

Sites that employ symbolic annihilation and erasure as their primary organizing strategy ignore the institution and experience of slavery altogether or treat them in a perfunctory way. Such treatment suggests that slavery and the presence, labor, struggles, and contributions of people of African descent were not important enough to be acknowledged. The second category, trivialization and deflection, includes those sites in which slavery and African Americans are mentioned, but primarily through mechanisms, phrasing, and images that minimize and distort them. Narratives and pictorial images that serve to demonstrate the benevolence of plantation owners and the affection of "faithful slaves" for these owners dominate this pattern.

The third strategy, segregation and marginalization of knowledge, is found at sites that include information about enslaved people but present it largely through separate tours and displays that visitors can choose to see or ignore, depending on their desire. "Black history" or "slave life" tours vary in format and content, take place less frequently than the main white-centric tours, and are less likely to be advertised. Interestingly, the presence of separate tours is a phenomenon primarily found in Virginia. These sites tend to develop information about slavery and African American history beyond minimal levels but do so in ways that maintain separate pathways to knowledge, with one subordinate to the other.

The fourth category is relative incorporation. At the few sites that fall into this category, the topics of enslavement and those who were enslaved are discussed throughout the tour. These sites are much more likely to raise issues that disturb a positive construction of whiteness and challenge the dominant themes that each state tends to present about its own history.

Finally, we have constructed what, in essence, is a residual category: in-between sites. These sites have moved beyond the first three categories but do not yet fall into the fourth; they are still quite conflicted in their representations of enslavement and enslavers, incorporating more information than many sites but doing so in a way that still valorizes whiteness and trivializes the experience of slavery. For clarification, we have included a site that falls into this category in chapter 7, where we discuss relative incorporation.

In addition to detailing the primary ways that elite white-centric sites deal with the institution of slavery, experiences of enslavement, and the presence of African Americans, we also visited a significant number of sites developed to share the experience, and honor the survival, of those people who were enslaved, and of African Americans generally. As mentioned earlier, we undertook tours of twenty sites that are organized by, and often for, African Americans. Some of these sites specifically are set up to explore the experience of those who were enslaved, such as the River Road African American Museum in Louisiana. Other sites that we have included focus on the history of African Americans in a specific area, such as Richmond, Atlanta, or New Orleans. These sites also exist as part of the contemporary tourism trade in their respective states; they are sometimes promoted as part of larger "African American history tours" and are mentioned in brochures along with other sites deemed as being of particular interest to those concerned with African American history.

These sites are not plantation museums in the sense in which we used the term earlier. They are not based on plantation "big houses" or other structures associated with the lives of master-enslavers and their families. Most of them are not organized around physical structures and/or buildings that actually existed during slavery, though many of them have significant artifacts from that period. Nor do these sites concentrate their focus on the lifestyles and achievements of elite whites. Rather, they are housed in locations that were secured after long effort, and they describe the lives and struggles of African Americans in general, both those enslaved and those legally free, with a particular focus on well-known individuals such as Booker T. Washington, Harriet Tubman, or Ellen Craft. In addition, many of these sites have their main focus on periods after slavery, in particular the civil rights movement. These Black-centric sites are included in this book because they stand in clear juxtaposition to the white-centric grand narrative of celebration, grandeur, and honor and because they demonstrate in a palpable and practical way a real alternative to the dominant perspective on slavery, southern history, and African Americans.

Theoretical Interventions and Linkages

Our work uses concepts and perspectives drawn from three primary literatures: studies of racialization, cultural studies, and work on collective memory. Our goal is to join ideas in such a way that we bridge gaps between literatures and contribute to all three.

First, we develop the notion of regimes of representation, drawn from cultural studies, and racialization, drawn from the literature on race and ethnicity, to argue that what is at work in plantation museums is a racialized regime of representation that strongly affects the national and regional collective memory and sense of identity. We also argue that the racialized regimes of representation at work across these sites are effective because they articulate with and reaffirm the racialized mythic life of the dominant white public in the United States: ideologies, images, and allocations of resources that construct African Americans and their experiences as inferior, white Americans and their experiences as superior and more worthy of consideration and focus. They also serve very centrally to reinforce gendered social and power relations.

We do not make any arguments about the intentions of the individuals who work at the sites we visited. Our fieldwork did not explore the workers' beliefs, attitudes, or ideologies, and therefore we cannot make imputations about such things. Further, we believe, as do others (Ansell 1997; Wellman 1993; Johnson 2001; Omi and Winant 1994), that the continuation of racially oppressive institutions and practices does not rely primarily on the intentions of some group of people we can identify as "racist." Instead, we believe that once racially oppressive systems have been put in place and accepted as normal, and particularly when they are surrounded by language that stresses racial neutrality, racialized disadvantage and advantage continue to be created by even well-intentioned people. However, we argue that the content, and silences or gaps in content, found at the sites we investigated are best understood as racialized strategies and discourses. These discourses draw on historical stereotypes derived from the institution of slavery and Jim Crow; they also draw on contemporary constructions and images that disparage African Americans and valorize white Americans.

The strategies that we have identified—symbolic annihilation, trivialization and deflection, segregated knowledge, and relative incorporation—relate to discursive framings and practices within the larger culture. For instance, symbolic annihilation (the dominant approach that we found, and one that is seductive in its normalcy within a white-supremacist system) is the museum equivalent both of the larger culture's outright erasure and denial of Black suffering at the hands of whites in modern culture and of the problematic "add-and-stir" approach to multiculturalism so roundly criticized by such people as Peter McLaren (1997) and Henry Giroux (1997, 2000). We argue that trivialization and deflection are linked to dominant stereotypes about African Americans, such as Blacks as dangerous, lazy, and content to be led by whites, as well as contemporary rightist discourses that deflect attention from the suffering of Blacks and instead frame whites and the South as "victims" of preferential treatment for minorities.

The third pattern or strategy, segregation and marginalization of knowledge, resonates with other segregated ways of knowing (and controlling) African Americans. Such segregation occurs through material practices such as housing and work segregation and through knowledge production and consumption that relegate learning about Blackness to a specific month (Black History Month) or to a body of literature (African American or ethnic studies) that is largely not incorporated into the white-centric knowledge base.

The practice or strategy of relative incorporation is more difficult to define; it does appear to parallel attempts to create integrated knowledge and practice. Not surprisingly, some sites that try to "do it better" still incorporate stereotypical images, and sometimes the coverage of slavery and those who were enslaved varies according to the docent leading a particular tour. On the other hand, some have considered the way framing is done at these sites to be more reminiscent of the "radical multiculturalism" advocated by Giroux, McLaren, and others. That is, they appear to have rethought the content and framing of the site more systematically than most of their brethren.

As we are demonstrating, each of these strategies is "linked in meaningful ways to the present social and political context" (Ansell 1999: 4). That is, the discourses and narratives we identify are important specifically because they are "inexorably tied to struggles for power and advantage in society. Far from being neutral, each discursive repertoire mobilizes a set of meanings about power and powerlessness, privilege and deprivation, advantage and disadvantage, deserving and undeserving" (p. 5). Our concern here is to make clear the racialized regime of representation and discursive strategies that exists across these sites.

In our use of the notion of racialization we are drawing from works that call attention to the way objects, people, and processes become identified as "racial" (Omi and Winant 1993; Miles 1989; Small 1994, 1997). Such terms highlight the fact that people, relations, and objects are never inherently about race, but rather become racialized through a social process of making meaning and allocating resources. We feel that such work is imperative, as it moves us beyond considering just the outcomes of an already racialized distribution system to demonstrating how racialization occurs on the ground level. Clearly, research that demonstrates segregation in housing, education, and employment is crucial for understanding the topography of racialized (and racist) outcomes; however, it is not enough. Additionally, it is important not to become fixated on the motivations or intentions of political or social actors. We believe that racialized discourses and practices continue to be shaped by a remarkable combination of factors, including economic profit, political gain, hostility to Black people, guilt, and so on. We believe there is a continuing need to identify the textures of racialized ideologies, including the marked gendered variations, the sites in which such ideologies are organized, and the consequences for those identified as white as well as those identified as African American. This analysis lends insights into the structures, institutional practices, ideological articulations of racism, and connective links with the past in the contemporary United States. That is, we contribute to the understanding of the social reproduction of racial oppression (Bourdieu 1984, 1992; Feagin 2000). We also make a substantial contribution to the developing body of literature called critical whiteness studies. Our contribution is in the richly detailed exploration of representations and erasures of the institution and experience of enslavement for peoples of African descent and the simultaneous elucidation of representational and rhetorical strategies that construct whiteness as moral, democratic, and superior. Few works explicitly demonstrate how these narratives are working simultaneously in the same representational, rhetorical, and physical space. The substantial empirical data that we bring to our theoretical interventions make for a compelling case.

Drawing on recent work in the field of social memory and collective identity, we argue that we should best understand the overall effect of the racialized discourses in effect at plantation museum sites as helping to construct and solidify a white public memory of valor, hard work, democracy, and grandeur. While there are sites providing counternarratives that disturb this white public memory (see chapters 7 and 8), they are few in number. The fact that so many sites engage in the work of "social forgetting" (Irwin-Zarecka 1994; Olick and Levy 1997) suggests, according to Irwin-Zarecka, that there are deep wounds and anxieties being "confined to oblivion"; this meets the present need, or at least the recent past need, of whites (the dominant group) to create a vision of the nation and themselves as noble and dissociated from racialized atrocities. Irwin-Zarecka, Olick and Levy, and others demonstrate the ways that both everyday and official remembering and forgetting serve political purposes and the needs of both community and individual identity projects. Irwin-Zarecka (1994: 94), writing about German and Polish representations of history, argues that the dilemma posed by German history—that of the integration of its horrifying chapters into what should essentially be an inspiring narrative—is the most acute version of a problem shared by many a collectivity. What is to be done with remembrance that involves shame, doubt, or feelings of guilt? How much presence should be granted to a morally problematic, challenging past? Can one be asked to commemorate mistakes and failures?

These are important and moving questions easily applicable to situations in other countries, such as the United States and its treatment of the institution of slavery and the genocide of American Indians. We will argue, and demonstrate, that the discursive strategies we have identified in the plantation museum industry of the South operate as they do because of the workings of collective identification, white guilt, and avoidance—and, in some cases, anti-Black hostility. We also argue that we must ask plantation museum sites, and other places where history is said to be taught, to commemorate mistakes and failures as well as achievements, and that we must give up aggrandizing situations and people and instead recognize the complexity (including engagement in brutal and atrocious behavior) that marks them.

From the literature on collective memory, specifically Irwin-Zarecka's and Olick and Levy's work, we also draw on the idea that how groups and institutions remember is strongly shaped by their own sense of themselves as victims. In this case, we found that many southerners who work as docents at these sites construct both the South and white southerners as victims—victims who lost everything and suffered immeasurably following the Civil War, victims of a "War of Northern Aggression" that brought uncouth and ruthless white northerners into their land, victims who have continued to be victimized by being misunderstood. Though victimization, in this case, is clearly a racialized discourse, by speaking of the South itself as a victim, white Southerners generally claim it in a way that erases its racialized location. In much the same way, plantations are sometimes referred to as "shrines" to which all Americans can look.

Our work also resonates with different strands of work coming from the museum studies field. For instance, our work, which demonstrates the elite and white-centric views presented at most plantation museum sites, dovetails well with work that demonstrates how museums have historically been related to processes of nation building (Ames 1992; Hoffman 1994; Prösler 1996) and expressions of elite class interests (DiMaggio, Useem, and Brown 1978; Karp, Kreamer, and Levine 1992; Zolberg 1992). As Urry (1996: 57) notes, "It is clear that the 'heritage' that mostly gets remembered is that of elites or ruling classes. It is their houses and estates that have been 'saved for the nation' by the National Trust and other preservationist organizations." He continues, "This produces a one-sided history which underrepresents the poor, those who lived in the north, women, slaves, the disabled, the middle classes, convicts, industrial workers, immigrants, Scottish, Welsh and people living in northern Ireland; and it conceals the social relationships of domination by which that ruling class exerted power." While he is speaking of Britain, the points he makes resonate with processes in the United States and certainly those found in our study.

We also align ourselves with those in the museum world who see museums not only as sites where outside processes are played out but as sites where knowledge and power are created. As Macdonald says, "Museums are never *just* spaces for the playing out of wider social relations. A museum is a process as well as a structure, it is a creative agency as well as a 'contested terrain.' It is because museums have a formative as well as a reflective role in social relations that they are potentially of such influence" (1996: 4).

Museums' very physical structures, the materials they house, and the people who enter them all create and reinforce certain normative practices (Bourdieu 1984, 1993; Hooper-Greenhill 1992, 1995). Of course, they are also imprinted with certain kinds of legitimacy that frame what they teach as "history" versus "heritage," where heritage is seen as being more folkloric and perhaps less factual than history. However, as many have argued, what gets accepted as history often is what comes from the dominant group—whether it be dominance in the arena of class, race, gender, sexuality, nationality, or something else. We hope that by writing not only about but *to* those sites that present plantation history, we encourage such sites to consider whether their efforts at education would be stronger if they were more inclusive and if they told of the experiences that enslaved people had there. We do understand that this will require much more work on the part of staff and volunteers; we don't think it will be easily accomplished. However, we believe the undertaking is imperative.

Methodology

Through our research it has become clear that there are multiple windows into the world of plantation tourism. We have attempted to look through as many as feasible using the most appropriate methods to do so. Therefore we have employed several methodologies in this project, including participant observation, interpretive methodology, and content analysis of a variety of different texts. We began site visits in 1996 and continued until the fall of 2001; over this time we visited many sites more than once and tried to have as many sites as possible seen by both Professor Eichstedt and Professor Small, as well as by graduate students. This gave us overlap in our data gathering and exposed us to different guides at the same sites.

When we first began this work, we did not conceptualize plantation museum sites based on the strict definition that we now use in the book. Instead, as we contemplated what shape the research would take, what kinds of issues we were interested in, and what kinds of questions we would ask, we explored representations of slavery in a variety of sites, including plantation museums based on original structures, regular history museums, history exhibits at regular museums, and Black history exhibits and museums. The vast majority of such sites had formal tours, either regularly scheduled or by arrangement; however, some of them were freestanding sites, that is, they were the ruins of plantations, identified by an official marker and available for viewing, but without any formal tours available. In addition, during the earlier stages of our work we visited a very large number of tourist information centers, including state welcome centers, county and parish tourist centers, and kiosks and booths in towns and cities. Overall, we visited hundreds of locations in our search for understanding how enslavement was represented.

Sites that do not fall under our narrow definition of plantation museums provide valuable supplementary data. In addition to the types of history museum mentioned in the preceding paragraph, which usually cover a wide swath of time, we consider museums of the Confederacy as well as museums of rural life that specifically focus on the seventeenth, eighteenth, or nineteenth century, since they cover the periods when peoples of African descent were enslaved and they frequently present themselves as being historical re-creations or reenactments of life during that era. Their inclusion or exclusion of the institution of slavery is an important indicator of what is considered germane to understanding a given time period.

At the start of our project we picked an arbitrary number of sites (fifty) that we wanted to tour in each state; in the broader definition of sites that speak to (or should speak to) enslavement, we far exceeded this number. We were committed to achieving a representative cross section of sites from all three states and to do this in a way that would provide us with the evidence necessary to characterize common patterns across the three states. At the same time, as we moved further into our work we narrowed our definition of a plantation museum site considerably. In selecting our sites, we used each state's official tourism guide, the American Automobile Association guide available for each region, and tourism maps. We also gathered brochures available at sites themselves. Through the cross-checking that such data gathering allowed, we visited all of the largest plantation museum sites in each state and as many smaller sites as feasible or available. We also included in this number sites that have been constructed to reflect or represent life during the years prior to emancipation. For instance, we visited composite sites that include original buildings brought from various locations to re-create a plantation or a rural village. While we did not visit every single site that falls within the purview of our narrow definition of plantation museum, from what we can determine we visited at least 80 percent of the available sites in each of our primary states (and sometimes far more). The breadth of sites covered and the fact that we often conducted multiple visits to the same sites have allowed us to identify important patterns in representational strategies. The sites we covered in other states (Alabama, Florida, Mississippi, South Carolina, and Tennessee) were not as systematically chosen as those within Virginia, Georgia, and Louisiana but rather were selected for their size and visibility. By touring these sites we were able to determine that the patterns we saw in our primary states were not unique to them; instead it is quite likely that the representational strategies we identify are spread across all of the states that have a plantation museum infrastructure.

The primary methodology employed was participant observation. The tours we went on at these sites constituted the first window through which we looked at each plantation museum. Such tours are an excellent way to access the meanings that are constructed by the staff of the sites. We provide data from fifty-four plantation museums in Virginia, twenty-nine in Georgia, and thirty-nine in Louisiana, including both private and public white-centric sites. All of the sites we attended are open to the public either on a daily basis or by appointment. All but a very small percentage of the sites require the payment of a fee to attend the tour and/or tour the grounds. At each of these sites we attended whatever tour was offered, watched an introductory film if available, toured the grounds, and explored the gift shop (further details of a typical plantation museum are provided in chapter 3). We also visited an additional twenty sites that are staffed and managed by African Americans in order to explore counternarratives that may be offered at these locations.

At each site we attempted to minimize our discussion with the docents who led the tours, instead observing the tour as it was presented. That is, we did not engage the tour guides and ask them questions about the institution of slavery during the official tour they provided. Our goal was to see what was included in a regular tour. We took extensive field notes during the tours, both docent-guided and self-guided, attempting to catch as much information about physical items on display as well as docent-provided information and information given on text plaques and/or automated voice-overs. The fact that we were taking notes sometimes made us stand out; other times it did not, as others there were also taking notes. If docents asked why we were taking notes, we explained that we were faculty with our universities and conducting research on plantation museums and the tours they offered. Normally tour guides did not ask about our note taking; sometimes docents told us that they figured we were either reporters or teachers, since "a lot of both come and do research."

While we usually did not explicitly engage the docents who led the tours, we acknowledge that our presence influenced the tours. For instance, the ways in which we are understood to occupy certain racialized, gendered, class-based, and national and regional identities influenced how we were treated and, quite likely, what each of us was believed to be interested in. For instance, the fact that Professor Small is a Black man with an English accent appears to have affected how docents interacted with him. At times, white docents appeared quite nervous upon finding a Black man on their tour; sometimes the fact that he spoke with an accent seemed to ameliorate their anxiety. There were tours at sites where docents used the word *slave* when speaking to Professor Eichstedt, who is a white woman from the northwestern United States, but when docents at the same site spoke with Professor Small, they used the word *worker* to reference those who clearly had been enslaved. At other times, when docents heard Professor Small's accent they began to assume that because he was from England he was an expert on, or at least greatly familiar with, certain architectural styles; some docents began professing their monarchist beliefs and their sadness that the United States became independent of Britain. Professor Eichstedt was also positioned in particular ways—as white, as nonsouthern, and as a woman. When docents asked where people on tours were from and Professor Eichstedt said California, she was sometimes referred to as a "Yankee in our midst" or was apparently assumed to know little or nothing about southern history. As a white person, Eichstedt was invited to imagine herself as a guest at various plantations in ways that Small was not. For instance, on tours Eichstedt attended that contained no people of color, white docents regularly said, "If you came here to visit, this is the room you would have slept in," or indicated the food "you would have eaten." On no tour that Professor Small attended was the inclusive language of "you" used. Additionally, gendering played a role; Professor Eichstedt was regularly assumed to be interested in the decorative arts produced by white women, while male visitors were often assumed to be interested in the maps and firearms that were sometimes displayed.

In addition to attending site tours, we also gathered an extensive collection of brochures and other tourist literature designed to draw visitors to the sites. These constitute a second window into the plantation museum industry. These pamphlets generally work to tell the potential visitor, in a limited space, what the highlights of a visit would be. We analyzed these brochures for content; specifically, we analyzed for content categories that arose out of our site visits and also looked for content that did not fit into already devised categories. These pamphlets will be discussed throughout the text. At plantation gift shops we purchased postcards that used plantation imagery and bought any books available about the site. Finally, we also bought and analyzed videos produced about specific sites as well as those that cover a large number of plantations (such as *Great Plantation Homes of Virginia*). What we have found is that the brochures and videos focus even more heavily on romance, grandeur, and architecture than do the tours themselves.

The use of grounded theory allowed us to develop categories from the data itself. That is, while we went to the sites with a particular interest in understanding what was being presented to the public, we employed the information provided at the sites themselves to develop the analytical categories by which we have organized our work. Based on these categories, we then engaged in content analysis of the brochures and films to see whether the same types of words, phrases, and images were employed in the textual representations specifically designed to attract tourists; we also looked for different categories that might be present in written text that were not present in the tours.

It is important to note that what we present is a picture of a particular moment in the plantation museum industry. We do not explore, for instance, whether any of these sites has changed its presentation over time, though it is clear that sites we present as being in-between or primarily employing strategies of segregation or relative incorporation have changed over time, in particular over the last ten years. We hope that further research will help capture the transitions that sites have gone through, as well as reveal how and why plantation museums made the decisions that shape their tours.

What is compelling is how many sites have *not* gone substantially further in discussing enslavement. How is it that, decades after the first civil rights legislation was passed and Black racial justice activism rocked the United States, most of the sites we explored still engage in symbolic annihilation and trivialization? That is an important question not only for the plantation museum industry but also for the other facets of social life, education, and regimes of representation that are deeply racialized. By drawing together the racialization literature with the literature exploring cultural practices and collective memory, we hope to provide a way to understand this and other cultural realms.

The book is organized into nine chapters. Part One, "History and Overview," provides the groundwork for understanding the organization of the plantation system as it existed prior to emancipation and the contemporary organization of the plantation museum industry. In chapter 2 we provide a brief history of slavery in each state, including when the state was colonized, by whom, and the effects of such colonization on indigenous populations; the demography of the state and an overview of the crops produced there; resident and nonresident ownership of plantations; and the state's relation to the Confederacy and experiences during the Civil War.

We also describe the primary organizing themes in each state's contemporary plantation museum tourist infrastructure. In chapter 3 we discuss the difference between private and public plantation museum sites and detail a typical plantation museum, including what is provided in the way of tours, videos, docents, and visual displays. Finally, we elaborate on the four discursive strategies for handling the institution of slavery that we will discuss in the following part.

Part Two, "Managing Slavery: Representational Strategies," provides detailed information on the plantations, organized around the four discursive principles of symbolic annihilation (chapter 4), trivialization and deflection (chapter 5), segregation and the marginalization of knowledge (chapter 6), and relative incorporation (chapter 7). Part Three, "Alternatives and Conclusions," provides a discussion of the counternarratives regarding the system of enslavement, the enslaved, and master-enslavers found at the Black-organized and -run sites that we visited (chapter 8), along with our final arguments regarding the meaning of this work and how we understand it to impact the contemporary understanding of collective memory in the United States and its racialization (chapter 9).

PART ONE

History and Overview

2 | Different States and Themes

The three states under consideration in this book, Virginia, Georgia, and Louisiana, were chosen for several reasons. These include the number of people enslaved in each state, the crops that were grown and the attendant methods of production, and the presence of plantation museums today. Understanding at least a bit of the history of these states is important, as it emphasizes the role of slavery in each state's development and helps locate the different stories that are now told about each state. In the following pages we will provide a very brief overview of the similarities of the states, the noteworthy specificities of each state's history, and a consideration of the experience of enslavement for those enslaved. We do not provide a social history of each site we explored, due both to the monumental nature of that task and to the complexities involved, but where possible we encourage readers to look at books provided by the sites themselves or at reference guides to the history of each state.

Themes and Issues in Southern Slavery and Plantation Life

To each of these three states slavery was crucial; it provided the labor that produced cotton, sugar, tobacco, and rice. The labor of enslaved people therefore provided the wealth that allowed the enslavers to live the lives they did. When the Emancipation Proclamation was issued in 1862, Virginia, Georgia, and Louisiana held a total of 1,284,789 enslaved persons, accounting for over 31 percent of all enslaved persons in the nation (Berlin 1974: 396–97, table A). All three states had seen their enslaved populations increase in size between 1850 and 1860—Virginia with an increase of 3.9 percent, Georgia 21.1 percent, and Louisiana 35.5 percent (ibid.: table C). An economically profitable system of trading in human cargo—the so-called internal slave trade—linked the three states together, buying and selling enslaved persons, disrupting entire families, and moving them hundreds of miles as the needs of individual master-enslavers dictated (Tadman 1989). The wealth held in the form of enslaved persons amounted to a very significant part of each state's wealth. For instance, in Georgia in the 1850s enslaved persons were being sold for $2,000 each, and their collective value was greater than that of all the state's lands and cities combined.

Agricultural production in these states covered the four major crops to be found in the South—tobacco in Virginia, cotton and rice in Georgia, and sugar in Louisiana. Virginia was the largest tobacco producer in the nation, as it had been throughout the nineteenth century (Klein 1971: 186–88). It was also the South's leading manufacturing state (ibid.: 239). Cotton was the largest crop across the South—in 1860 the southern states produced 5,387,000 bales of cotton annually (Franklin and Moss 1998: 124). On the eve of the Civil War, three-quarters of all enslaved people in the South were employed in the production of cotton (Faust 1991: 13). Georgia led the nation for many years in the production of cotton, though it was surpassed by western states, including Louisiana, in the last decades before the war. In addition to cotton, Louisiana was also a key producer of sugar, an important product not only for the state but for the nation as a whole. At the start of the Civil War Louisiana had the second highest per capita wealth in the nation. Louisiana was also important because it contained New Orleans, which was, after New York, "the largest antebellum port of entry in the United States. There arrived 120,000 immigrants between 1852 and 1855, more than a fourth of all those reaching the country in this period" (Shugg 1939: 39). All three states, therefore, were important for their roles in the fledgling Union and for the ways that slavery was manifested within them.

There are, of course, several important similarities between the states. For example, in each state the land that was farmed by whites (and by the Africans and African Americans whom they enslaved) was taken from existing indigenous populations that in many cases were decimated by European illnesses, massacres, or forced relocation (Zinn 1999; Takaki 1990). Of course, slavery and plantation agriculture were also central to each state as

economic, political, and social institutions. The entire body of southern society, almost from the very start, was dominated by slavery. Plantations were
its backbone, and the profits that flowed from the crops grown there were
its lifeblood.

The states shared the presence of a very strong and overwhelmingly male
plantocracy that ruled southern society and politics. One of the South's
foremost authors reminds us that "as a distinct slave society, the antebellum
South developed its fundamental social, cultural, intellectual, gender and
political relations under the aegis of the slave system" (Fox-Genovese 1988:
55). Planters dominated southern society from early on, fending off the
power of the English aristocracy in early Virginia and then the power of the
English state in the War for Independence. Their power was rooted in economic dominance in the South, maintained through an interlocking network of households and the institution of marriage, and was expressed
through extensive political involvement at the regional, state, and eventually federal levels.

The lifestyles of master-enslavers and their families in the three states
were dominated by paternalist morality, gendered ideology, and aristocratic
codes of honor borrowed from Europe and transformed in the context of
local conditions. Aspects of civil society, such as the architecture of public
and private buildings, music, theater, art, and extravagant consumption patterns, referenced and often imitated European patterns. Finally, the perva-
siveness of racisms of different kinds cemented over many of the class and
ethnic divisions that were at the base of what became white society. By ma-
nipulating philosophical, moral, and Christian ideologies, southern planters
were able to circumvent what others saw as insuperable and inexcusable
contradictions between the rhetoric of freedom and equality and the practice of enslavement and class oppression.

Wealth and Ownership of Enslaved Persons

The number of master-enslavers was not large in any period, not even just
before the end of slavery. For example, in 1860 there were about 385,000
master-enslavers, distributed among 1,516,000 free families. Thus nearly
75 percent of all free southerners had no connection with slavery through
either family ties or direct ownership. Furthermore, "of the twenty-four
percent of white southerners who were members of slaveholding families,
49% of these families held less than five enslaved people, while only 12%

owned more than twenty enslaved people" (Faust 1991: 12). This last number is important, since the holding of twenty people is generally accepted as the minimum number a planter had to have for his or her site to be considered a plantation (Vlach 1991: 21–22; Stampp 1964: 30). The number of enslavers varied across states: In Virginia, one-fourth of families owned enslaved persons, whereas in Georgia two-fifths of families and in Louisiana one-third of families enslaved others (ibid.: 30). Of these master-enslavers a full 338,000 (88 percent) owned fewer than twenty enslaved persons (Franklin and Moss 1998: 123). What this means is that "the planter aristocracy was limited to some ten thousand families who lived off the labor of gangs of more than fifty slaves. The extremely wealthy families who owned more than a hundred slaves numbered less than three thousand, a tiny fraction of the southern population" (Stampp 1956: 30–31). Looking at it in percentage terms, "in 1860, only 2.7 percent of Southern slaveholders owned 50 or more slaves," and "a mere 0.1 percent of slave owners held estates of 200 or more slaves" (Kolchin 1983: 101). Only the most elite had the lavish lifestyles represented in movies such as *Gone with the Wind*. John M. Vlach argues that while the "grand plantation was an atypical landscape for whites, it was for enslaved blacks, on the other hand, a significant and common environment" (1991: 23). Historian John B. Boles explained the apparent paradox by using a theoretical group of just ten slaveholders. Of those ten, Boles suggested, imagine

eight owning two slaves apiece, one owning twenty-four, and the tenth possessing sixty. Obviously most slaveholders (80 percent) would own fewer than five slaves, but most slaves (84 out of 100) would reside in units of more than twenty. Such an imaginary model suggests what the numbers reveal. In 1850, when 73.4 percent of the slaveholders held fewer than ten slaves, exactly 73.4 percent of the slaves lived in units numbering more than ten. Over half, 51.6 percent, resided on plantations of more than twenty bondsmen. These figures were more pronounced in the Deep South, and still more so in 1860, when fully 62 percent of the slaves in the Deep South lived in plantation units, and one-third on really substantial plantations of more than fifty slaves. (Boles 1983: 107)

This is important because it suggests the importance of large holdings for enslaved African Americans and their experiences creating familial and community life.

Class Inequality among Whites

Wealth in the South was highly concentrated, and inequality, even among whites, very pronounced: "The average wealth of slaveholders in the Cotton South in 1860 ($24,748) was 13.9 times the average wealth of non-slaveholders ($1,781); slaveholders [who accounted for 25 percent of the population] owned 93.1 percent of the region's agricultural wealth" (Kolchin 1983: 180). Because of these inequalities, and because so few whites directly owned enslaved persons, means had to be found to sustain active support among all whites for plantation slavery, as master-enslavers were afraid that poor whites might heed the abolitionists' calls. Racism—or rather, racisms of different kinds—was pervasive, and provided the glue to hold white society together. In his analysis of racism, Fredrickson argues that "the urgent need to ensure the loyalty of the non-slaveholding white majority caused them to emphasize it increasingly as they mobilized the southern states for secession and civil war" (1981: 161). "An uncompromising commitment to white supremacy was thus a central and unifying component of the separate southern identity that crystallized on the eve of the Civil War" (ibid.: 162).

Codes of Honor

While the colonizers of Virginia and the other colonies eventually shook off what they perceived as English political oppression, they evidenced no desire to discard English culture or ideology. They maintained English elements of class and political inequality as well as moral and civil ideologies, including Christianity. The ruling elites in Virginia in particular also maintained British cultural tastes in architecture, dress, and music. In maintaining an exemplary civil society, white southerners in general, and elites especially, held closely to a distinct set of values considered by many to be a specific "code of honor."

> The Southerner was convinced that life should be ordered by certain well-defined codes of conduct that were a part of the cult of chivalry. Horsemanship and skill in the use of arms, so indispensable to successful living in the South, fitted conveniently and prominently into the cult of chivalry. Respect for and protection of white women were aspects that seemed to increase in importance as the problem of sex and race become more complicated and as the maintenance of racial integrity became a part of the program. (Franklin 1964: 34)

Finally, for the southerner "nothing was more important than honor. Indeed, he placed it above wealth, art, learning, and the other 'delicacies' of an urban civilization and regarded its protection as a continuing preoccupation" (ibid.: 35).

Violence and a warm embrace of a strong martial spirit provided protection for this code of honor. Franklin indicates that dueling "was widespread throughout the ante-bellum South" among the elite; among the powerless, violence took the form of brigandage, bullying, and fighting. Southerners took pride in this code of violence, especially where it was seen as central to the defense of the honor, integrity, or courage of a gentleman or the reputation of his ladyfolk.

In addition to militarism, a specific gender ideology was at the heart of this code. The defense (and control) of white elite women was paramount in planter society. Fox-Genovese tells us: "The figure of the lady, especially the plantation mistress, dominated southern ideals of womanhood. That slaveholding ladies were massively outnumbered by nonslaveholding or small-slaveholding women challenges any easy assumptions about the relation between the ideal and reality but does not undermine the power of the ideal" (Fox-Genovese 1988: 47). She continues: "The voluminous papers of educated women display a clear and often militant defense of their class privileges and their distance from lower-class white as well as black women" (ibid.: 97). Rich white women were encouraged to disdain working-class white women and Black women of all statuses—enslaved or legally free—and were rewarded for doing so (Fox-Genovese 1988; Clinton 1982).

Fox-Genovese argues that "southern slave society consisted largely of a network of households that contained within themselves the decisive relations of production and reproduction" (1988: 38). In general, "southern society on the whole remained a conservative, tightly knit, hierarchical, and closed system" (ibid.: 37). Marriage was its foundation and the conduit of its intergenerational success. Women married young: "The median age of marriage for southern women (taken from a sample of planters born from 1765 to 1815) was twenty, whereas the median age for men was twenty-eight. This contrasts dramatically with statistics on northern planters, for whom the median age of marriage for women was twenty-four, for men, twenty-six" (Clinton 1982: 60). Furthermore, "cousin marriages and marriages to the siblings of dead spouses helped keep wealth 'within the family.'" Planters gave generous gifts of land and enslaved persons to their children: "as a rule, sons received land and daughters, slaves; sons, of course, almost always received the larger shares" (ibid.: 37).

Other gendered and racialized aspects of southern life were prostitution and profligacy. Nowhere was this more common than in New Orleans. By 1788 the practice of open concubinage of women of color—particularly those of mixed origins, most frequently called "quadroons"—was widespread. The children from these relationships grew in number. The Spanish were considered somewhat more considerate of "mulatto" children, and provided for them better than the English did (Sterkx 1972: 63). These children were able to build up wealth, including ownership of enslaved persons, in ways, and in numbers, unparalleled elsewhere in the United States.

Lifestyles

Expensive goods, imported from Europe and elsewhere, characterized the lifestyles of southern elites. Most were bought with the profits from trading, breeding, and working human chattels. There were rich parties for birthdays and weddings, and travel to Europe for fun or education. For example, Charles Manigault, one of the wealthiest Low Country master-enslavers, with plantations across South Carolina and Georgia, went on frequent international tours (Dusinberre 1996). Many planters escaped the summer heat and malaria by going to Savannah or Charleston, or to New Orleans or Natchez; others in the "southern heartland" had "permanent residences in a local village or town" (Fox-Genovese 1988: 107).

The master-enslaver elites built elaborate and expensive plantations when they were able. They imitated classical and neoclassical European styles and tradition—in the names of towns (Athens, Paris, Rome, Geneva), in the styles of buildings (Greek Revival, Gothic), and in their homes. The most important structure, actually and symbolically, was the "big house"—"the term generally used to designate the planter's home," says Clinton, "regardless of its size" (Clinton 1982: 17). Clinton continues:

The style and size of these homes varied from region to region and period to period, but generally plantation houses were substantial two- or three-story structures. Most had spacious receiving halls on the ground floor. Dining rooms, parlors, libraries, music rooms, and sitting rooms were located off the central hall; bedrooms and nurseries, on the upper floors. Many mansions had porches on both upper and lower stories. Most homes were equipped with fireplaces in every room. A handsome staircase in the center of the house was often supplemented by a back stairs for servant use. (Ibid.: 18)

In addition to the big house, there were outbuildings such as barns, stables, workshops, and warehouses. There were slave cabins at "a convenient distance from the master's home," and many planters also had nursery and hospital facilities (ibid.). Most big houses had a detached kitchen, and the larger ones had separate smokehouses and storehouses.

The rich had luxury goods in their homes and had "house slaves," and their children had "expensive clothing, expensive horses and expensive educations" (Harris 1985: 82). Newlyweds were often provided with "dining tables, chairs, sideboards, settees, rockers, four-poster beds, necessary chairs (with chamber pots hidden beneath the seat bottoms), chests of drawers (sets of drawers with handles, which fit on top of one another for easy transport), silver, china, pots and pans, and sometimes family portraits and heirlooms" (Clinton 1982: 25).

The picture just painted is one of great luxury and privilege; it would be easy, given the images presented in popular culture, to believe that travel and luxury were the norm for white southerners, or even white enslavers. However, "only the very wealthiest slave-holding households remotely approximated the physical luxury and ease attributed to them in the romantic legend that was strong even then but would grow stronger in the days of 'the Lost Cause'" (Fox-Genovese 1988: 105). While largely mythological, this vision nevertheless drove—and, we argue, continues to drive—the current representations of enslavers.

Defending Slavery, Employing Racism

The defenders of slavery, particularly the master-enslaver aristocracy, found themselves occupying positions hard to defend in a country that was using libertarian doctrines to argue for its independence from Britain. They evaded the sprit of the Declaration of Independence by drawing on arguments that stressed the importance of private property over a "slave's rights to liberty" or claimed that Africans and African Americans were not fully human (Fredrickson 1981: 143).

From the very start, ethnocentrism and racism were central; they were ideologies that were flexible across geographic space and over time, and they became increasingly important as the nineteenth century progressed (Gossett 1965). In general, master-enslavers emphasized the moral and intellectual inferiority of Blacks, with a particular emphasis from the start on their status as heathens. "The masters sought to legitimate their authority by emphasizing their benevolent paternalism, the alleged Christian motivation of the enslavement of blacks" (Clinton 1982: 14). In addition to making arguments about the civilizing and soul-saving function of slavery, enslavers also framed those enslaved as incapable of self-government and content in their subordination. Clinton points out: "Planters sentimentalized to the point of caricature the image of happy darkies singing in the fields—omitting all reference to whips, chains, brands, maiming, selling families apart, and rape, among the numerous atrocities allotted to blacks only" (ibid.: 14). Racism was used not only to justify the treatment of people of African descent but also to justify the dislocation and eradication of indigenous Americans.

Another dilemma white elites circumvented was any advocacy of egalitarianism among whites in a context in which only 25 percent of whites owned enslaved persons. They escaped the class implications of this by drawing on racism. "An ideological marriage between egalitarian democracy and biological racism pandered at once to the democratic sensibilities and the racial prejudices of the 'plain folk' and was thus well suited to the maintenance of inter-class solidarity between planters and non-slaveholders within the South" (Fredrickson 1981: 154–55). Many elite slaveholders denied the idea of equality among all whites but considered racism to be useful. America was founded as a democratic nation, but planters were themselves controlled by European class traditions, aristocracy, and inequality. They embraced freedom for themselves but imposed slavery on Africans and subordination on white women and working-class whites.

The Experience of African Americans in the Preemancipation South

The experiences of enslaved African Americans varied across time and place and would be impossible to summarize in a brief accounting. For a more complete understanding of the experience of enslavement, we encourage readers to turn to the extensive literature that exists on this topic (Campbell and Rice 1991; Stampp 1964; Genovese 1968; Blassingame 1979; Morgan 1975; Fox-Genovese 1988; Kolchin 1983; Rawick 1972). What we present here is merely a basic overview.

African Americans began to be permanently enslaved in the United States in 1640 in the state of Massachusetts. This racialized enslavement continued in the North through the mid-1830s, though northern states gradually started enacting emancipation laws beginning in the 1790s. African Americans continued to be legally enslaved in the South until 1862, and many were held in bondage through the end of the war in 1865 (indeed, there is much evidence to suggest that enslavers kept some enslaved people in bondage even after the war by deliberately not telling them about the Emancipation Proclamation or that the war had ended). By the 1860s there were almost four million enslaved people in the United States. This number should be understood for what it is: the number of enslaved people alive at this point. Millions more had been enslaved over the course of the previous two centuries, and at least one-third of those stolen from Africa had died during the dreaded Middle Passage to the Americas.

The experience of enslavement varied with the context in which it was carried out. For instance, African Americans were enslaved to work in factories and urban centers and on farms and plantations. Some lived in circumstances where they were the only enslaved African American living with a family of whites, others in situations where 95 to 100 percent of the resident population were enslaved. Different laws were passed in different places to curtail enslaved people's movement, their ability to congregate, and the legality of learning to read and write; such laws became more common during the 1800s as white fears of Black revolt increased and as tensions over the issue of slavery mounted between the North and the South.

There is considerable documentation of the experience of enslaved African Americans. Prior to the 1960s most evidence was based on information provided by whites; since then, we have substantial data from Blacks, which provide more accurate and telling insights into the lives of the enslaved. These data come from two primary sources: narratives written during the period of enslavement, particularly those written as antislavery tracts by enslaved people who escaped, and interviews undertaken in the 1930s with those who had been enslaved. The interviews were conducted by both Black and white researchers hired by the Works Progress Administration and were extensively edited (usually by white administrators) and then gathered in a number of volumes. Themes that stand out in these accounts include labor that went from "can see to can't see," or sunup to sundown; the inability to make fundamental decisions about one's life; fear of having one's family sold apart; and the sexual exploitation consistently faced by enslaved women, particularly those who worked in the main houses. Stories of horrific violence, including whippings, brandings, maimings, and killings, run throughout these accounts. While some economists have argued that it was economically irrational for master-enslavers to injure those who performed labor for them and in whom they had invested a great deal of money, repeated accounts of brutality belie this claim. Also, this claim assumes that humans make choices primarily based on rational calculations, although we know that individuals make decisions based on a wide variety of factors, including religious beliefs as well as emotions such as fear, lust, vindictiveness, hatred, and power. These motivations often led enslavers to act in ways that were economically irrational and dangerous to those they enslaved.

While those who were enslaved were clearly profoundly mistreated during slavery, it is important to acknowledge that even in these circumstances, enslaved people created family lives and cultural traditions that helped them survive. The success of Black culture varied with their location, whether smallholdings, plantations, or cities and towns (Reidy 1992: 81). The combination of various cultural influences in the context of powerlessness produced the cultural matrix that became unique to the South. Africans, and increasingly African Americans, sought to retain and adapt aspects of the African cultural practices they and their ancestors had brought with them. The cultures created among enslaved Blacks, among legally free people of color, and between the two affected not only Black life but white life as well. Both the environment and the economic system exerted an influence on the culture of Blacks, and of whites too—for example, dance songs, work songs, and religious and burial chants were all part of the African musical cultural heritage imported and transformed in various U.S. slave cultures (Smith 1985: 166). This is the process that many have labeled creolization; one well-known example is the Gullah dialect, found along the Georgia coast (ibid.: 161, 172). Cornel West (1993) and others note that valued Black cultural traditions such as signification and expressive oral traditions enabled the enslaved to communicate about their work, the location of the master-enslaver, and events happening off the plantation in ways that whites did not understand. But enslavers, who also served as local, regional, and national politicians, sought to control even these activities—various localities outlawed drumming, dancing, and other practices.

At its core, the experience of enslavement in the United States was that one's life was not one's own. The enslaved individual had no control over where he or she lived, whom he or she served, the conditions under which he or she served, or what that service included. Enslavement was at its base an economic institution, so fundamentally this meant that enslaved persons' labor was not their own. Except in rare circumstances where enslavers allowed those they "rented out" to keep part of the wages they earned, enslaved persons received no compensation for the labor they provided. It was this stolen labor that provided the foundation for the wealth of the master-enslavers.

The commonalities outlined above—the experiences of the enslaved; the general distribution of wealth and enslaved people; the gendered codes of honor, upheld by violence, that southerners employed; the lifestyles of the very wealthy; and the arguments used to defend slavery—are important to understand. While we have presented only a brief overview, we hope that it has suggested some of the ways that slavery across the South was in some ways a uniform phenomenon. However, it is important to note that these general trends are punctuated by state differences. These differences arise from the different groups that settled various regions at different times, the various crops and climates associated with each region, and the shape that enslavement took in each physical and political context. They also varied in large measure in response to the numbers of Africans and African Americans enslaved and their particular responses to that enslavement. These differences then created other differences—for instance, in political and social life and a given state's experience during the Civil War. Again, while the coverage we provide here is necessarily brief, we seek to draw attention to the unique attributes of the states and how they affected the experience of enslaving and enslavement. These differences are frequently acknowledged and manifested in the current plantation museum infrastructure in the contemporary South. And, as further chapters will show, such differences are often exaggerated or distorted to meet contemporary needs.

The History of Virginia

Not only was Virginia the first colony to be settled, it was also "the largest and most influential state in molding the slave institutions of the North American continent" (Klein 1971: viii). After the failed Roanoke experiment of the 1570s, the first permanent European settlers arrived at the start of the seventeenth century. During their first several decades there, the settlers were preoccupied with surveying the immediate vicinity of the

Jamestown area; negotiating with and positioning themselves vis-à-vis the indigenous population (including significant armed conflict); trying to ensure adequate supplies of food and the necessary clothing and shelter; and, importantly, trying to identify or invent a product that would provide the much sought-after commercial profit.

Virginia borrowed many of its early laws and much of its protocol of slavery from its English neighbors in the Caribbean. The colonization of what became Virginia reflected the increasing strengths of merchant interests alongside aspirant English individuals. Early initiatives and the financing of Virginia were largely the work of England's merchants and those with commercial interests. Along with them, it was English adventurers—both those with wealth and those without—who were the early settlers of the colony that was to become Virginia. The Crown was reluctant to invest the necessary capital in financing these initiatives, though it sought to reap rewards from taxes and did so in large measure, especially as tobacco became the dominant crop.

When the English arrived, their experiences with the Native Americans were uneven. The indigenous inhabitants were about forty small tribes in the Chesapeake Bay region (Nash 1992: 55). The natives that the English had the most initial contact with were organized into a confederation led by Chief Powhatan. The English were already inclined to see Native Americans as heathens and savages; some were inclined to try to "save" them, while others sought to exterminate them. The English, despite varying outlooks, were dominated by a desire for land and profits and quickly developed the hegemonic position that Indians were a threat to be contained or destroyed. Conflicts became increasingly severe and the English increasingly barbaric in their attacks. There is no doubt that racism and ethnocentrism against people of color were central here. As Morgan points out, the English perpetrated atrocities against Native Americans—for example, flinging children into the river and shooting them in the head—that they did not do to the French or Spanish (Morgan 1975). Over the course of the following centuries Native Americans were increasingly controlled, marginalized, subordinated, or removed. The English (and eventually American) desire for land, and the massive growth of civil society, left little place for Native Americans. If it wasn't entirely true that all white settlers believed the only good Indian was a dead Indian, the majority of the English were inclined toward that end of any continuum of views that might have existed.

As white settlement continued, the number of English increased rapidly, especially after the first decades. By 1790, the time of the first census, there were 442,117 whites in Virginia, and the population grew to 1,047,299 by 1860 (Klein 1971: 236, table 5). The majority of the English settlers belonged to the working class. For a period England saw Virginia as a dumping ground and sent "political prisoners, debtors, economic discontents, laborers and religious dissenters" (ibid.: 167). Other settlers were members of the aspirant commercial class. A central factor in the nature and extent of migration was the headright system, by which anyone could transport a person—including himself—to the New World and was entitled "to receive fifty acres of land free for each individual taken across," including indentured servants (ibid.: 169). By the fourth decade of the seventeenth century between fifteen hundred and two thousand indentured servants were arriving in Virginia annually (ibid.: 170). The headright system continued for whole of the century and enabled a strong yeomanry to develop alongside planters (ibid.: 172).

In 1619 the first "Negroes" arrived and "appear to have been treated as indentured servants" (ibid.: 40–41) who could gain their freedom, own property, and vote. Driven by their desire to control a labor force, and borrowing from the Spanish precedent, white Virginians quickly turned to the enslavement of Africans. Heavy importation of human cargo from Africa began after the 1640s, and increasingly a distinction was made between "servants" and "slaves" (ibid.: 41). Klein reminds us that "in Virginia, chattel slavery was created entirely by the customary, judicial, and statutory decision of colonial origin" (ibid.: 39). He continues, "As there existed no precedent for Negro slavery in English common law, the Virginians, through their customary, judicial, and statutory practices and decisions, thus created their own slave regime" (ibid.: 40). Though they tried, white Virginians were less likely to enslave Indians because they were nomadic, were particularly effective at avoiding capture, and were less likely to survive intensive agricultural labor (ibid.: 43). Increasingly African Americans lost rights—the right to "self-preservation and security," trial by jury, freedom of movement, and marriage (ibid.: 48–49). Furthermore, "manumission was made as difficult to execute as possible," and the lives of free Blacks "made as precarious as possible" (ibid.: 50). Most stringent were laws against miscegenation; the mixed-race children of white women were sold into bondage. White women who had sexual relationships with Black men suffered heavy fines or five years' servitude.

Peoples of Color

The number of people of color, particularly those enslaved, increased dramatically over the decades. By the end of the seventeenth century, enslaved Africans were the bulk of the labor force on Virginia tobacco plantations (Klein 1971: 174). The importation of human cargo, particularly from Africa, expanded throughout the eighteenth century, and England became the prime supplier of enslaved humans (ibid.: 176). The headright system also applied to Blacks, so as white Virginians increased their ownership of human property, they also increased their ownership of land.

In 1790 there was a total of 305,493 people of color in Virginia, including 292,627 enslaved people and 12,866 who were legally free. This was "more than double the number of slaves in any other state in the union" (Klein: 186). A total of 34,026 master-enslavers, who represented 7.6 percent of the white population, held this population of enslaved people. At the start of the Civil War Virginia's population included 548,907 people of color (490,865 enslaved and 58,042 legally free) (ibid.: 236, table 5). By 1860, however, the percentage of the white population that enslaved others had fallen to only 5 percent (55,063 people) (ibid.: 186). Note that while the percentage of individual slave owners is low, 25 percent of families were involved in enslaving others. The median number of people enslaved by master-enslavers was 18.8—that is, 50 percent of master-enslavers owned more than 18.8 enslaved persons, while 50 percent owned fewer than 18.8 (ibid.: 187).

In 1790 the "free colored" were only 4 percent of the total population of color. While their numbers rose slowly, they still amounted to only 11 percent of the total population of color in 1860 (ibid.: 123). Legally free people of color suffered greatly, being "degraded, despised and dispersed" across the state (ibid.: 253).

The overwhelming majority of Virginia's enslaved persons worked in tobacco (ibid.: 177). Without a doubt, and despite some variations at the start, monocrop plantation agriculture dominated Virginia's commerce, both before and after independence. Tobacco was stumbled upon after an unsuccessful search for other goods and crops such as silk and grapes, but "so quickly did Virginia leaf find a profitable market that by the end of the third decade of the 17th century tobacco had achieved its position of dominance over the Virginia economy that was thereafter never seriously challenged." (ibid.: 165).

The late colonial and early national periods saw geographical expansion and soil exhaustion and the "growth of a vital hinterland" (ibid.: 185). This led to the growth of the crucial intermediate Piedmont region. "Once the first communal organizations had been dissolved, however, and the power of the Indians finally broken, the colonists dispersed over a vast area, their plantations racing along the rivers (James, York, Rappahannock, and Potomac) towards the falls" (ibid.:. 28). The tramontane frontier developed an entirely new economy based on corn, wheat, and other nonplantation crops, but the intermediate Piedmont region tended to reproduce the plantation system of the Tidewater (ibid.: 185).

Many of the families of planters who became leaders in Virginia emigrated to Virginia in the mid-1600s. These included the first Carters, Lees, Randolphs, and Byrds (Dabney 1971: 46). According to historians, other influential families included the Harrisons, Pages, Wormeleys, Burwells, Masons, Beverleys, Gymseses, Carys, Nelsons, Diggeses, Ludwells, and Fitzhughs. Dabney writes:

> As an example of how a single marriage involving such families could affect the life of the colony, the commonwealth and the nation, consider the direct descendants of William Randolph of "Turkey Island" and Mary Isham of "Bermuda Hundred," who were wed in the middle 1670's. The list includes Thomas Jefferson, John Marshall, and Robert E. Lee, not to mention "Light-Horse Harry" Lee, Edmund Randolph, Peyton Randolph and John Randolph of Roanoke. (Ibid.: 47)

The chief architect of the Carter family fortune was Robert "King" Carter, born in 1663. By 1700 he was already one of the largest freeholders in the Northern Neck of Virginia, and when he died in 1732 he left a vast fortune, including over a thousand enslaved persons (Dabney 1971). His sons continued his plantations throughout the eighteenth century; repeated intermarriage with other wealthy families, such as the Hills and Lees of Virginia, ensured that much wealth stayed within the (extended) family.

Most of the powerful planter families in Virginia "derived from English merchants and traders or were intimately connected with them" (Klein 1971: 172–73). For example, William Fitzhugh, who was considered a member of the aristocracy, was a longtime trader before becoming a planter. Others who created plantations, despite their backgrounds, soon joined this aristocracy.

As mentioned previously, the powerful individuals among the early settlers of Virginia and the Carolinas sought to emulate English life. English forms of government were quickly modified to suit local conditions, including planters' need to have greater control over their commercial interests than might be allowed if they had remained in England. They controlled the local political machinery and dominated the church to such an extent that bishops from England would not go there and regarded them with disdain (Klein 1971). As detailed previously, it is also clear that the local elite reproduced much of what they felt was important in English life, such as homes, furniture, music, and other cultural forms.

Slavery and tobacco cultivation provided the foundation of wealth for Virginia's elite enslavers. In particular, the Tidewater and, to some extent, Piedmont regions of Virginia were devoted to tobacco growing. Unfortunately for the planters, by the late 1700s the soil was largely depleted. While Edward Ruffin and others advocated crop rotation to replenish the soil, many large holdings became dramatically less productive. Farming in the Shenandoah Valley and other lands that butted up to the Blue Ridge Mountains tended not to be organized around tobacco; on plantations in this region where enslaved people worked, multicropping was the norm.

According to some sources, as the land became less prosperous and the population of enslaved persons grew, Virginia and other northerly slaveholding states entered a new trade: They sold enslaved people into the Deep South (for example, Louisiana and Georgia) to meet the ever-increasing need for labor to service cotton (Tadman 1989). Virginia's role in this has led some to call it a "breeder state," that is, a state where the number of enslaved people was purposely increased with the goal of selling offspring to master-enslavers in other states. This practice created great fear among the enslaved population, as they always stood at risk of being sold south, particularly if they worked in the fields. Countering this view is the work of Robert Fogel (1989), an economist who argues that most of the movement of enslaved people west and south was of those who accompanied their migrating owners. He also argues that the sale of enslaved people accounted for only 1 percent of the revenues for Virginia and Maryland and therefore it cannot be argued that these were breeder states. This debate regarding the role of slavery in Virginia in the fifty years leading up to the Civil War is noteworthy, since different contemporary sites in Virginia make reference to the sale of enslaved Virginians to the Deep South and suggest that Virginia should be understood as a breeder state.

Virginia and War

Virginia's roles in the Civil and Revolutionary Wars, as the state tourism board today likes to emphasize, cannot be understated. Virginia was the home of numerous Revolutionary War patriots who fought to free the colonies from Britain's rule. The Virginian Patrick Henry gave his "Give me liberty or give me death" speech to the Virginia Convention in Richmond. Richard Henry Lee (ancestor of Robert E. Lee) carried Virginia's resolution that "these united colonies are, and of a right out to be, free and independent states" to the Continental Congress in 1776. Thomas Jefferson drafted and signed the Declaration of Independence; other Virginia signers were Carter Braxton, Benjamin Harrison, Richard Henry Lee, Francis Lightfoot Lee, Thomas Nelson Jr., and George Wythe. When it came to setting up a new government and constitution, Virginians were likewise in the forefront. George Washington presided over the Philadelphia convention convened in 1787 for the "sole purpose of revising the Articles of Confederation" (Dabney 1971: 169). Other prominent Virginians in attendance included Edmund Randolph, governor of the state, and James Madison, who became known as the "father of the Constitution." Jefferson also drafted the Constitution, and George Mason drafted the Declaration of Rights, which became the blueprint for the Bill of Rights (Dabney 1971). Not all of these Virginians supported the ratification of the Constitution during the Virginia Convention of 1788, however; foremost against ratification were Patrick Henry, George Mason, James Monroe, and William Grayson.

In the Civil War, Virginia also played a central role. The state both contained the capital of the Confederacy, Richmond, and was bordered immediately on the east by Washington, D.C., the capital of the Union. This location meant that Virginia saw fighting for the full four years of the Civil War, unlike most other states. According to the National Park Service's Civil War Sites Advisory Commission (1997), Virginia saw 123 battles, the most of all the states that saw fighting. The state suffered a great deal of physical destruction during the war. Furthermore, Virginia split into two parts—Virginia and West Virginia—over the issue of secession from the Union; in many cases relatives did indeed fight relatives, as white families split over loyalty to the South or the North. The central role played by Virginia in the Civil War is not lost on tourism and public parks agencies. Virginia has a very extensive Civil War History Trail for visitors to explore, including major and minor battle locations, Civil War reenactments, and museums. This focus on the Civil War, along with the framing of Virginia as the birthplace of American democracy, provides the primary lens through which Virginia is interpreted.

The History of Georgia

As early as the 1500s the Spanish established a number of missions in the region that was to become Georgia. The British began to settle parts of the region between Florida and South Carolina in 1717, and as the century progressed, leaders in philanthropy, religion, economics, and imperialism joined together to exclude Native Americans and create the English colony of Georgia in the 1730s. The initial intention had been to establish a colony that would act as a buffer zone between English South Carolina and the Spanish in Florida as well as to produce silk, wine, and olive oil for Britain. Georgia was one of the few mainland colonies to receive direct government support, and the king and his ministers expected commercial and strategic advantages for the British Empire. However, the colony lacked the experience, the proper climate, and the capital base required to produce these goods. Blacks and slavery were initially excluded from the colony, though slavery was legally embraced in 1752 (Gray and Wood 1976; Coleman 1977; Bartley 1983; Wood 1984). The colony remained the poorest and smallest of the king's North American possessions, and it continually faced economic hardships.

The first two governors of the Royal Province of Georgia saw Georgia's problems as threefold and interrelated: lack of wealth, lack of people, and lack of defenses. By 1741, though more than twenty-eight hundred settlers had migrated to the colony, its population was less than half that size (Bartley 1983: 3), as its people drifted to other colonies to seek their fortunes. Dispossessing the Native Americans of their land and turning to the enslavement of Africans as the solution to their problem, the white colonists transformed Georgia into a prosperous economy based on enslaved labor, all for the benefit of whites. In addition to the English, other groups of Europeans arrived at various times, including German Protestants, Moravians, Scotch Highlanders, Scotch Irish from Ireland, and small numbers from Italy, Switzerland, and Wales. A number of English Jews arrived in 1833. Whites also came from elsewhere in the American colonies, including a group of New England Puritans in 1750, and others from Virginia and the

Carolinas in the 1760s. By 1750 there were two thousand whites and over a thousand Blacks in the colony.

When Governor Wright arrived in 1760 Georgia comprised roughly one million settled acres. During Wright's tenure over six million additional acres were added. Wright himself soon owned eleven plantations and 523 enslaved persons. Lieutenant Governor John Graham held twenty-five thousand acres and at least 240 enslaved persons; the president of the governor's appointed council, James Habersham, "held ten thousand acres and 198 enslaved persons." By 1773 sixty people owned twenty-five hundred acres or more, with twenty individuals holding in excess of five thousand acres. "These sixty men, who comprised fewer than 5 percent of landowners, held more than 50 percent of Georgia's slave population" (ibid.: 6).

Land was taken from Native Americans in a variety of ways, including warfare, outright theft, and legally sanctioned treaties, many of dubious nature (for instance, the signing of the Treaty of New Echota by the Cherokee Major Ridge, which gave away Cherokee land and led to the Trail of Tears). The stolen land was then distributed to whites in various ways, involving the headright system and lotteries.

The importation of enslaved Africans provided white Georgians with the labor that allowed them to clear, plant, and harvest the land taken from the Indians. Slavery was made official in 1752. By 1761 Georgia's population was around ten thousand, with over six thousand whites in that number. By 1773 Georgia's population was estimated at thirty-three thousand (45 percent of whom were enslaved), a figure almost ten times what it had been two decades earlier. By 1776 Georgia had forty thousand people, with slightly more whites than Blacks. Increased production of rice, indigo, and other crops provided the colony with foreign exchange and generated among some families a burgeoning prosperity. The consolidation and expansion of the cotton economy further fueled the population increase. Georgia could claim 162,000 people (36.5 percent of whom were enslaved) by 1800, and 340,000 (44 percent of whom were enslaved) by 1820 (Coleman 1977: 10).

Until the abolition of the international trade in human chattel in 1808, many of the enslaved Africans brought to Georgia came via the West Indies. After that date the enslaved population increased primarily though self-reproduction and legal and illegal imports from other states. By the 1850s there were 381,682 enslaved people, well over 40 percent of the state's population. By 1860 the total population of Georgia reached 1,057,286, with 591,550 whites and 465,698 Blacks, of whom 462,198 were enslaved (ibid.: 413; Smith 1985: 104). The vast majority of those enslaved worked in agriculture, most in cotton. There were over thirty-five thousand enslaved persons in rice cultivation, and about twenty thousand enslaved persons in towns.

In 1860 the legally free population of color numbered thirty-five hundred, one of the smallest of any state in the Union (Berlin 1974). Free Blacks were highly concentrated geographically, with over 50 percent living in fifteen counties, including those within which the cities of Savannah and Augusta were located (Sweat 1957).

Among Georgia's whites there was substantial inequality, both between those who owned enslaved persons and those who did not and within each of those two groups. The 1850 census indicated that 38,456 families owned enslaved persons. The overwhelming majority of enslavers were white men; there were some white women owners, and a tiny number who were people of color (see Sweat 1957). The vast majority (97 percent) owned twenty-nine or fewer enslaved persons, but 1,154 (3 percent) enslaved more than thirty. Most white Georgians lived in rural areas; less than 10 percent of the total population of the state lived in towns in the 1850s, and only Savannah, Augusta, Columbus, and Macon had populations over three thousand (Wallenstein 1987: 10). Savannah was the largest town in Georgia, with a population of 14,622 in 1850 (ibid.: 12).

Crops

When the colony of Georgia was first established, it consisted of a thin strip of land along the coast. The expansion of Georgia brought farms to the rich uplands, where farmers could grow profitable cash crops. Early sources of income were lumber, cattle, and trade with Indians. By the 1790s white settlers had poured in from Virginia and North Carolina and established tobacco culture, which quickly transformed Augusta into a thriving tobacco center and sharply increased Georgia's exports. Soon, however, cotton virtually drove tobacco from the fields. Cotton had always been around but did not become profitable until Eli Whitney perfected the cotton gin in 1793. In 1791 Georgia produced a thousand bales of cotton; in 1801 the figure was twenty thousand bales. Soon it produced more cotton than anywhere else in the world. After 1840 Georgia fell behind the booming cotton states in the West in absolute terms, but its production continued to rise. The rapid increase in cotton cultivation had tightened the grip of slavery, which some whites had hoped was a dying institution, upon the South.

Georgia led the south in manufacture of cotton goods and was second only to Virginia in the manufacture of woolen articles in 1860. Many of the cotton mills were in Savannah. In 1848 there were eighteen mills employing 544 people, including enslaved and free people of color (Johnson 1980: 420). By 1850 Georgia marketed approximately half a million bales, and in 1860 more than seven hundred thousand.

As the white population grew, so too did differences in class position, nationality, and religion. The number of wealthy master-enslavers grew substantially, and by the last decades of slavery "the top one-fifth owned 90.1 percent" of enslaved persons (Wallenstein 1987: 1). Planters would commonly leave their estates and live elsewhere, either locally or heading to Savannah or Charleston, South Carolina, for short periods, especially during the heat and disease of the summer (Smith 1985: 7), leaving the plantations to continue operations in their absence.

Among the wealthiest master-enslavers in Georgia were Thomas Butler and Charles Manigault (the latter spent much time in South Carolina). Stretching across the Low Country of South Carolina and Georgia, the Manigaults and the Heywards, both enslaving families, were intricately intermarried (Dusinberre 1996: 31). Gabriel Manigault, the son of a Huguenot immigrant, founded the family fortune, and when he died in 1781 he was reputed to be the wealthiest man in the commonwealth (ibid.). Charles Manigault, Gabriel's grandson, married one of the Heyward daughters and consolidated his fortunes in several plantations. Heyward has the dubious distinction of being the largest master-enslaver in U.S. history—Phillips calls him "the greatest of all rice planters" (1966: 249). At his death in 1851 Heyward left an estate that included 2,087 enslaved persons (ibid.: 250). Manigault was one of the richest enslavers—he had several huge plantations, hundreds of enslaved persons, and elegant mansions in South Carolina and Philadelphia (Dusinberre 1996).

Close by one of the Manigaults' plantations were the Butler family's holdings. Major Pierce Butler, who was born in Ireland, arrived in America in 1774. He married a rice plantation heiress and built a "handsome home on St. Simons Island and finally a great house in Philadelphia where he died in 1822" (Phillips 1963: 259). At his death his grandsons, Pierce and John, jointly inherited his estate. In the mid-nineteenth century they had a large plantation on Butler's Island, and other properties on St. Simons Island and elsewhere. Pierce Butler was responsible for the largest sale of enslaved persons in U.S. history—in 1859 he sold 429 enslaved persons at the slave market in Savannah, Georgia, offering a silver dollar by way of compensation to individuals in the families that he separated. The sale was spurred by his gambling debts, which had to be paid off (Phillips 1966: 251; Dusinberre 1996).

While these planters lived lavish lifestyles, those they enslaved clearly lived quite meagerly. On the subject of providing food for enslaved children, Roswell King Jr., the overseer at Pierce Butler's plantation, boasted that "it cost less than two cents each per week, in giving them a feed of okra soup with pork, or a little molasses or hominy, or small rice" (Smith 1985: 117). (Roswell King Sr. later moved north in Georgia, where he founded the town of Roswell.) In addition to having great social power, these master-enslavers also wielded substantial political power. For example, in the 1849–50 legislative session, four-fifths of all senators and representatives were master-enslavers, and a majority held substantial numbers of enslaved persons. Similar statistics can be cited for the judiciary (Wallenstein 1987: 21).

The economic expansion of Georgia produced the most immense profits for massive master-enslavers, but there was also considerable success for small farmers, who shared in the wealth and racialized status. Cotton "democratized" slavery among whites, at least for a time: "Ordinary white farmers could, and did, acquire slaves and even plantations'" (Bartley 1983). Yeoman farmers numerically dominated the state; they usually lived simply in rural areas, with sufficient goods and with little sophistication. The towns had a small artisan class, which matched the yeomanry in social and economic standing. Both artisans and yeoman farmers usually had little formal education but were independent-minded and valued their vote at election time. These people were the backbone of much of Georgia's development. Rich whites dominated, "but political reality required subtlety rather than brute force. Accordingly, planters established bonds of reciprocity and paternalism with white citizens of lesser means" (Reidy 1992: 48–49). Despite the imbalance of economic and political power, powerless whites always had a stake in the system. The privilege of white skin was the hegemonic apparatus that cemented the enslavement of Africans. Poor whites' adherence to the system was in part facilitated by the fact that cotton production was easier for small farmers to undertake than production of tobacco or rice.

While certain forms of honor, decency, and gentility carried a high premium within the planter elite, such attitudes were in short supply when it came to their treatment of the enslaved. Master-enslavers and mistress-enslavers, and whites in general, were brutal and violent, malicious and aggressive, exploitative and oppressive. This was most commonly the case in regard to the productive and reproductive labor extracted from the enslaved. And it saw frequent expression in sexual violence and rape (Giddings 1984; Jones 1986). A prime example is David Dickson, who in 1840 owned six enslaved persons; by 1849 he owned fifty-three enslaved persons and 2,010 acres of land, making him one of the largest enslavers in the county. He was also one of the county's most distinguished gentlemen, according to local (white) opinion (Leslie 1995: 36). Amanda, his daughter of mixed origins, became infamous when, after both the end of legal slavery and a long fight with his white family, she inherited his substantial fortune. Her mother was Julia Frances Lewis Dickson, one of the persons that Dickson enslaved. When Amanda was born in 1849, David Dickson was forty years old and Julia was thirteen (ibid.: 37). It was not a romantic relationship; Amanda was the product of rape. This is a frequently cited case because of the legal battle and the huge amount of money involved. There were, of course, many other rapes about which we hear very little.

Like elite white enslavers across the South, those in Georgia drew on racism to garner the support of economically poor whites who did not participate as owners in the system of slavery. As in other places, they wove together religious, political, and emerging scientific justifications for the enslavement of African Americans and the forced expulsion of Native Americans. The civil society developed by elite white Georgians was similar to that in Virginia, with the following exceptions. As noted earlier, the seasonal absence of master-enslavers was common in the coastal region. Second, there was more variance in the cultural groups that made up the dominant white grouping than in Virginia. Like elites in Virginia, however, elites in Georgia also created grand homes and lived lavish lifestyles. They also were heavily involved in government and were therefore able to guide Georgia to secede in 1862.

Georgia was the fifth state to declare secession from the Union. According to numerous sources, the Union government's strategy was to cut the South into manageable, isolated pieces. By doing so, it would be able to restrict the movement of supplies to the Confederate army. In this light, Georgia was very important—it was the second largest state east of the Mississippi and had the most developed railroad system in the Confederacy. A total of 125,000 white Georgians participated as Confederate soldiers in the

Civil War (Bragg 1987; Bryan 1953). Several notable generals and military leaders also came from Georgia, not to mention Alexander H. Stephens, a lawyer, state senator, and vice president of the Confederacy.

Union naval forces blockaded ports such as Darien and Brunswick without much resistance; however, it took a battle at Fort Pulaski to win control of Savannah in April 1862. Savannah was a very important Confederate city, but unlike others was virtually untouched by the fighting and destruction for a good portion of the war. Land battles didn't begin in Georgia until September 1863 (the Battle of Chickamauga). Of course, the Civil War event imprinted on Georgia's memory is Sherman's "March to the Sea." General William Tecumseh Sherman was made commander of the military division of Mississippi in 1864 and was ordered by Ulysses S. Grant to "create havoc and destruction of all resources that would be beneficial to the enemy." It was these orders that led to the widespread destruction that Sherman's army perpetrated as it moved through Georgia, destroying crops, buildings, storage facilities, and railroad lines. With 18,797 troops, Sherman began the Atlanta campaign on May 4, 1864, and captured the city on September 1, 1864. From Atlanta, which Sherman fortified and used as a military encampment, he began his advance to the coast. Sherman left Atlanta with sixty thousand troops in November 1864; he set fire to munitions factories, railroad yards, clothing mills, and any other targets believed to be a resource for the Confederacy. The fires that he started frequently burned out of control and spread to other buildings. (Such a scene, of course, was immortalized in *Gone with the Wind*.) The March to the Sea took a month; Savannah surrendered to Sherman two days before Christmas 1864. The army "marched to Savannah in two huge columns, leaving devastation in their wake" (Briskman 1998). Sherman's march is the Civil War event most commemorated in Georgia's history.

Another important aspect of the state's history is the Andersonville prisoner-of-war camp. This infamous camp, built in June 1864, housed a total of forty-five thousand Union prisoners over the course of the war, of whom thirteen thousand died of conditions related to contaminated water, severe overcrowding, and lack of adequate food and shelter. At one time there were thirty-two thousand Union POWs, while the camp was designed to hold thirteen thousand.

As in Virginia, the history of the Civil War is publicly marked in Georgia, and a substantial part of the tourism industry is related to tracing the Civil War. There are, for example, tours specifically designed for those who are interested in Civil War history, including tours of the Andersonville camp.

Louisiana

Native Americans had lived in the area that was to become Louisiana for at least ten thousand years before they set eyes on a European. They had diversified into various ethnic and linguistic groups, had developed several extensive civilizations, and numbered at least thirteen thousand by the start of the 1700s.

The first Europeans to arrive in the area came down the Mississippi River. In 1542 Luis de Moscoso de Alvarado floated past what was to become the site of New Orleans (Wilds, DuFour, and Cowan 1996: 6). It was over one hundred years later, in 1682, that the vast area that became Louisiana was given its name by René-Robert Cavelier, Sieur de La Salle, who came down the Mississippi River from Canada and claimed the land for his king, Louis XIV (ibid.: 7). The French increased their activities, taking footholds in various places and giving French names to the territories. Some of the names were of officials, and others were of private investors, as with Antoine Crozat, who gained a commercial monopoly on the colony in 1712 and was reputed to be the richest man in France (ibid.: 9).

The following decades saw competition and conflict among the French, Spanish, and British seeking a foothold along the mighty river, and the territory changed hands several times. The French had it from the 1680s through 1762; during this time they founded Natchitoches in 1714 and made New Orleans a center of activity in 1718. In 1762 Louisiana was ceded to the Spanish, who returned it to France in 1800. The United States, after many of its residents settled there, becoming the majority in many parts, eventually purchased Louisiana in 1803 for $15 million. Congress created the Territory of Orleans in 1804, which approximates the boundaries of the present state of Louisiana (ibid.: 28).

After initial settlement by the French, the following decades saw the arrival of various ethnic groups, who came either voluntarily or by force. For instance, France sent various reprobates from the correction houses, along with untrained soldiers. Other less savory individuals joined them, including many who called themselves gentlemen. The period 1718–28 saw the arrival of Germans and the importation of human cargo in the form of Africans. Acadians arrived after being expelled from Canada by the British;

some drifted in during the 1760s, and in 1785 a group of fifteen hundred arrived from France, where they had settled some fifteen years earlier. More Germans arrived in the 1820s, along with a varied assortment of other ethnicities, including Irish and Portuguese. Spain subsidized the arrival of two thousand or so Canary Islanders, the largest group of Spanish-speakers to enter the colony at this time (ibid.: 25). The population increased slowly under the French, rose dramatically under the Spanish, and continued to do so under the Americans.

The first enslaved Africans were imported into Louisiana from the West Indies in 1712 (ibid.: 61). The colony saw the first large importation of human cargo in 1719, when 451 Africans arrived on the ships *Aurore* and *Duc de Maine*. Another 1,500 arrived in the following two years. They were central to the survival of the colony, doing its backbreaking work, clearing the wilderness, and bringing important agricultural knowledge for planting rice and indigo (ibid.: 23). Thereafter, along with importations of human cargo, the domestic trade in human chattel played a large role in Louisiana's economy, with many thousands sent to the state from Virginia and South Carolina (Tadman 1989). There were large slave markets in New Orleans and in Alexandria. Pirates also played their part: "Lafitte sold as many as four hundred in a day at his hangout on Grand Terre" (Wilds, DuFour, and Cowan 1996: 63).

During the 1700s the population of Louisiana varied widely. During both the French and Spanish periods, people of African origins consistently outnumbered whites. For example, in 1788, "only twenty years after Spain assumed full control, Louisiana's population had mushroomed to 39,410, which included 19,737 free persons and 20,673 slaves" (ibid.: 25). This general ratio held throughout the next seventy-five years; throughout this period, people of African descent were always in the majority. The ratio of Blacks to whites during Louisiana's early history was much different from that in the other two states under consideration. The balance shifted slightly during the 1800s under U.S. rule; however, the proportion of Black residents, both enslaved and free, remained much higher in Louisiana than in the other two states.

During the occupation by the French, the Spanish, and even the Americans, legally free people of color in Louisiana were able to avail themselves in far greater measure of opportunities denied their counterparts elsewhere in the United States. More mixed-ancestry people were manumitted by their white fathers than elsewhere, or were manumitted for service. And they had responsibilities denied to legally free people of color elsewhere in the United States—the Spanish had militias consisting entirely of legally free people of color, and in many periods free people of color were called upon to apprehend fugitive enslaved people. In this way, Louisiana developed a unique system of manumission, combining French, Spanish, and English customs and regulations (Sterkx 1972: 118). The number of legally free people of color grew substantially over the decades, from 7,585 in 1810 (ibid.: 95) to 18,647 in 1860 (Foner 1970: 407, n. 1).

Many legally free people of color in Louisiana attained economic success, with the majority working in some skilled occupation (ibid.: 407). Most were in agriculture. For example, in colonial Louisiana "free coloreds were overseers for many white planters, and in New Orleans and other towns they were the tradesmen, the mechanics and the owners of small businesses" (ibid.: 416). Some acquired substantial amounts of property and wealth. Several became plantation owners and were as successful as Jean Baptiste Bienville, a "free Negro planter whose estate was valued at almost 14,000 pesos in 1802" (ibid.). At the end of the first decade of the nineteenth century, says Berlin, "no other Southern state had as large a class of free Negro planters as Louisiana, and no other Southern city had as active and as educated a free Negro professional elite as New Orleans" (1974: 130).

A small number among them reached levels of comfort that, in some cases, rivaled what prominent whites enjoyed. For example, in Iberville Parish in 1830, the largest number of enslaved persons held by a free person of color was forty-six. In St John the Baptist Parish, three people of color had fifty-two, forty-nine, and thirty-eight slaves, respectively (Sterkx 1972: 134). Also, Marie Thérèse Coincoin, whose Melrose Plantation is currently part of the Louisiana tourist infrastructure (and was visited for our project), owned over a hundred enslaved persons. This level of ownership by legally free people of color was quite rare, and overall the percentage of legally free people of color who owned enslaved persons was very small, less than 1 percent of all owners. Despite benefits of various kinds, legally free people of color were still seen as inferior to whites and were subject to many restrictions, particularly after the Americans took control.

Crops

Cotton had been grown in Louisiana since the 1740s, but as elsewhere, Whitney's cotton gin made it highly profitable. Substantial expansion of cotton cultivation began after 1795, and in the first several decades of the nineteenth century master-enslavers and their human property poured into the Mississippi Valley. Many Americans moving to Louisiana settled in the north of the state, which became one of nation's big cotton-producing regions. Cotton prices, which ranged from 22 to 44 cents per pound in 1801 to 33.9 cents in 1817, helped drive the pursuit of cotton (Malone 1992: 21). By the 1850s cotton production in Louisiana was surpassed only by Alabama and Mississippi.

Most enslaved labor in Louisiana in the 1820s worked in upland cotton, but a favorable sugar tariff in 1828 moved some cotton planters into sugar production. Sugar cane was introduced early in the territory's history. By the 1790s sugar cane was widely grown, and by 1803 there were at least eighty-one sugar plantations operating in Louisiana. The temperate climate and fertile soil of the Mississippi River delta was ideal for sugar's long cycle of cultivation. Dispossessing Native Americans of their land and enslaving Africans and African Americans for their labor provided the other necessities. By 1815 Louisiana was producing ten million pounds of sugar per year; this doubled to twenty million pounds by 1818 (ibid.). The explosion of sugar plantations continued over the next decades, and by 1830 there were 691 estates; by 1849 Louisiana surpassed all other states in sugar production (ibid.). In 1853 Louisiana produced almost fifty million pounds of sugar, and in 1860 cotton production was nearly eight hundred thousand bales, at four hundred pounds each (Wilds, DuFour, and Cowan 1996: 72).

The records for profits in sugar production brought with it another vital statistic: "For all of its inhabitants, Black and white, Louisiana was the deadliest state in the Union during most of the antebellum period, and the low-lying, semitropical sugar parishes were the most disease-prone in the state" (Malone 1992: 53). Yellow fever took over fifty thousand lives in New Orleans alone during the twenty years before the Civil War. A fatal epidemic in 1853 accounted for twelve thousand of these (Shugg 1939: 53).

In Louisiana in 1860, 71 percent of families did not own enslaved persons (ibid.: 24). Of those who did, in the antebellum period "three in five slaveholders had less than ten Negroes" (ibid.: 27). After them there was a middle class who "owned plantations of less than five hundred acres and from ten to forty-nine Negroes" (ibid.: 27). As with the two other states under consideration, there were more farms than plantations in Louisiana. For example, "in 1850, only about two in five agricultural holdings could be called plantations; of 13,422 properties, 4,205 raised over five bales of cotton and 1,558 had sugarhouses." By 1850 86 percent of Louisiana master-enslavers reported owning fewer than twenty enslaved persons, though probably no more than 70 percent of Louisiana's enslaved persons lived in such units (Malone 1992: 60). Large properties—that is, properties where fifty or more people were enslaved—became more prevalent in Louisiana in the 1850s. In 1860 48.4 percent of enslaved persons in the state lived in units of fifty or more (ibid.:65). Most planters found that units of fifty to one hundred were the most effective; if they had more than a hundred, they would start a different farm with a separate overseer. Where Louisiana differs from the other two states is in having more plantation units with larger numbers of people enslaved on them. In Virginia the median number of enslaved persons on a plantation in 1860 was 19.3; in Georgia it was 26.4 and in Louisiana 49.3 (Kolchin 1983: 244, table 5).

Most of the wealth and power in Louisiana, as in other southern states, was concentrated in the hands of a small group of planters and commercial and professional magnates. A small upper class had most of the wealth and controlled most of the commerce and plantation agriculture in Louisiana. Shugg indicates that "about one in thirty-seven families was a member of this powerful group" (1939: 27). He points out that "the sons and daughters of fifty families were each said to be worth more than $100,000, and of nearly a hundred more, over $50,000" (ibid.: 27–28). Louisiana had from half to three-quarters of all millionaires in the United States prior to the start of the Civil War. Louisiana was then much wealthier overall than either Virginia or Georgia. As with the other states, economic power gave rise to political power. Shugg argues that "together the planter and merchant, black belt [rural plantations] and city, ruled the state. While planters held the upper hand, filled many offices, and set the tone of public opinion, city lawyers occupied the larger share of offices, represented the merchants, and withal served their planting clients as well" (ibid.: 155).

Who were these powerful master-enslavers? One of them was John Burnside, who "on the eve of the Civil War owned six thousand acres of land and more than a thousand slaves, and was accounted one of the richest men in the South, worth two million dollars." Another was Duncan Kenner, a sugar planter, "one of the largest slaveholders in the South." Still another was Governor Paul Herbert, "a descendent of poor Cajuns, who won for himself a magnificent plantation and political honors" (ibid.: 32).

The rich, particularly the urban Creoles, enjoyed cultural tastes and patterns that were the envy of the nation. There was an established French opera (ibid.: 35), circuits of balls and Mardi Gras celebrations, Old World architecture in the city's homes, and "ceremonious Catholicism" (ibid.). French culture dominated for long periods, but Anglo culture increased its strength over time and transformed New Orleans into a "Protestant stronghold" in the later years before the Civil War (ibid.: 63).

Codes of conduct among the elite in Louisiana had much in common across the state; however, there were regional differences related to the ethnicity and language of the local population. In general, Anglo-Americans and their culture tended to be imposed (and often resisted). Creoles were dominant in the southern part of the state, including New Orleans; Cajun practices held sway in the southwestern region, and Anglo farmers dominated the northern sections of the state.

Gender ideology was strong, as was racism. Both served to suppress any challenge to white Anglo patriarchy. Poor whites did not directly express class hostility through organized resistance but did express race prejudice; the general feeling was that they might be poor, but they were free and had white-skin status. This entitled them to look down on Blacks with contempt. "Race prejudice, in other words, filled the void of class hatred" (Shugg 1939: 30).

In 1860 Louisiana's economy (which was wholly dependent on external markets) was producing impressive profits for its master-enslavers. Cotton and sugar prospects seemed boundless to the master-enslavers; rice production had increased, tobacco production had almost doubled, and towns were growing throughout the state (Malone 1992). This fact meant that, in general, Louisiana became involved in the Civil War with less fervor than states such as Virginia or Georgia. Shugg argues that "Louisiana, unlike South Carolina, was never a protagonist of Southern and State rights. The strongest economic and social ties bound this state to the nation" (157). However, wealthy master-enslavers were strongly in favor of secession, and they were joined by merchants and others with large economic interests. As the threat became one against not only the economic power of the master-enslavers but also the integrity and sovereignty of the state, other groups were brought in, many of them under tremendous political pressure. Shugg (1939: 169) argues that it was agitation by a minority—the "planting and commercial plutocracy" on behalf of "a slaveholding philosophy"—that took Louisiana out of the Union. Most people were "either opposed or indifferent to secession, but altogether helpless in any event to resist it" (ibid.: 169).

Louisiana sent a considerable number of men to war, most of them rank-and-file soldiers. Around fifty-six thousand white men marched to war—a number that was equal to "one seventh of the total white population, and embraced all white men between the ages of eighteen and forty-five" (ibid.: 170–71). However, only half of them volunteered—the rest became soldiers after the enactment of conscription. Louisiana also sent officers: Two of the Confederacy's eight full generals were from Louisiana; both P. G. T. Beauregard and Braxton Bragg had gone to West Point and fought in the Mexican War. Beauregard headed the men that began the war by opening fire on Fort Sumter in April 1861. Many thousands of white men who did not want to fight for the Confederacy fled to the swamps in the south of the state. At the same time "more than 24,000 Louisiana Blacks—more than from any other state—served with the Union army" (Wilds, DuFour, and Cowan 1996: 41). Interestingly, one of the North's premier military leaders, William T. Sherman, had been the superintendent of the Louisiana State Seminary of Learning in Pineville when the state left the Union. He resigned his position (ibid.: 42) and headed back to Ohio, where he eventually volunteered to act as a leader in the Union forces.

Louisiana suffered many casualties during the war. The North saw New Orleans as a vital strategic point, and the city "was captured by Farragut on the first of April, 1862, and garrisoned with troops under Butler the first of May." It then became the base from which the federal government "reconquered and reconstructed Louisiana" (Shugg 1939: 184). Shugg adds, "No state in the South, unless it be Virginia, South Carolina, or Georgia, suffered more than Louisiana" (ibid.: 191).

When the Civil War started, Louisiana had the second-highest per capita wealth in the nation, and its property was valued at $602 million in 1860 (Wilds, DuFour, and Cowan 1996: 63). Tremendous damage was done during the Civil War, and the "plantations were ruined" (Shugg 1939: 192); real property had lost two-thirds of its value, one-third of the land was no longer under cultivation, and two-fifths of sugarhouse machinery and farm implements had been destroyed. In general, sugar was hit worse than cotton. Shugg summarizes: "Of more than 1,200 large estates that harvested the cane of 1861, only 180 were struggling to get along in 1865" (ibid.: 193). In addition, the cities were also hard hit economically. In sum, when the war ended Louisiana had "less than half its former wealth" (ibid.: 194). By 1880 the value of its property was only $422 million, and the state was ranked thirty-seventh in per capita wealth out of a total of thirty-eight states (Wilds, DuFour, and Cowan 1996: 64).

At least 350,000 enslaved persons in Louisiana were emancipated by the end of the Civil War, and the majority of them continued working for their former master-enslavers. The federal government largely abandoned them; there was to be no forty acres and a mule. White supremacist organizations developed, and the following years and decades saw pervasive gratuitous violence against Blacks, including a number of massacres (Wilds, DuFour, and Cowan 1996: 50). As in the other states, Reconstruction was short-lived, and white southerners were given freedom to reinstitute wholesale racial oppression within several years of the end of the war.

As we demonstrate in later chapters, the sense that Louisiana suffered greatly during the Civil War is a potent, and commonly used, framing device at plantation museums in the state. While there is much less focus on specific battles of the Civil War in Louisiana than in the other two states, there is far greater emphasis there on the damage that the war did to the state. At the same time, there is a stronger focus on the ethnic diversity of Louisiana and on the "grand, romantic, and luxurious" civil society that flourished in the state. These foci have legitimate roots in Louisiana's history; however, we argue that the enslavement, resistance, and survival of people of African descent could be equally legitimate themes.

Conclusions

This chapter has provided an overview of some key social, economic, political, and cultural features of Virginia, Georgia, and Louisiana. While all three states were initially established as colonies by Europeans and eventually came to be dominated by the English, they were created and framed in different historical periods and were subject to the influence of different historical forces. These influences gave rise to structural, cultural, and ideological differences across the states in the course of their historical trajectories. Significant differences include the demographic ratios of whites and enslaved persons, the plantation crops cultivated, the distribution of class status among the white population, and the size and distribution of agricultural units of different kinds. Yet they share many features with regard to patterns of racialization—in particular, the centrality of enslaved African and African American labor in their growth, the plantation economy, and the formulation and elaboration of increasingly virulent ideologies of racism. And at the same time as the master-enslavers distanced themselves from what they saw as oppressive and autocratic political systems in Europe and embraced their own version of democracy, they continued to admire, revere, and imitate European cultural traditions.

What should be clear by this point is that for all three of the states the enslavement of people of African descent was foundational to economic and social life for the entire white population. Working-class whites did not benefit to the same degree as the master-enslaver class, who also controlled the political process, and some argue that the institution of slavery economically injured those whites who did not own enslaved persons. However, all whites participated in and took benefit from the white-skin privilege, which was one of the ideological bases of the entire system of slavery.

3 ⫼ Overview of Plantation Sites and Tourism

This chapter is divided into two sections. In the first section, we detail the variations in size and organizational structure of the plantation museum sites we visited. We also argue that there is a notable relationship between organizational structure and the rhetorical strategies most commonly employed. The second section of this chapter provides an introduction to plantation museums in general and describes the information that visitors generally learn on tours provided at these sites.

As we detail, tours overwhelmingly focus on aspects of antebellum white southern life that maintain a vision of the genteel, honorable South. This framing relies on the language of romance, wealth, honor, and the chastity of white southern women and is created through a focus on architecture, furniture, and accoutrements such as paintings, chandeliers, candelabras, dishes, and so on, which all demonstrate the taste and refinement of the white elite; an additional and equally important focus is on the codes of conduct that guided family life and social interaction. This discourse is highly gendered, and we argue that such gendering provides a foundation for asserting the morality of the white enslaving class.

This chapter, then, provides a grounding in the way that the bulk of plantation museums present themselves to visitors. In chapter 6 we discuss sites that offer separate tours providing information about slavery and those enslaved; however, at such sites the main tours continue to have the foci that we describe in detail here. Such framing, we argue, is part of a racialized regime of representation that presents the preemancipation South as genteel, honorable, and gracious and generally disregards the fact that the enslavement of human beings provided the foundation that the society of white enslavers rested upon.

Size and the Public/Private Distinction

We include several types of buildings under our definition of a plantation museum site. The first type, and the one most frequently covered in this book, is a site based on physical structures that were originally used as part of plantation complexes during the period of slavery. This includes the so-called big house or mansion along with a range of outbuildings (kitchens, coach houses, overseer's houses, barns, smokehouses, cribs for storing crops, slave cabins, and garden structures such as wells, gazebos, or teahouses). The buildings may be either on the original plantation grounds or at a different location. A variation of this is what we call composite sites, in which a number of original buildings are brought from different locations to construct a so-called typical plantation. The Antebellum Plantation in Georgia and the Rural Life Museum in Louisiana are examples of this variation. A second type of structure is a mansion or townhouse that was built in a town relatively close to the plantation and was occupied by master-enslavers and/or their families in summer (to avoid heat and disease) or for special holiday celebrations. These can be found in such places as New Orleans, Louisiana; Natchez, Mississippi; Savannah, Georgia; and Charleston, South Carolina. Each of these different types of sites works to represent the life of the whites who occupied them in the colonial, federal, or antebellum period.

Throughout our work we have explored plantations of widely varying sizes and organizational structures. Historically, a plantation was distinguished from a farm by the size of the enslaved population; scholars use the term *plantation* to refer to an agricultural unit with twenty or more enslaved people. It was believed that when a farmer could command the labor of twenty enslaved people, he would be able to cease laboring on the farm himself and instead become a planter, that is, someone who managed, planned, and oversaw the workings of the plantation (Vlach 1991). A few of the sites we include, most commonly town or city homes that were owned by master-enslavers and regularly inhabited by them, did not have twenty-plus resident enslaved people. However, there were usually enslaved people present in such houses, the wealth of the owner was based on enslaved labor, and these buildings are some of the most frequently visited sites in the tourist infrastructure of the New South, since they are located in easily accessible urban areas.

Most plantations that are open to the public today as tourist sites are places where substantially more than twenty people were enslaved. Most sites, in fact, had at least forty enslaved people; this speaks to the classed nature of historic preservation. These are sites that elites have identified as worthy of saving, since an elite view of history favors their own activities as those that shaped the nation or region. The activities of the remaining 95 percent of the population have generally not been considered worthy of representation.

In addition to noting the predominance of very large plantations among those sites organized as plantation museums, we have categorized them by organizational structure (that is, ownership and management). We identify six types of structure; three are variations on public ownership, and three are differing forms of private ownership (see table). First let us consider public sites. The term *public* refers to sites that are substantially funded by public monies and staffed by government employees. There are three levels at which such sites are organized: city, county, or regional; state; and federal. There are relatively few sites that are the property of a city, county, regional, or even state government. Out of our whole sample, only 17 percent are managed by city, county, or state governments. (See the appendix for a listing of sites.) There are also very few sites organized and run by the federal government, via the National Park Service; Virginia has more National Park Service sites than the other two states. Only 4 percent of all plantation sites in our study are run by federal government agencies, but they should not be overlooked, since our analysis suggests that, in general, public sites are more likely to incorporate a greater amount of substantive information on slavery than privately organized sites (we take up this point in chapter 9).

Private sites, like public ones, can be differentiated along several lines. For instance, private sites can be owned by a single family and used as a moneymaking enterprise. In all of the plantation sites we visited that fit in this category, the owners occupied the home. In these cases, decisions about what to include in the tours are generally made either by members of the family or in some cases by persons they have hired to manage this part of their business. We have defined these sites as private for-profit sites. In general, these and bed-and-breakfast sites are the least likely to incorporate information regarding the institution of slavery.

Table 1

	Public			Private		
	State	Local/ County	Federal	Private Nonprofit	Private For-Profit	Bed-and-Breakfast
Virginia*	1	7	5	28	9	4
Georgia	4	4	0	14	2	5
Louisiana	3	2	0	9	13	12

*Two sites, Colonial Williamsburg and Carter's Grove, are a combination of for-profit and nonprofit.

The bed-and-breakfast (B&B) sites, which are more common in Louisiana and Georgia, are intriguing, since people come specifically to stay in an old plantation home. That is, these sites advertise themselves not as historic homes but specifically as plantations, and their promotional literature emphasizes the ability of visitors to "step back in time" and experience "the grandeur of the South as it used to be." The brochure for Tezcuco Plantation in Louisiana states: "Listed on the National Register of Historic Places, Tezcuco offers a unique glimpse of life during its antebellum days. . . . Guides in antebellum dress will take you back to an era of bygone days." Chretien Point Plantation, also in Louisiana, provides an elaborate description of what a B&B visitor might experience:

> Truly Chretien Point is the most charming and livable of all Louisiana Plantation homes. When one imagines the elegance of Louisiana plantation life, one is visioning Chretien Point. History, serenity, location and size epitomize the treasure that is Chretien Point. . . . The setting is cool and serene with beautiful live oaks, pecan, cherry, pine, mimosa and tallow trees gracing the grounds adding to the unique elegance of the plantation.

Georgia also has its share of B&B lodgings organized around plantation motifs. These include White Columns Plantation, Inn Scarlett's Footsteps, and the Grand Wisteria Plantation Bed-and-Breakfast. The advertising from these sites references *Gone with the Wind*, beauty, grandeur, and the notion of returning to bygone days.

As part of this experience, most B&Bs surround visitors with antiques. For instance, Edgewood Plantation in Virginia is described this way in a brochure on James River plantations: "Edgewood's Gothic Revival archi-

tecture features 7,000 square feet of antiques, charm, romance & history."
Antiques are presented as signs of wealth and taste—attributes that visitors
may partake of, at least vicariously, by visiting the sites.

The final category of private ownership is that of a private nonprofit
foundation. Nonprofit status is not uncommon, though as the table above
demonstrates, it is more frequently found in Virginia than in the other two
states. Such foundations are chartered as tax-exempt groups to raise money
and obtain grants for the restoration and running of one or several homes.
For instance, the Association for the Preservation of Virginia Antiquities
was founded in 1899 "with the purpose of rescuing Jamestown from decay."
Today the association operates thirty-four historic properties in Virginia,
including a number of plantation museums. An important national organization is the National Trust for Historic Preservation. The trust owns and
runs twenty historic sites across the country; of these, four are in Virginia
(three of which are plantation museum sites) and one, a plantation museum,
in Louisiana. There are other groups that organize such sites—for instance,
the Colonial Dames Society (formed in 1890) owns and operates more than
forty historic sites across the United States and assists in managing another
forty-odd sites; included in both categories are plantation museums such as
Gunston Hall in Virginia. The United Daughters of the Confederacy also
owns and administers a number of sites (including several plantation museums), all of them in the South.

Other nonprofit foundations have developed specifically around one
property. Examples of this include the Mount Vernon Ladies' Association
in Virginia, and the River Road Historical Society in Louisiana (which operates Destrehan Plantation). These organizations tend to be staffed primarily by volunteers, mostly middle-aged or elderly white southern women.
This is a crucial point, because the whiteness of the volunteer staff reflects
the racialized nature of the interests attached to these house museums. In
those cases where Black women have worked as docents, they have been,
with one exception, paid staff, not volunteers. This fact itself arises from
and reflects racialized inequalities in the United States, for as the literature
on philanthropic organizations and volunteering shows (Tiehen 2000;
Hodgkinson et al. 1992), women are much more likely to volunteer than
men, and people of color are less likely than whites to volunteer. However,
some evidence shows that when socioeconomic status is controlled for,
African Americans participate more than whites and other racial minorities
(Auslander and Litwin 1998; Palsi and Korn 1989). In the case of house

museums, however, West (1999) argues that their genesis was with the preservation movements organized by white women, who legitimated their move into the public realm by focusing on the topic of domesticity.

While the degree to which representational strategies varied by organizational structure was not dramatic, there is a stronger pattern of distribution of representational patterns by state, as can be seen in the accompanying table. Symbolic annihilation is clearly the dominant strategy employed at plantation museum sites (55.7 percent of all sites: 42.6 percent in Virginia, 72.4 percent in Georgia, and 61.5 percent in Louisiana). What is interesting here is that there is a significant difference in the proportion of Louisiana and Georgia sites that employ symbolic annihilation compared to Virginia sites. Plantation museums in Georgia and Louisiana are much more likely to simply not discuss enslavement or discuss it very minimally. Sites in Virginia are apparently more likely to discuss enslavement; however, they are also more likely to engage in trivialization.

Those sites listed as primarily employing trivialization and deflection (27.0 percent of all sites: 35.2 percent in Virginia, 17.2 percent in Georgia, and 23.1 percent in Louisiana) use tropes and imagery such as that of the happy/grateful slave or good owner. All such sites also use symbolic annihilation; that is, there are only a limited number of mentions of the enslaved, and at least one or more of these mentions trivializes slavery and/or positions the enslaver as a good owner. Note that together, symbolic annihilation and trivialization account for approximately 83 percent of sites across the three states. Also, a number of the sites that use segregation or relative incorporation as a primary strategy use trivialization and deflection as well (the figures are noted in the table); their use of this secondary strategy is discussed in chapters 6 and 7, respectively.

The category of in-between sites (9.8 percent of the total) serves to recognize that some sites are no longer trapped in symbolic annihilation and trivialization as their primary organizing strategies but also have not reached relative incorporation. They do a somewhat better job incorporating issues of enslavement and work to complicate the dominant narrative to some extent while at the same time relying on trivialization and euphemisms. For instance, Melrose Plantation in Louisiana was the home of a family that came from the union of an enslaved Black woman and her white owner, who legally freed her and the children they had together. (They also had children together after she was legally freed.) This woman and her descendants

Table 2

	Symbolic Annihilation	Trivialization/ Deflection*	Segregation	In-Between	Relative Incorporation	Total
Virginia	23	19	4 (2 also use deflection)	5	3 (1 also uses deflection)	54
Georgia	21	5	1 (also uses deflection)	2	0	29
Louisiana	24	9	0	5	1	39
Total	67	34	5	12	4	122
% of all sites	55.7%	27.0%	4.1%	9.8%	3.3%	100%

*Sites listed in this category also engaged in symbolic annihilation and trivialization.

then went on to enslave a substantial number of other people, whose labor they appropriated to secure their wealth. While the words *slave* and *slavery* were used around twenty times during each of the tours we took at Melrose, the frequency is misleading, because the story told at this plantation museum is one of wealth and of the successes of the family; there is very little here that addresses the experience of enslaved people.

A very different example of an in-between site is Gunston Hall in Virginia. Gunston Hall has undergone somewhat of a transformation over the last several years. When we first visited the site in 1997 and 1998, the site was characterized by symbolic annihilation. Also present was trivialization through images of happy/grateful slaves. Gunston Hall had a "slave life" tour, but it was offered relatively infrequently. Since then the site has incorporated a discussion of enslavement into its framing much more consistently, though we found on recent tours that this varies according to which docent is conducting the tour. It is clearly beyond the more exclusionary categories, but not quite to relative incorporation.

In addition to considering representational distribution by state, we also considered distribution by organizational status. What is apparent from this analysis is that no for-profit sites (except the mixed sites of Colonial Williamsburg and Carter's Grove) went beyond symbolic annihilation and trivialization. While some of the public sites still are organized through symbolic annihilation and trivialization, they include among their number sites that are either segregated or relatively incorporated. For instance, the two Georgia sites that we identify as either in-between or segregated are both public sites. In Virginia, the Carlyle House, which we define as engaging in relative incorporation, is regionally owned and administered. In Louisiana, one of the in-between sites, Kent Plantation Home, is a state site. So there is some slight preponderance of public sites among the categories of segregation, in-between, and relative incorporation. However, at public sites one is also quite likely to find stories that trivialize enslavement (for instance, the Alexander Stephens site in Georgia, and Chatham Manor and Arlington in Virginia). Symbolic annihilation was most likely to be found at private sites, particularly bed-and-breakfasts, though sites run by private nonprofit organizations varied considerably—some are in the in-between stage (such as Destrehan Plantation in Louisiana and the Archibald Smith Plantation House in Georgia, which is owned by the city of Roswell and managed by a nonprofit), while others fully engage in symbolic annihilation and trivialization. For-profit sites, then, are the least likely to incorporate any meaningful discussion of enslavement and are the most likely to put a very positive and valorizing spin on the white enslaving families who inhabited the plantations' mansions.

In some cases, we believe, this reflects the perceived interests of the visitors, as sites that are privately owned and exist to offer a "respite from the stressful world" would appear to have much less impetus to incorporate a potentially troubling discussion of slavery. It also reflects the amount of oversight that sites experience, as privately owned sites are far less likely to have external committees specifying particular issues that must be addressed. When asked, docents at private for-profit sites have volunteered that they believe white visitors come because they want to see pretty things and that these visitors aren't really interested in the topic of slavery or the lives of those who were enslaved. Additionally, smaller sites, even some public ones, have indicated that they have not incorporated information on slavery because none of the staff has taken it on as an area of interest. That is, these sites rely on individual staff to map out their own areas of interest and incorporate their research into the site's interpretation. This point reemphasizes how important the race, gender, and geographical origins of the docent actually are. If no individual picks slavery as his or her topic of interest, it is unlikely that it will be covered. These factors all affect the framing of the sites and the relative lack of incorporation of a discussion of slavery. They lead instead to the whitewashed image of the South presented at these sites.

Plantation Tours Overview

The vast majority of the plantations we visited, whether public or private, provide a common format for visitors. First, most plantation museums have a gift shop where guests can purchase site-specific and general southern memorabilia. Next, most sites include an introductory video designed to teach visitors about the history and layout of the property. Third, approximately 90 percent of sites offer tours led by a docent; the remaining number have self-guided tours. In most cases, guided tours cover only the contents of the main house and possibly the kitchen. Outbuildings and gardens are generally toured without the guidance of a docent. Through such standardization of format the representations—and silences—around slavery become taken for granted. It also demonstrates the ways that later plantation museum sites emulated their predecessors (such as Mount Vernon and Colonial Williamsburg).

Gift Shops

Gift shops are a staple in the plantation museum industry, offering a selection of southern memorabilia as varied as books, dolls, crockery, and wall hangings. The massive gift shop at Nottoway Plantation highlights the science of commercial planning: Visitors are required to enter the site through the gift shop and are thus encouraged to make a purchase. The Oak Alley Plantation gift shop is extensively stocked, like many gift shops throughout the three states, though Oak Alley's includes the only on-site ATM that we saw at these sites. At a couple of sites the gift shops are in what used to be slave cabins. This is apparently the case at the National Park Service's Arlington House, the home of Robert E. Lee; when Professor Eichstedt asked, after leaving the main house, if there were any such cabins left, a docent said that the gift shop was housed in a former slave cabin, but interestingly, there was no notation on the building to indicate that this was the case.

Examples of site-specific merchandise include coffee mugs with the logo or image of the plantation, books on the plantation or on the enslaver, dishes with the family crest or the same design found on the family's china, cookbooks from the plantation, magnets with images of the plantation, and postcards depicting various rooms in the house (at most sites photography inside the homes is prohibited) and aerial views of the estate. Some sites also

Sign outside Loyd Hall Plantation, Louisiana.

have books that describe the site and/or the white inhabitants in detail or provide copies of personal papers of the enslavers. For instance, at the Mary Washington House in Fredericksburg, Virginia, visitors can buy a copy of her will. In addition to trinkets that specify the plantation itself, most plantations also sell general books and videos about either plantation homes (such as *Virginia Plantation Homes* or *Louisiana's Plantation Homes: The Grace and Grandeur*), the South in general, or southern cooking. Also to be found at numerous sites are copies of the Confederate Articles of Secession and books that detail the Civil War and the roles of various famous southern generals and politicians, as well as Confederate flags and other Confederate paraphernalia. Many sites also have paper dolls of Confederate heroes and/or children from the pre–Civil War South. A large proportion of the sites that sell Confederate artifacts also sell the flags and hats of the Union.

A significant number of sites also have "negritude memorabilia," or portrayals of Blacks that replicate stereotypical images. For example, Berkeley Plantation in Virginia sells "mammy bells," with a gingham cloth skirt over the bell and the handle painted to represent a black face with white eyes and a red mouth, all topped off with a kerchief. Apparently these bells are designed so that one can signal a servant, who in this case is presented as a Black woman. Such memorabilia is much more common in Louisiana than in Virginia or Georgia; at least 30 percent of Louisiana sites sell cookie jars or salt-and-pepper shakers that feature stereotypical images of Black men and women. Such objects are found at Tezcuco Plantation in Louisiana— ironically, in a gift shop that adjoins the River Road African American Museum (discussed in chapter 8), which educates visitors about the experience of enslavement. Some sites also have figurines of grinning Black children eating watermelon or playing with cotton bales. Many sites sell postcards depicting a range of outrageous and offensive stereotypical images, such as black children with wild hair and rolling eyes about to be eaten by crocodiles. These images compound the problematic representations of African Americans found in other locations at the sites.

Videos

Introductory videos, which range from eight to thirty minutes, provide aerial views of the mansion, sweeping landscape images, and a general overview of life on the plantation as the site depicts it. A point stressed in most videos is the social or political importance of the wealthy or famous white people who lived at and/or visited the site. The narration in the videos also often stresses that the plantation should be understood as a significant site of national cultural remembrance. For instance, the narrator's voice in the video at Stratford Hall in Virginia says, referring to Virginia and presumably Stratford, "For Americans, this is sacred ground," "Most of the ideas that make America great came from this small corner of America," and, at the end of the video, "By coming to Stratford, the home of the Lees, you will come to understand in a personal way the unique character of men and women who changed the course of America." Videos rarely deviate too greatly from the framing that is presented during tours. It is rare to see any images of African Americans in them, though, as in the Stratford Hall video, voices speaking in "Black dialect" are overheard, usually discussing chores or the labor they are performing.

Black memorabilia for sale at Tezcuco Plantation in 2000. The presence and sale of such images reinforce stereotypical racialized understandings of African Americans among white consumers.

Tours

Most sites (90 percent) also include a guided tour, usually led by a white woman docent between the ages of thirty-five and seventy. The vast majority of the docents we encountered were born or raised in the South, as we deduced from biographical information they volunteered about themselves and from their accents. There were instances where white docents were younger or male, but this was uncommon. There was also a very small number of instances when an African American woman docent led the tour. We saw Black women docents leading white-centric tours at Oak Alley Plantation, Greenwood Butler, Loyd Hall, and Melrose Plantation in Louisiana, and at Stratford Hall in Virginia. These docents usually presented the same script and did not provide additional or different information than their white counterparts. The exception to this was at Callaway Plantation in Georgia, where the African American tour guide discussed how visitors looked to her to provide additional information on the experience of enslaved African Americans.

Across the sites we toured, very few staff dressed in period clothing, though there were exceptions. At the same time period clothing is very common in the illustrations in leaflets handed out to describe plantations and also on the front covers of videos, especially those for sale at the sites. For example, period clothing is worn by people—especially attractive young white women, representing the image of the southern belle, dressed in extravagant gowns in front of white-columned houses—in the leaflet for the Cannonball House (Macon, Georgia), that for the Archibald Smith Plantation Home (Roswell, Georgia), and the general leaflet on Roswell, Georgia. Presumably these images are produced to attract white visitors to the area. While it was not common to see staff wearing period costumes, there were more white women dressed in fancy hoop-skirt gowns in Louisiana and Georgia than in Virginia. Even when so attired, docents almost never engaged in first-person interpretation. The few exceptions to this pattern were a state-run site in Virginia, Pope's Creek Plantation (the birthplace of George Washington), and very large sites such as Colonial Williamsburg and Carter's Grove in Virginia. It should be noted that at Pope's Creek, the docents dressed in working clothes and not in grand antebellum style.

There are also sites that offer self-guided tours, often with the help of maps and audiocassette players. At some sites the narration is done from a first-person perspective. For example, when Professor Small visited the Rosedown Plantation House in St. Francisville, Louisiana, visitors received a map, and at various locations there were speakers and cassette players that provided a short narration by a person from the period of slavery, such as the plantation doctor, the plantation cook, or the owner. At other sites, such as Montpelier in Virginia, most of the recorded narration is provided in third-person style—that is, the narrator describes the locations and artifacts from the position of some external observer. Still other sites had no guided tour; instead visitors receive a map of the property and then read text plaques placed along the way. This type of self-guided tour was found at Virginia's Red Hill, Georgia's Jarrell Plantation, and the Antebellum Plantation at Stone Mountain when Professor Eichstedt visited in 2001.

Both docent-guided and self-guided tours tend to focus on several primary topics: architecture, furniture and antiques, wealth and/or status of the white family who owned the house, elite family lifestyles, famous (white) people who lived or visited there, and/or famous events such as the Revolutionary or Civil War. Much of this is presented via a larger framing of the "genteel South," including a focus on hospitality, generosity, and romance.

Guided tours run anywhere from twenty-five to seventy-five minutes. Usually a visitor, after paying the entrance fee, is directed to wait in the visitor center (if the site has one) and view the plantation's introductory video. If there isn't a video, or after the video has finished, the guest is told to proceed to the front porch of the main house to wait for the next tour to begin. Tours usually start on the front porch of the house, where the discussion of the plantation as a crop-producing site and a beginning discussion of the architecture takes place. While standing on the porch the docent can point to various outside features (such as fields) and explain the house's location in relation to the closest waterway. For many years travel by water was quicker and safer than travel by land; therefore the most elaborate architecture commonly faced the waterway, from which guests would arrive. Additionally, the location of the nearest waterway was vital to most plantations, as they relied on boats to move their product from plantation to market. Rivers were also an important method of moving enslaved people into interior regions of both Louisiana and Georgia, though this was mentioned at only one site.

After explaining some of the basic information about the location of the plantation, tours usually move into the main house. Docents lead visitors from room to room and explain various features of construction, the uses of various rooms, decorative additions, and how numerous artifacts fit into the daily life of the master-enslaver's family. These pieces all add together to create a vision of an elite, genteel South.

Architecture and Interiors: Beauty and Grace

Every white-centric site that we visited discusses the architecture and exterior elements of the plantations. Many of them discuss the construction of the main buildings, with a particular focus on the house occupied by the enslaver and his or her family. The architectural features of the buildings, the original method of construction, and any subsequent changes are usually noted in full detail. During tours, the docents make reference to the kitchen and whether or not it was still standing; in most cases kitchens were built a short distance from the main house. Where the plantation museum site still maintains a significant garden, this is also described, sometimes in detailed printed guides visitors use for self-guided garden and outbuilding tours.

The interiors of the houses are described in great detail. The description includes the walls and ceilings, the doorways and windows, and the specific furnishings in rooms such as bedrooms, bathrooms, living rooms, larders, and closets. The staff also explain the particulars of paint, wallpaper, and plaster used to embellish the homes and add to their magnificence.

ARCHITECTURE   While all sites discuss architecture, the majority of sites advertise themselves in relation to their structural design. For instance, the Hay House, in Macon, Georgia, describes its architecture as "a renaissance treasure against a southern backdrop." From Mississippi's Springfield Plantation brochure comes the following:

> Built in 1786–1791 during the Spanish Domination of West Florida (Mississippi) by Thomas Marston Green, Jr., wealthy planter from Virginia[,] SPRINGFIELD is one of the first houses in America to have a full colonnade across the entire façade and is the first such mansion to be built in the Mississippi Valley.

Unlike most early buildings, which we are told do not "retain their original interiors," "SPRINGFIELD remains almost entirely original, including magnificent Georgia-Adams-Federal woodwork and mantels hand carved in Virginia in the 18th century." It continues: "SPRINGFIELD, still a working plantation after more than two centuries, offers the beauty, elegance, and romance of the Colonial South during the colorful days of Spanish rule."

From Virginia, Sherwood Forest Plantation brochures note:

> The house, circa 1730, is Virginia Tidewater in architectural design, and is the longest frame dwelling in America. . . . Greek Revival features, added by the President [John Tyler] and his young bride, Julia Gardiner, are evidenced by lattice, columns, and pilasters on the porches while cornices, mantles and carved medallions grace the formal rooms of the house.

Through visiting these sites one can become quite familiar with different architectural styles, such as Colonial, Federal, and Greek Revival. When we toured the sites, we were taught about the emphasis in Federal style on symmetry and balance. This is explained to visitors through the discussion of doorways that don't lead anywhere but are provided for visual balance, or through noting how houses were constructed with an even number of rooms on either side of a central hall to provide structural balance. Greek Revival homes, we are told, are noteworthy for the large columns on the front of the house.

The architectural details provided can be quite substantial. A good example comes from the leaflet produced by the town of Milledgeville, Baldwin County, Georgia, to describe the history and range of buildings in its historic district. On the town's Historic District Tour visitors have the opportunity to view a range of styles, including

> "Gothic," "Carpenter Gothic," "Gothic Revival," "Traditional brick," "Plantation Plain with later additions of porch, columns and pediment," "Federal with regional adaptations," "Federal Transitional with later additions of Greek Revival," "Federal with Victorian additions," "Federal/Early Greek Revival," "Milledgeville Federal," "Milledgeville Federal with Victorian additions," "Late Georgian, Greek Revival portico," "Neo-Classical," "Classical re-revival," "Victorian," "English Tudor," "Greek Revival," "New England Folk," "Georgian with a variety of Victorian additions," "High Federal with Italianate details," "High Victorian," "Victorian with Second Empire Clock Tower."

Each building noted on the map is presented with a drawing of the house and an address.

Visitors are also educated about construction processes and materials, including the unique features of regional architecture, and sometimes details of buildings used to house the enslaved. Details cover the diverse array of materials used to construct these impressive mansions and the effort and cost that went into locating, purchasing, and transporting the materials. For example, at Madewood Plantation in Louisiana researchers learned that there are six hundred thousand bricks in the house and that all of them were made on the property. At Belle Grove in Virginia docents explained that the marble found in the main parlor and dining room is from the Massachusetts quarry that is the source of the marble used to construct the United States Capitol. Guides regularly discuss the massive beams that support the home as well as the thickness of the walls. In Virginia docents frequently explained to us that many homes in the state were constructed out of pine and then provided with faux finishes that made them appear to be built of oak or other more expensive woods. Many homes have large columns constructed of brick that were then covered with plaster and painted to look as if they were made of marble or another stone. In Georgia, we were told at the Hay House in Macon how expensive the Italianate home was to build, $120,000, while most houses built in the area were Greek Revival homes that usually cost $15,000–$20,000 to construct. In Louisiana we repeatedly heard how horsehair (or hair from another animal), mud, and moss were blended to make bousillage, the material used to construct the walls of many Louisiana plantation homes. All sites, if applicable, stress the ways that the owners tried to make the homes appear more elaborate by applying faux finishes to simulate the look of more expensive woods or marble.

Staircases and their construction appear to be of particular interest on plantation home tours. This may be because staircases can be pointed to as a thing of beauty and grace. For instance, the staff at Shirley Plantation remarked that the staircase appears to be "flying" or "hanging"—attaching the staircase to only one wall and using a series of wrought-iron straps and rods to suspend it causes this visual effect. At several sites, the docents explained how a stairway's banister is made out of one continuous piece of wood. We also were told how specific staircases were used in different films about the Old South. For instance, at Chretien Point in Louisiana, both visitors who attend the guided tours and those who read the promotional brochures learn that the rear hall contains "the fabulous staircase copied for 'Tara' in the movie *Gone with the Wind*." Finally, we were also asked at numerous plantations to note the difference in step width between many of these older staircases and those of the contemporary era. At some locations this difference in width is attributed to the smaller feet of "people from the past, who were much smaller," contrasted with the larger feet of people today.

The discussion of architecture is often framed by tour guides in ways that highlight the ingenuity of the master-enslavers. Staff detail how owners built their houses with doors across the hallway from each other not just for visual symmetry but also to allow cooling summer breezes to flow through the house. The public is educated about the development of windows that reached to the floor and could be opened so that they served as doors through which people could access the balconies and porches.

From our tours we learned that while Virginia plantation homes made good use of cellars, homes in Louisiana almost never had such spaces because the ground was swampy and saturated with water. So in Louisiana we saw examples of the use of large olive jars placed into the earthen floor as storage units that kept food cool. At another site in Virginia we were educated about the ingenuity of the owner who installed a hollow space under the wooden flooring near the doors to pull cooler air into the home. Docents taught us that residents of plantations didn't waste space—halls were used as rooms where people danced and slept. We also heard conflicting stories about the presence or absence of closets. For instance, most homes, we were told, did not have closets built into them. The majority of the staff at these sites said that closets were absent because they would be counted as an additional room for taxation purposes. Other sites highlighted the presence of closets at their sites and noted that they were installed specifically to demonstrate the owners' wealth. A few other sites, however, informed us that closets were not taxed and that such an explanation for the lack of closets is myth.

As part of these tours visitors learn about the extensive reconstruction efforts that either private owners or private or public entities have engaged in to restore the site to as authentic a representation as possible. While clearly this relates to the interior decorations, it also refers to the architecture. At numerous sites the guides describe how stairways have been ripped out, porches removed or rebuilt, and indoor plumbing removed to return the house to the state it was in during the period that is being interpreted. At a number of sites parts of the walls have been pulled away so that visitors can see the type of construction used to build the house and so that the docents can discuss how construction practices differ from those employed today. How many remaining panes of glass are original to the house was also detailed. These panes would then be pointed out as we moved through the house; their age being notable because of the way that glass settles over time, a process that causes multiple ripples throughout the glass.

Much of the framing of these discussions of house structure allows docents to emphasize the master-enslaver's ingenuity or note how a particular plantation owner may have employed the same architect or craftsperson as another homeowner who was more famous. For instance, at Belle Grove in Virginia docents recounted how Isaac Hite married Nelly Madison of Montpelier in 1783 and "acquired a 483-acre tract of land that would become Belle Grove." Hite wrote to James Madison and asked after the architect who built Monticello, since he was much impressed with the architecture. The guide suggested that we note the "Jeffersonian influences" as we moved through the house. Architectural discussions also stress the quality of homes (and furniture) constructed in the past. Architectural discussions, then, provide a primary focus and grounding for tours.

PLASTER AND WOODWORK   Another important piece of plantation museum tours is the discussion of moldings on the walls and ceilings, frieze work, wallpaper, and any other such decorations. The discussion of medallions (plaster decorations usually attached to the ceiling or above doorways) and other moldings are used as an occasion to note the wealth and taste of the owners. Such decorations are discussed in all forms of media surrounding the plantation museums. For instance, a promotional brochure for Tezcuco, in Louisiana, states:

> Antebellum Greek Revival Architecture had reached its height of interior embellishment during the period Tezcuco was built. The ceiling cornices and center rosettes in this house have marvelously executed plaster detail and all the interior doors and window sashes still have the original false graining (called "faux bois" by the French) which was painstakingly painted by hand. The galleries are adorned with wrought iron in the traditional grapevine pattern.

A brochure for Kenmore Plantation in Virginia describes the house and plasterwork in the following way:

> Here, a skilled plaster man created three of the most beautiful rooms of the colonial period. Legend says that George Washington, who often visited Kenmore, even helped design the plaster decorations. The 18th century craftsmanship would be embellished in the years after the Civil War. The splendid work seen today is a rare example of the artistry of two centuries, combined in great beauty and harmony.

Plaster work throughout the sites, then, is presented as an important facet of what makes a home "notable." Staff regularly note how they are able to determine what rooms were likely used for what purposes by the absence or presence of certain types of decoration. For instance, rooms that were private, which were generally only entered by the family (and enslaved people), were believed to be plain and without elaborate frieze or medallion work. Conversely, rooms with a great deal of medallion work are believed to be more public spaces—spaces by which visitors, both in the past and in the present, were to be impressed.

PAINTINGS AND CANDELABRAS   Other features discussed by docents are accoutrements such as paintings, chandeliers, and candelabras. Most privately operated plantations had a number of paintings on display; some had drawings or photographs. These paintings are usually of plantation owners from the period under interpretation—for example, Thomas Butler of Georgia and Charles Manigault of South Carolina and Georgia. However, if the site is privately owned and occupied, then there are often paintings of subse-

Medallion at Loyd Hall plantation. Frieze work,
medallions, wallpaper, and other ornamental displays of
wealth are often described in detail during plantation
museum tours.

quent and current owners as well. Many sites contained portraits of Confederate heroes such as Alexander H. Stephens, Robert E. Lee, and
Stonewall Jackson. Bulloch Hall, in Roswell, Georgia, has paintings of
Martha (Mittie) Bulloch Roosevelt, mother of President Theodore Roosevelt. These paintings often provide the opportunity to discuss the web of
kinship that tied together elite families of the South or to draw attention
to the fact that a not particularly well known white family was in fact related
to the Lees, Washingtons, Jeffersons, or other famous political and social
leaders. At Shirley Plantation we learned that the second wife of Charles
Carter gave birth to Anne Hill Carter, who became the mother of Robert
E. Lee.

   The discussion of paintings also allowed tour guides to share knowledge
of painting techniques from the past. At Shirley Plantation we learned of
the artist John Walston, who was rumored to have painted bodies on can-
vases while in Boston and then added the specific head for a painting when
he visited a plantation. This allowed the artist to produce a higher volume
of portraits; it also accounts for why a number of portraits show people with

very similar-looking bodies. Sometimes the more famous people are fictional, as in the case of Scarlett O'Hara and Rhett Butler, whose paintings and pictures adorn the walls of the now defunct Road to Tara Museum in the Antebellum Plantation complex at Stone Mountain, Georgia.

A few sites advertise themselves, at least in part, in relation to the extensive collection of paintings they hold. The owner of Chelsea Plantation, for instance, says that Chelsea (located in the Tidewater region of Virginia) is the "largest repository of eighteenth-century portraiture," though most of its portraits are on loan to Colonial Williamsburg. In Louisiana, both Oaklawn Plantation and Oakley Plantation, which is advertised as the "Audubon site," display a major collection of Audubon paintings and prints. Both portraiture and Audubon's paintings of birds fall into classical definitions of fine art. Contrasted to fine art is the genre of painting known as primitive art, which is highlighted in several sites in Louisiana. For instance, both Melrose and Beaufort Plantations have numerous paintings by the famed primitive artist Clementine Hunter (see chapter 5 for how Hunter was discussed).

In addition to paintings, some sites display maps from the time period under interpretation. These maps indicate not only the inhabitants' sense of space but also the extent of the owner's land holdings. In some cases a map is considered particularly noteworthy because it was drawn by a famous person such as George Washington, who worked as a surveyor early on.

Many sites also display chandeliers and candelabras that may have been original to the house. These accessories are almost invariably designed to display the taste and wealth of the person who lived at the site. In some cases, these accoutrements are designed to display the taste and wealth of the current owners. For instance, Oaklawn Plantation, which was the home of Mike Foster, governor of Louisiana, in the mid-1980s and again in the 1990s, contains numerous examples of chandeliers, candelabras, and other paraphernalia designed to highlight the status of the governor. On the tour, Professor Eichstedt and her graduate student assistant, Katherine Huffstutter, were told to expect it to be a "big ooh and ahh day" as they saw the governor's various holdings. The docent, a white woman in her early fifties who was wearing period dress, told us that the walls were sixteen to twenty inches of solid brick and that the ceilings were fifteen feet high. She also explained that the home was completed in 1837 and that it was built by slaves (this was one of four mentions of slaves on the tour). She noted that the owner who lived here after the Civil War found it "impossible to get help to run the plantation" and sold the plantation to a New York company that used the land to plant sugar cane; the house itself stood empty and neglected until a young steamboat captain named Barbour, who showed "lots of courage, vision, and determination," set about restoring the home in the early 1900s. After a few more transfers of ownership the plantation was purchased by Mike Foster in 1985. After we were informed of the history of the house, we proceeded through a typical tour where furniture, accoutrements, and possessions were explained. Included on the tour were the following: a hand-blown gas-operated glass chandelier from Venice (one of only three in the world); a two-hundred-year-old tapestry depicting a garden in Versailles; a mantel made from black and gold marble from the Alps; a collection of Fabergé eggs (including one purchased in 1999); a Louis XIV desk that had been owned and used by Napoleon; a chair from Napoleon's castle; Wedgwood ware and cranberry glass; one of the "South's most complete collections of Audubon prints"; a "very old chandelier—one of the oldest," made of pierced bronze, that "came from a castle in Europe"; an extensive carved duck collection; a two-hundred-year-old French Baccarat crystal chandelier that we were told we "must imagine how beautiful it is when lit"; very rare Belgian black marble; vases from the 1840s; Louis XIV mirrors; a soup urn from the 1740s; emu-egg purses; a Waterford crystal collection; consoles from 1804 and 1815; Venetian hutches from the 1600s; hand-carved Italian chairs from the 1830s; a Louis XIV "bull cabinet" made out of ebony and inlaid with tortoiseshell; "unicorn" chairs; an 1830 sideboard that the docent explained is also called a huntboard because when the men were out hunting the "women stayed home to have sandwiches and drinks ready for them"; and numerous paintings and prints. In this case, as in many others, these objects, especially those that are rare and very expensive, were highlighted and discussed in depth.

FURNITURE   Another primary focus of the plantation tours is the furnishings. Furnishings, like fancy plasterwork and accoutrements, are presented as a sign of taste and of wealth. Staff at the sites pay particular attention to pieces that were owned and used by the family that is being interpreted. However, if few pieces were actually owned by the family under discussion, docents are very likely to mention that the furniture includes expensive "period pieces" and that the staff of the site worked to ensure that the pieces on display are from the appropriate era. If the maker of the piece is considered a famous artisan, that fact is noted.

Additionally, visitors are told detailed stories at many sites about how the group or individual responsible for the restoration of the plantation made special efforts to obtain original furniture. These discussions sometimes note the luck of the organization but more often than not cite the hard work of some in obtaining the furniture and the charity of others in donating it. As we noted above, particularly noteworthy is furniture that is original to the home and that can be linked to a famous person. One of the most striking examples of the importance of making links between furnishings on display and famous people in Virginia can be found at Chatham Manor, a National Park Service site. One room is designated the "morning room" and has a number of portraits of the home's owners and several pieces of furniture. One of the pieces of furniture is a large wingback chair with a cushion on it. The text next to the chair asserts:

> The wingback chair, in front of you, dates to late 1700's. A circular hole cut into the bottom of the seat identifies it as having been a chamber chair. According to family tradition, George Washington, the Marquis de Lafayette, James Madison, James Monroe, Washington Irving, and Robert E. Lee all used this chair.

This chamber chair is on display because a number of Revolutionary and Civil War heroes and other famous individuals all used it to defecate. What is not addressed, either in relation to this chair or in relation to chamber pots (except at two sites out of all of those we visited), is whose job it was to empty the chamber pots; instead the focus is on the novelty of having to go to the bathroom in one of these devices. This detail always captures the interest (and horror) of children on the tours.

It is important not to downplay the significance of furniture for these sites or their visitors. Since much of the tour guides' discussion (at least 30 percent) is dedicated to the antique status of various pieces of furniture, we must assume that antiques are a major draw for visitors. Additional evidence to back up this supposition is provided by the numerous comments overheard throughout our tours of the sites in which other visitors specifically asked about the history of particular pieces of furniture. While furniture and other accessories provide the vehicle to demonstrate the wealth and taste of master-enslavers, other material artifacts such as dishes, tools, and kitchen utensils provide a way to discuss both the wealth of owners and the creativity displayed by people living in the eighteenth or nineteenth century. What is noteworthy is that in only a few cases is that ingenuity attributed either to those who were enslaved or to free Africans and African Americans.

Because it is not specified, it seems that the ingenuity is to be attributed to the white owners and not to those who performed the labor. Instead, at some sites we were explicitly told that the staff "knows" that certain furniture was built on the plantation by servants because "of its crude nature." This belies the fact that many sites have furniture created by master craftsmen who were enslaved and whom the owner leased out to other whites.

DISHES, TOOLS, AND KITCHEN UTENSILS   At approximately three-quarters of the plantation sites china or flatware is displayed, either on the dining room table or in china cabinets. If the dishes were original to the family or from a famous maker, such as Wedgwood, this was noted. If not, it was usually explained that the displayed china or dishware reflects a pattern seen on shards of pottery found on the plantation. Dishes, it was noted at several sites, were used to display wealth. At one site, when the visitors entered the dining room the docent pointed out that all the bowls were turned upside down on the table and asked us what we thought was the reason for this practice. One white woman visitor suggested that it was to keep flies off the bowls. While the docent agreed that turning the bowls over would keep flies off, she said that the practice enabled guests who ate at the table to see the mark of the artisan who made the dinnerware. This was, the docent suggested, the same as the contemporary practice of having visible designer labels or logos on clothes.

Unlike dishes, most tools and utensils were designed not to signal status but to be functional. Therefore, except in the case of such items as tea caddies, ceiling fans, or bell systems for calling servants, most functional utensils are displayed in the less public spaces of the home, such as bedrooms (where one finds chamber pots, heating pans for the beds, shaving kits, and an occasional washtub) or the kitchen. Where tea caddies exist, they are almost always pointed out, because being able to purchase tea was a sign of wealth. Tea caddies were crafted out of fine wood and are today expensive antiques. When discussing them, docents usually noted that the tea caddy would be locked and the key held by the mistress of the house, since tea was quite expensive. This piece of furniture, then, while technically functional, is represented primarily as an antique. Other functional items, such as kitchen utensils, are discussed in terms of their uses, not their antique status.

Kitchen utensils are discussed in approximately 95 percent of all tours. The collections of kitchen utensils under discussion at these sites are quite extensive. For instance, at most sites kitchen utensils on display include

Fire screens, portraits, mantels, and furniture are often
the focus of plantation tours. Across all the sites studied,
furniture alone is mentioned thirty-one times as often as
enslaved people.

Dutch ovens, spider pans (frying pans with legs), toasters that are flipped by
the cook's toe to ensure that both sides of the bread are browned, waffle
irons, mortars and pestles, butter-making churns, wooden blocks on which
beaten biscuits are said to have been made, apple presses, and so on. Dried
or drying herbs are often hung from ceiling beams, sugar cones from which
sugar would be scraped are displayed, and representations of the types of
foods that might have been used as raw ingredients are on view. Overall,
tools discussed by docents provide some entry into understanding how the
foods the plantocracy ate were made or preserved. What is missing from

most sites is a sustained dialogue about who performed the labor that made possible the lifestyle of the master-enslavers. Instead, as we note below, much discussion of material artifacts provides the basis to elaborate on such things as elite family lifestyles.

ELITE FAMILY LIFESTYLES   Almost every white-centric site discusses the details of the everyday life of the master-enslaver's family and the relationships between family members and famous individuals, events such as the Revolutionary War and Civil War, or local politics. If appropriate, staff discuss famous people whom the family knew and who visited the plantation home. The tropes used to highlight these issues vary across the states. For example, in Virginia, which frames itself as the "birthplace of democracy," the primary focus is on the men who participated in the framing of the United States' system of government. The Shirley Plantation brochure, for instance, notes, "Since colonial times, Shirley has been a well known center of hospitality. The Hills and Carters entertained the Harrisons, Byrds, Lees, Washingtons, Tylers, and other prominent Virginians." In Georgia, famous men and events such as General Sherman's "March to the Sea" are highlighted. However, in Georgia the most common famous "event" is the movie *Gone with the Wind*. References are made throughout the state to Margaret Mitchell, the author of the novel, or to the host of fictional characters and the real-life actors who played them. Interestingly, the movie's characters stand in for real-life famous people, and in the collective myth of Georgia, they often take on a life of grandeur, glory, romance, and tragedy that amounts to something larger than the events of real life. In Louisiana too, wealth, grandeur, affluence, and opulence are highlighted; and the veneration and aggrandizement of wealth are all the more accentuated by comparing the unique richness and wealth of the state's master-enslavers in the antebellum decades—there were more millionaires on one road in this state than in the rest of the country, it is said—with the extent and depth of deprivation, loss, and calamity ushered in by the Civil War. At the same time, we also have a far greater emphasis on the ethnic differences between segments of the population—here, Anglos, Creoles of mixed French and African ancestry, and Cajuns—than in any other state we visited. These ethnic differences come out clearly when one visits, say, the Oakley Plantation at the Audubon State Historic Park, the Laura Plantation, and the Acadian Village.

Grandeur, wealth, and refinement of taste are primarily highlighted through the discussion of the furniture and accoutrements that we noted above, but also important is a discussion of consumption patterns and the leisure activities of the enslaving class. For instance, staff almost always detail what plantation owners and their guests ate. Curators at many sites have set up the dining rooms so that the china and silver are displayed for visitors. At a significant number of sites, plastic examples of food that might have been served are also on view. These settings provide the occasion to discuss when and what the master-enslavers and their guests ate. Visitors learn that the largest meal of the day was dinner and that it was served between two and four o'clock in the afternoon. Docents explain that the dinner experience usually lasted at least two hours and consisted of multiple courses. Children rarely, if ever, ate with adults, and certainly not if guests were present. The exception to this was that when young women were considered old enough to wed (ages twelve through sixteen), they were invited to the table, where they could be introduced to guests.

At approximately 97 percent of all sites, the leisure pursuits the master-enslavers engaged in are explained in detail. For instance, we learn that music was a favorite pastime, and many tour guides indicate that "girls were expected to play to entertain the family and guests." Many sites also have card tables set up with a game in process. Both the card-playing abilities and ingenuity of owners are explained. At 80 percent of sites that had card displays the docent asked the visitors what looked different about the cards from those we see today. The answer (provided by either a visitor or the docent) was that the cards did not have printed numbers. This was always used as an occasion to note how those players had to be quick enough to figure out the number on the card without having it printed for them. Dancing was also a passion for the enslaving class. Here architecture and leisure blend together as staff explain that hallways were at that time designed not only to facilitate the movement of breezes through the house but also so that dances could be held in them. At sites in Virginia we are also taught how the Virginia reel can be better understood if we know that this was a dance to be performed in central hallways, not in grand ballrooms.

Through the discussion of leisure time the gendered nature of social life in the preemancipation South is elucidated. Like other attributes of southern life, the extent to which this is discussed varies from state to state. For instance, in Virginia, while there is discussion of the gendered nature of household labor and the fact that white women did most of the interior decorating, much of this is framed through narratives of famous white male leaders. Dolly Madison's famed hospitality is linked with James Madison's political activities; likewise, Julia Gardiner's decoration of Tyler's Sherwood Forest and her love of music are linked with her support of her husband's presidency and the fact that she instituted the playing of the song "Hail to the Chief" while she was First Lady. In contrast, at least 70 percent of Louisiana and Georgia sites engage in very heavy gendering that acts as an anchor for a discussion of family and social life. Docents note that there were separate rooms for women and men and that after dinner the men would settle down to smoke cigars, play cards, and talk politics while the women would retire to another room. What exactly the women were doing in this other room is rarely noted. The exception to this was at Tezcuco Plantation in Louisiana, where a white woman in full southern-belle regalia showed the visitors the gentlemen's parlor and said that ladies couldn't stay there because "ladies, our ears are too delicate." She then winked and said that she was "sure the older ladies drank their own whisky and smoked their own cigars."

Gendering in a few cases was highlighted by the exception to the rule. For instance, at two sites in Louisiana white women tour guides told stories of white women who had lived in the house and who had violated the gendered rules of conduct. On Professors Small and Eichstedt's separate visits to Chretien Point Plantation in Louisiana, the docent told stories of a white woman named Felicité who owned the plantation at one time. Felicité, whom the docent described as the "first liberated woman," "wore britches, rode astride [a horse], smoked, and played poker with men." The guide explained that Felicité increased her land holdings from five thousand acres to ten thousand and the number of enslaved people from one hundred to five hundred. At Montpelier in Virginia the mistress-enslaver was noted for holding salons where interesting thinkers and literary people gathered. It was noted that her salons were quite the event and were places where women and men spoke about politics together. Again, the story was told with an air of awe—here was a woman who broke with some of the period's public expectations concerning women.

These transgressions of male space by independent women serve to highlight the very gendered, and rigidly controlled, nature of social and familial life. What is intriguing is that the ways these transgressions are told suggests that the criteria of equal opportunity for women today are being read back into the past, so that while male contemporaries of these women likely would have viewed them with derision, disdain, and/or alarm, the women's actions are seen through today's lens of equal opportunity as desirable and laudable. These women are presented as being ahead of their time for challenging the boundaries that constrained them such a long time ago.

Another fact of gendered plantation life that a predominately female staff explain is how many of these white women died in childbirth. Visitors find out that a great many of the master-enslavers on these plantations, especially large plantations, had more than one wife over the course of their lives. This was because the first wife, with very few exceptions, had died giving birth. This information is often given in far more detail in leaflets and booklets handed out or sold at the sites. For example, at Bulloch Hall in Roswell, a forty-page booklet that is available for purchase provides detailed overviews of the history of the Bullochs, related families, and the hall itself. In this book readers learn that James Bulloch, who came from Glasgow, Scotland, in 1729, had a total of four wives. Tour guides also regularly mentioned the survival rate of the master-enslaver's white children. Through this discussion of the deaths of the white children, visitors are told that boys and girls were unlikely to be distinguished in dress prior to the age of one or two, and that "boys were treated as if they were girls until it was clear that they would live through childhood. Then they were separated and given a different education."

We also learn, through discussion of family and the presentation of artifacts, of the gendered ways that boys and girls played and learned. Girls' rooms are almost always decorated with dolls that have a pale or peach-colored cloth or porcelain skin. Some of these rooms also have black dolls displayed. These dolls are, not surprisingly, dressed differently than their white counterparts. They have kerchiefs on their heads and are usually spatially separated from the white dolls in the room. A representative example of this is one room where there was a black doll with a gingham dress and kerchief in a doll crib, and four white dolls in nicer dresses sat around a tiny china tea set on four tiny chairs.

The boys' rooms, by contrast, have animal skins, books, toy rifles, jacks, and similar items scattered about. Unless there is a separate schoolroom or schoolhouse at the site, it is usually in the boys' room that visitors are told of the schooling practices on the plantation. We learn that the master-enslaver's white sons would be given their first lessons on the plantation and then at a certain age either be sent overseas to finish their schooling or be sent to a prestigious college such as William and Mary in Virginia. Here it is usually noted that girls were unlikely to be formally schooled—at least above basic levels. There are some interesting differences here, though, between the Creole (French) and Anglo plantation owners in Louisiana. At Creole sites it is often noted that under French law women were able to own property and conduct business. Therefore, we are told, Creole daughters were more highly educated than their Anglo counterparts and Creole women had more rights (such as the right to own property, enter into their own contracts, and so on) than those women who were ruled by law descended from English tradition.

We did not, except at Melrose Plantation and Beaufort Plantation in Louisiana, at Monticello in Virginia, and through the "Other Half" tour at Colonial Williamsburg (discussed in chapter 6), learn about the possibility of the master-enslaver having children who were enslaved, even though this is well documented. At Louisiana's Melrose Plantation the fact of race mixing provided the genesis for the founding of the plantation itself. Melrose was founded by Marie Thérèse Coincoin, an enslaved woman who in 1767 was leased to a French man named Augustine Metoyer, who became the father of eight (or ten) of her children. He bought and freed Marie and their first son, and in 1787 he gave her land. She then purchased enslaved people of her own and used the money she made to buy and secure the freedom of her other children and grandchildren. As the African American docent noted on the tour, "She was a slave, her children were slaves, but she still used slaves as a workforce." The other site in Louisiana where race mixing was discussed was Beaufort Plantation, where a painting of a mixed-race young man and his white father provides the opportunity for the docent to discuss both the painting and whom it is believed to represent. The docent assures us that the painting has no relation to anyone in the family that lives there; instead, it is a painting of Asher Nathan, whom she describes as a "Jew from New Orleans" who had an affair with a Black woman. He loved the son and wanted him to have a better life, so he bought his freedom. Because they were under the Napoleonic code, the father was able to give the son "money and prosperity." The family apparently didn't like the area and "moved back to New York." This sort of painting is, according to the guide, quite rare and was displayed in a show at the Metropolitan Museum of Art in New York City. She went on to note that this practice, of "aristocrats mingling with Blacks," was not uncommon. The issue of such union were "mulattoes," who, she told us, "like to be called Creoles"; "some of them are very good-looking; they're as light as we are." This is an example, she said, "of how we are rich in heritage in this area." Finally, the public controversy over whether Thomas Jefferson fathered children with the enslaved Sally Hemings has brought the issue to the forefront in Monticello's interpretation.

While these mentions of relationships between white fathers and Black mothers suggest a world where the strict racial boundaries of social life were to some extent breached, overall presentations of white family life exclude the possibility of mixed parentage and instead present white family life as "only white." That is, not only is the possibility of crossing racial boundaries excluded, but the ways that close interactions with enslaved people created room for particular kinds of family life are also left out of the story. White family life, then, is generally presented as highly structured, particularly for women and girls, and as the crucible in which young white elites absorbed the expectations of their society. Given that most tour guides at these sites are white women, it should be noted that such family arrangements are not always presented as desirable. In fact, as we will discuss in the next chapter, white women in particular are presented as hardworking and often overburdened. While these representations of white women in the South tend to stress some amount of limitation and control, the discussion of romance, a major framing device for these sites, presents southern life as rich and desirable.

The Romantic Urge in a Romantic Era

As noted above, romance is a central theme of the plantation tours in Louisiana and Georgia (it plays a less significant role in plantation tours and advertising in Virginia). The discursive strategy of romance has two primary dimensions. First, we use the term *romance* to note the discussion of particular romantic relationships that occurred on the sites. For example, docents across the states discuss the romances of specific individuals and provide details of such events as engagements, marriages, and duels. Related to this is a general framing of most or many of the issues discussed in tours—the aspirations and wishes of lovers, young and old; the pride and integrity of men competing for the hands of beautiful southern belles; the trepidation and courage of those facing great personal loss. Second, we use the word to refer to the labeling of the plantations themselves as beautiful, scenic, evocative backdrops for lovers, with European architecture and furniture, and resplendent perfumed gardens. They are presented as sites of peace, tranquility, melancholy, and sometimes mystery, and are marketed as places for contemporary visitors to spark their own romances or to escape to bygone days. Often, too, events from the past are used to signal the appropriateness of plantation museums as romantic sites.

When visitors attend tours at plantation museums, docents present various facts of the romantic lives of the master-enslavers. We are told of great passions and loves and how various people had pined away after losing the great love of their life—often to disease, but sometimes to war or politics. For instance, in Louisiana at the Alexander Moulton House, in an upstairs bedroom there is a picture of Anne Elizabeth Moulton (1844–1910). The text below the picture says that, "thwarted in her desire to marry a northern general, she donned a widow's black dress for the rest of her life, which caused most people in the community to think of her as an eccentric." At Evelynton Plantation in Virginia we learn of Evelyn Byrd, whose betrothed went to England and died there; she then "grieved herself to death" over a period of years.

We also learn of courting rituals among enslaving elites. For instance, the male docent at one Virginia plantation told of the white male practice of giving a woman a mirror as a gift. If she turned it glass side up, it meant she was interested and the suitor should continue his pursuit. If she turned it glass side down, it meant she was not interested in his attentions. We were told that this is where the term "turned down flat" originated. At a site in Louisiana we were told that if a white man approached a white woman at a ball or event and put a piece of ice in her drink, it indicated his serious interest in her, since ice was such a precious commodity. Further, if they weren't married or engaged, "she should catch him immediately because it meant he had a lot of money." The link between money, courting, and marriage was made at several sites across the South. For instance, at several sites throughout the three states we were told how young women would test the quality of their engagement rings by scratching their initials into the windowpanes. If they could scratch the glass, then they were sure that the stone in the ring was really a diamond and that the suitor was worthy of marriage. At Shirley Plantation, a privately owned and run Virginia site, we were told that this tradition continues to the present moment. At some sites we were also told of elaborate weddings held in various houses and how, for a fee, contemporary couples can hold their own weddings in a "lovely and historic home."

These stories of individual romances, either of enslavers or of contemporary visitors who can rent the plantations for their own wedding, are nested within a larger romantic framework that operates across all three

This roadside sign for Edgewood Plantation in Virginia
is indicative of the romantic framing of plantations,
particularly those that are primarily organized as bed-
and-breakfasts.

states. Much of the advertising for plantation museums, particularly those
that are also bed-and-breakfasts, focus on themes of romance and relaxation.

Tezcuco's brochure exhorts visitors to "relax under majestic Oaks, drift
back through the years and enjoy a quiet evening for a vacation, honey-
moon, anniversary, birthday or just a get-a-way," while Shadows on the
Teche's brochure tells us that "it has everything a Southern plantation house
should. Big White pillars. Beautiful furnishings. Live Oaks dripping Spanish moss. But there's something special here," which is the extensive documentation that was found in the attic of the home. The Myrtles, a bed-and-
breakfast also found in Louisiana, presents itself in the following manner
on its brochure:

The history of the South will always provide us with tales of romance and mystery. The saga of the Antebellum South and a lifestyle that will never be forgotten lives on at this grand mansion. A first glimpse of the mansion with its magnificent double dormers and lacy grillework of the 120-foot veranda envelopes one with a complete sense of peace and tranquillity.

Finally, Oak Alley suggests that we "enjoy her beauty and dream of her rich past." While at Oak Alley guests can "experience a bygone era in the South's most beautiful setting."

A more extensive example of romantic imagery is provided on a Web site for Asphodel Plantation in Louisiana:

THROUGH THE MISTS OF TIME IN PLANTATION COUNTRY

It is early morning and a light fog hovers over the fields and streams near St. Francisville or down the shady reaches of the Great River Road. The air is crisp and clean and your feet lead you onward over the dewy grass where Audubon might have walked and sketched wild turkeys and wood ducks for his famous *Birds of America*. Or they may lead you beside roadways where horse-drawn buggies once carried ladies in rustling silk gowns. . . .

Eagerly, your eyes search the landscape. In the distance it slowly emerges, indistinct and large: a hovering whiteness through the moss-draped oaks. As you draw closer you see the massive columns and experience a rare sense of wonder. You are in Plantation Country, a setting for the recent movie *Interview with the Vampire*. Is this the present or have you eluded time and logic and somehow slipped back to days gone by? . . .

. . . Plantation Country is a pocket of mystery, elegance and majesty, of historic towns and rural customs, of the rich delta lands and the culture of the people who drew their life and wealth from the alluvial soil. (Asphodel Plantation 2001)

The imagery suggests a dreamy place that erodes visitors' normal sense of time and duty. Entering this area, visitors are to imagine being swept along, if not physically, at least emotionally. This type of phrasing is common throughout the plantation museum world, particularly at sites that advertise themselves as bed-and-breakfasts.

Romance and melancholy often go hand in hand at these sites. Many sites use ghost stories to suggest a mood of melancholy and a history of tragedy. These ghost stories inform visitors of great passions, including anger, rage, jealousy, and love, that transcend time—so much so that the presences of

At Loyd Hall Plantation in Louisiana, this former plantation kitchen is used to house two bed-and-breakfast units. Supposedly one of the units (on the left) is a regular site of hauntings, possibly by the enslaved cook who lived above the kitchen in the loft.

those wronged refuse to leave the site. Some locations not only tell visitors ghost stories when they tour the grounds but advertise the hauntings to prospective guests. While Virginia and Georgia sites have "ghost tours," particularly during the Halloween season, Louisiana sites feature the most developed and elaborate ghost stories.

For instance, the African American docent at Loyd Hall Plantation provided extensive discussion of hauntings. The docent said that she had many of her own ghost stories from having worked there for twenty-eight years. She spoke of seeing things out of the corner of her eye, having the hair on her arms and the back of her neck stand up, hearing the piano being played when no one was there, and seeing a rocking chair that rocks when no one is seated in it. She also spoke of the cat in the house suddenly focusing on something that no one can see and following it around the house while its fur stands on end. She explained that at least four people had been killed in the house. The first was William Loyd, who was hung by Union troops after they found out that he was playing Union and Confederate troops against each other during the Civil War. Inez Loyd, the niece of William, threw herself to her death from a third-story window when her fiancé was killed. The third death was of Harry Henry, a Union soldier who deserted and hid in the attic. Members of the family found him up there and struggled with him over his gun, which went off and killed him. The family buried him under the house in a shallow grave to hide his body; they were afraid of getting in trouble with federal troops for killing a Union soldier. The final death recounted was that of Sally Boston, a "slave nanny" in the home who "nursed everyone—soldiers from both sides." She was probably poisoned, we were told, and guests and staff sometimes see "a glimpse of a woman all in white who they think is Sally." The guide said that though the house is haunted by these ghosts, there is "nothing evil" in the house; however, when staff members set the tables there is always something that goes missing and is later found in other rooms. Also, photographs have been taken that show figures and shapes "that shouldn't be there."

The docent also noted that two visitors at the bed-and-breakfast have woken up to find the walls of their room vibrating and the bed moving with them in it. This room, we learned as we moved about the property on the tour, is one of the two rooms constructed out of the original plantation kitchen, a place where the enslaved cook probably slept. The docent felt that there are ghosts all over the property and that these "people died very violently, not at peace, and they're still looking for something at Loyd Hall . . . they're not ready to go." The docent believed they "watch over [Loyd Hall] and protect it, because there is nothing negative there. "

Perhaps the most dramatic story of hauntings comes from the Myrtles, a private bed-and-breakfast plantation in St. Francisville, Louisiana. When we began the tour the white woman docent explained that the Myrtles was ranked as the thirteenth top haunted mansion in the United States. It is haunted by three people that can be identified. The first ghost is that of Chloe, an enslaved girl who was caught eavesdropping by the owner, Judge Woodruff. To punish her, he had her left ear cut off. In retaliation for this maiming, she poured the "equivalent of arsenic into a birthday cake," and several family members died. Two of those who died were Judge Woodruff's daughters; along with Chloe, who was killed for poisoning the family, they haunt the house and property. The docent shared several stories about these ghosts and their hauntings. For instance, guests often see the ghosts; in fact, 70 percent of the guests come specifically because the house is haunted. She also explained that the house has had numerous owners and that this turnover is primarily because of the hauntings. The owners at the time we took the tour had bought the home in 1992, lived in it for only two weeks, and then left. One of their children, age three, would repeatedly talk to people that no one else could see, and when the family went out the child would be extremely distressed and want to know why they had left his "little sister" behind. The parents worried that he had formed a relationship with the spirit of one of the little girls. He also would ask "why his little sisters got to swing on the chandeliers but him and his little brother didn't get to."

In addition to these ghosts, the docent explained that the original white owner of the property, David Bradford, also known as "Whiskey Dave," "created a lot of ghosts" because he came here, drove off the local Natoma Indians, and destroyed the burial ground that had been located on the site. The Natoma people, the docent said, would place their dead on raised platforms so that they would decay naturally. When Whiskey Dave came, he "took all of the bones and threw them off the property into heaps and just left them there." The docent suggested that these people might also be haunting the property.

These stories of hauntings provide substance to the framing of the South as a melancholy and deeply emotional place. Along with the more general framing of romance and stories of long-ago loves, they suggest the deep passions felt by southerners of the past, and call for visitors to come and create their own "special memories." Of course, what is generally left out of this discussion (except in a few ghost stories) is the tragedy of enslavement that always lay within reach of those lovely, and loving, enslavers.

Grounds Tours

In addition to videos and guided tours that detail the lives, loves, and interior surroundings of the enslaver's family, most sites have some form of grounds tours. These are usually self-guided tours aided by a map of the site; guided tours of outbuildings are quite rare. The only outbuilding, or dependency, likely to be interpreted by a docent is the kitchen. Grounds tours generally include a number of different buildings, including kitchens, gazebos, smokehouses, icehouses, laundries, and an occasional garden shed.

At most plantation museum sites we visited, the original kitchens were built away from the main house to prevent fires—a fact that is explained at virtually every site that has such a kitchen. Additionally, sites that have kitchens within the main structure note that this is an anomaly because of

Typical kitchens on plantation museum tours feature implements like those used to prepare food during the period being interpreted. Kitchens were often the only places where the presence of slaves was noted.

the threat of fire. The occasional home has a "warming kitchen," that is, a kitchen where food was brought from the outside kitchen to be arranged on the china and kept warm before being presented to the master-enslavers. In most cases, homes with interior full or warming kitchens do not have interior stairs from the kitchens to the upper floors. Instead, as docents explain, the servants would carry the food outside and up an exterior flight of stairs in order to enter the home on the floor that contained the dining room. Both exterior and the few existing interior kitchens provide an opportunity for docents to relay what are apparently meant to be amusing stories, such as how those carrying food were required to whistle from the time they left the kitchen to the time they entered the dining room to ensure that they did not eat any of the food they carried. We describe several of these stories in the following chapters.

In contrast to the main house or mansion, few discussions occur regarding the materials used to construct the exterior kitchen, though most sites do note that the floor of the kitchen was almost invariably made of dirt. If bricks were added at the site, the docent informs the visitors that these bricks would not have been there in the time period she or he is interpreting. At several sites visitors are told that the cook would have slept in the loft above the kitchen, though in all but one case the upstairs was closed to visitors. Some plantation museums, such as Longfellow Evangeline in Louisiana and Pope's Creek in Virginia, have reconstructed the plantation's kitchen, since the original burned to the ground in the past.

In addition to comments about the floor, the only other comments about construction of kitchens center around the cooking hearth. Visitors are often told to pay attention to the large size of the hearths and to imagine cooking in this manner. Tour guides at some sites ask visitors to imagine "how large a fire you could build in a fireplace of that size" and then proceed to explain that, in fact, cooking was done over several small fires that were made in the hearth, as a single huge fire would not serve the purposes of the cook.

In fewer cases kitchens have, in addition to the main hearth, smaller baking ovens built into the hearth. When these are present staff talk about the difference between Dutch oven baking and that done in the smaller wall ovens. As noted earlier, however, the main topic in all kitchens is the variety of tools used to prepare food.

At a limited number of sites there are, in addition to kitchens, other outbuildings that have survived and which are included as part of the grounds tour. At sites with such structures, text is often provided, either on the building or through brochures. The smokehouse at North Bend in Virginia is an example of a typical representation. It is hung with pieces of smoked meat, such as a haunch of pork. At the bottom of the smokehouse is a large pit where the fires were made, and very often the beams of the smokehouse (from which the smoking meat hung) show char marks from the fires of the past.

Icehouses, when included on tours, provide another opportunity to point out the ingenuity and wealth of the master-enslavers. In Virginia and Georgia icehouses are usually deeply dug cellars or wells into which large chunks of ice would be lowered. In Louisiana, because of the threat of flooding and because of soft soil, they were built aboveground. In Virginia the ice was generally cut from a nearby lake or pond and dragged on sleds to the icehouse. These large chunks of ice would be packed with sawdust or straw and would sometimes last the summer. In Louisiana, ice would be brought from as far as Canada down the Mississippi River. Several sites in Louisiana mention this practice, undertaken especially for special parties and occasions, and note that such behavior helps indicate the status and wealth of the owners.

Laundries are relatively rare on plantation museum sites; only four sites that we visited have them. These locations set up the laundries with washing cauldrons and posts for hanging the laundry to dry. Indeed, labor is explicitly marked at laundries; however, who carried out the labor is generally obscured through the use of the passive voice or the use of the term *servants* rather than *slaves*. At laundries, as at other outbuildings (with the exception of icehouses), the focus is on the task performed rather than the construction or significance of the building itself.

One final type of building that may be present on a grounds tour is a slave cabin or, if the site is in a town, servants' quarters. There are relatively few sites across the South that still have standing slave quarters. For example, in Virginia there are such cabins at approximately 31 percent (sixteen) of the sites we attended. However, only six out of the sixteen sites actually interpret these as structures that housed enslaved people. At the others they serve as gift shops or garden sheds, or simply stand as empty, uninterpreted buildings. Georgia and Louisiana have similar percentages of plantation museums with standing, though not necessarily interpreted, slave cabins. In Georgia, the Cannonball House has quarters that housed enslaved people and are now used as a Confederacy museum. And while Louisiana has similar numbers of sites with slave cabins, relatively fewer are actually interpreted as such—at four of the sites the cabins serve as something else (housing for contemporary workers, bed-and-breakfast units, or storage), while at the other three sites, the cabins are not interpreted either by docents or by text. The one site that does interpret the cabins is the Kent House. There are also servants' quarters in the Gallier House in New Orleans, though the framing here is via the term *servants* and there is no explicit mention that the structure housed those who were enslaved. On the tour of the Southdown Plantation in Louisiana the docent first suggested that they have slave cabins but later admitted that they were really huts build to house Black workers in the 1930s.

This relative scarcity of remaining cabins seems to stem from multiple factors. First, many such buildings have simply fallen down. Quarters for enslaved people were almost always poorly built wooden structures and were not designed to last any significant length of time. Other quarters were destroyed, along with numerous other outbuildings, during the Civil War. Still others may have been destroyed deliberately after the Civil War because they were reminders of certain unpalatable aspects of the past. Finally, docents at a couple of sites suggested that "no one would have thought to preserve those buildings; they weren't important." These various factors help explain why only approximately 25–30 percent of sites have slave quarters on their property, and an even smaller percentage have them as part of their interpretive efforts. Sites at which the cabins have been abandoned or are used for storage space (the latter was the case at Nottoway Plantation) often did not allow visitors to view them; other sites indicated that they intended at some point to make the cabins part of the tour but had not done so yet.

In only a few cases is the construction of slave buildings discussed, usually when the construction or materials are in some way distinct. For instance, along the Georgia coast, visitors are informed of the materials involved in making tabby buildings: lime, shells, and sand. Tabby was used to construct storage sheds or slave cabins. There are several poignant and evocative examples of tabby ruins on Butler Island, Georgia, from the Retreat Plantation owned by Thomas Butler. These buildings include the ruins of what was once a hospital for the enslaved. The fact that the ruins of the hospital are now located in the middle of the parking lot at the Sea Island Golf Club and can be viewed amid brand-new Mercedes, BMWs, and Cadillacs is striking. In the next chapter we look at how slave cabins are discussed in more detail.

Gardens

While visitors are not often explicitly encouraged to view whatever vestiges of slave cabins are left standing, they are generally encouraged to visit the gardens of plantation museums sites. In fact, the extensive array of flowers and the elaborate layout of gardens are central to many of the plantation museums we visited (for instance, Stratford Hall, Kenmore Plantation, Rosedown Plantation, and Hofwyl-Broadfield Plantation). Gardens serve throughout the plantation museum tourist industry to signal the emphasis on beauty and order that the plantocracy was believed to share, and to implicitly valorize the contribution of plantation slavery to contemporary visitors' pleasure. Additionally, gardens link the plantation to the general surrounding area and its idyllic beauty. Most sites encourage visitors to tour the gardens after they have finished the main tour. Gardens are highlighted in the videos, with many beautiful aerial shots, and in the range of leaflets, many with photographs, that are handed out free of charge. Some sites emphasize the gardens as one of the most beautiful aspect of the plantation. For instance, Rosedown Plantation, in the West Feliciana region of Louisiana, places the gardens as a central feature of the self-guided plantation tour. The brochure that advertises St. Francisville, Louisiana (produced by the West Feliciana Parish Tourist Commission), says, "Glorious, century-old gardens at *Rosedown* and *Afton Villa*,inspired by the fabulous gardens of 18th century France, have been restored to their original grandeur. In spring, camellias and azaleas bloom in profusion amidst stunning, moss-draped oak alleys and glass statuary." Both Hofwyl-Broadfield and Barnsley Gardens in Georgia also boast impressive gardens. At several sites in Louisiana, sugar cauldrons, once implements of backbreaking and oppressive labor, have been transformed into picturesque containers for water lilies, thereby erasing the labor of enslaved persons that marks these tools. There are several of these cauldrons across the grounds at the Rural Life Museum in Baton Rouge, Louisiana, and at the Kent House in Alexandria, Louisiana. The presentation of gardens works to draw visitor attention again and again to beauty and tranquility. Gardens are also used to signal the activity of enslavers; for instance, the brochure for the Audubon State Commemorative Area tells readers that "restored formal and kitchen gardens adjacent to the house demonstrate the early Louisiana plantation owner's tendency to re-create formal beauty in their wilderness environment." The fact that this tendency to re-create beauty was coupled with the systematic exploitation of enslaved people is simply not discussed.

Museums and Formal Displays

Most sites also had a designated museum or series of displays where family and era artifacts were displayed and placards provided descriptions of life on the plantation. The size of these displays varied dramatically; in some cases there was information provided along the hallway visitors traverse to enter the video viewing room, while in others there were specific rooms set aside for large photographs, miniature reconstructions of the plantation as it existed during the specific time period under consideration, and a variety of family artifacts. For example, Stratford Hall in Virginia, the birthplace of Robert E. Lee, has a fairly significant display in addition to the house tour and video that are provided for tourist consumption. The Longfellow Evangeline site in Louisiana also has a display in its main visitor center that covers a range of topics, including how sugarcane and indigo were grown and harvested. At Berkeley Plantation in Virginia there is a small display in the basement that contains bullets and various artifacts from the property. At all sites, the displays generally continue the main representational strategy (symbolic annihilation, trivialization, segregation, or relative incorporation) found throughout the rest of the site.

All of the components we have described above work to construct an image of the preemancipation life of white enslavers in the South as honorable, refined, gracious, beauty-loving people. There are very few wrinkles that mar the surface of the genteel southern way of life presented in these plantation museum packages. It is only when sites work to incorporate discussions of enslavement that the pretty picture gets disturbed. It is no wonder, then, that the primary ways that enslavement is discussed serve to erase, minimize, or trivialize the fact and experience of slavery.

Conclusions

What should be clear from the proceeding discussion is that each plantation museum comprises a number of different components. The components usually support a common racialized regime of representation in which plantations are presented as white places of honor and romance and where the presence of enslaved African Americans is generally elided. As you will see as you move through this book, each of these components contributes to visitors' understanding of the site under scrutiny. Where there are apparent contradictions between a strategy embodied in one component at a site and that embodied in another, these contradictions will be discussed.

We should reiterate again that we understand that there are multiple ways to interpret the information presented at these sites. We understand that staff at these sites believe themselves to be doing the best job possible with the resources they have available to them and that their interpretation of what is important at these sites may differ from ours. Again, our goal is to understand the patterns we find across plantation museum sites and to locate these patterns in relation to what we regard as a general racialized regime of representation, with distinctive aspects and emphases, that is common to the plantation museum industry as a whole. While site docents clearly know a lot more about the specifics of their site, locale, or district than we do, what we bring to the analysis of individual sites is the benefit of substantial evidence collected across an extensive geographical terrain. While we don't deny the effort that went into organizing these sites, we do suggest that the patterns we find across the sites are powerful and noteworthy and can be profitably understood as a racialized pattern, or regime, of representation. We characterize this racialized regime of representation as consisting of a general discursive framework (the fundamental elements all sites share), distinctive rhetorical strategies for managing the topic of slavery and those who were enslaved, and particular regional narrative styles that bring a local flavor to the discussions. Here and in chapter 1, we have highlighted the common aspects of the discursive framework. In the following chapters we turn our attention in far more detail to the rhetorical strategies used to organize and represent the topic of slavery.

Overall, white-centric plantation museum sites employ strategies for handling or managing a racialized past and present that add up to a pattern of obfuscation and mystification. That is, through a range of strategies and practices, rhetorical devices and pictorial images, the importance of slavery in the growth of the southern and national economy, as an underpinning of southern white gentility, and as a condition upon which U.S. democracy was built is obscured. In the following chapters we explore these strategies more fully and offer specific examples of how they are enacted at plantation museum sites; in chapter 8 we explore counternarrative and transcoding strategies employed at the Black-centric sites we visited.

PART TWO

Managing Slavery: Representational Strategies

4 | Symbolic Annihilation and the Erasure of Slavery

Our primary concern in this chapter is the way sites are structured so that the institution of slavery and the presence and personhood of those enslaved and of legally free African Americans are either completely erased or extremely minimized. This erasure and minimization are achieved via a number of rhetorical devices and practices that are found in tour guides' comments, in the many artifacts in the homes (portraits, wall plaques, personal items, and so on), promotional literature, leaflets, and videos. Since much of what we explore is the absence of a discussion of slavery and those enslaved, presented here is a picture of what is discussed and identified by tour guides and highlighted in promotional literature or videos. Our argument is that what is present, combined with what is absent, is part of the discursive formation of a genteel (white) South. We argue that the best way to interpret this erasure and minimization is as an example of symbolic annihilation, which suggests that slavery and people of African descent either literally were not present or were not important enough to be acknowledged. Drawing on the work of Amy Ansell (1997), we also argue that this discursive practice constitutes symbolic racism. That is, while the explicit degradation of African Americans through "old-fashioned" racism has decreased, new forms of racism, including more subtle forms of framing racialized talk, have developed. In this case neither slavery nor the people enslaved or their contributions are allowed into the organizing framework.

Coupled with this symbolic annihilation of enslavement and erasure of the presence of both enslaved persons and most working-class whites is a simultaneous aggrandizement of the white elite master-enslavers who resided at these sites. Additionally, the detailed accounts of the lives, hopes, ambitions and experiences of the white elite plantocracy are very gendered; the distinctions between white men's and white women's spheres are highlighted throughout the tours. Through the stories told in videos, in printed material, and by docents, white residents are represented as hospitable, generous, moral, and democratic.

Clearly the simultaneity of repression and elevation is not restricted to these sites; oppression is always already present (Beauvoir 1953; Fanon 1967; Memmi 1965). What we demonstrate in this chapter is its explicit occurrence in the plantation museum industry. The pages that follow develop the concept of symbolic annihilation, detail the content of white-centric tours, and exemplify the specific rhetorical practices of symbolic annihilation by making detailed references to a range of sites across Virginia, Georgia, and Louisiana. We also highlight how in each state the symbolic annihilation of slavery and enslaved persons is achieved by drawing upon the narrative styles that prevail in that particular state—that is, the birthplace of presidents and the Civil War in Virginia, *Gone with the Wind* and the Civil War in Georgia, and the tragic losses of the Civil War and eighteenth-century ethnic difference in Louisiana. We provide detailed information from sites in two ways. First, we describe tours, leaflets, and videos from some of the larger sites that demonstrate this concept and capture variations in narrative styles across the states. Second, we provide representative examples from other sites that best exemplify symbolic annihilation. Collectively, this evidence provides insights into the substance and texture of sites that operate through the concept of symbolic annihilation. We conclude the chapter with a discussion of the constructions of whiteness found at these sites.

The Concept of Symbolic Annihilation

Symbolic annihilation constitutes a powerful rhetorical and representational strategy for obscuring the institution of slavery. The concept of symbolic annihilation was developed in the 1970s in the works of George Gerbner (1972) and Gaye Tuchman, Arlene Kaplan Daniels, and James Benét (1978), who argue that women are subject to symbolic annihilation in the media when they are either absent, trivialized, or condemned for taking non-stereotypical gender roles. Tuchman, Daniels, and Benét write, "The paucity of women on American television tells us that women don't matter much in American society" (1978: 11). Others have used the concept of symbolic annihilation to explore or label the lack of representation of a variety of groups, including gays and lesbians (Kielwasser and Wolf 1992), all women (Gilmartin and Brunn 1998), and Native Americans (Merskin 1998). None of the other treatments of symbolic annihilation significantly develop the concept past what was laid out by Gerbner and by Tuchman, Daniels, and Benét. In other words, most authors accept the original definitions and apply them to situations where subordinated groups are absent from, or marginalized within, media representations.

We use the concept of symbolic annihilation to reference both the erasure and marginalization of slavery, the enslaved, or legally free African Americans within the plantation museum industry, as evidenced by what information is included and excluded from guided or self-guided plantation tours. At the same time we expand the concept of symbolic annihilation by describing some of the strategic rhetorics employed to enact it. For our purposes, we consider symbolic annihilation to occur in cases where slavery and the enslaved are either completely absent or where mention of them is negligible, formalistic, fleeting, or perfunctory. Generally this strategy occurred at sites that mentioned slavery or the enslaved three or fewer times. However, as we'll demonstrate, some sites that mention slavery three or fewer times also employ the strategy of trivialization and deflection, which we discuss in chapter 5.

Plantation museum sites across the South deploy a repertoire of devices and representational strategies in the category of symbolic annihilation, such as:

- Exclusive focus on the material and social life of the plantocracy, even though these people usually represented a tiny fraction of a given plantation's population
- Absence of any mention, acknowledgment, or discussion of slavery, the enslaved, or African Americans
- Mention of the enslaved or Blacks in a perfunctory and fleeting way, usually in a throwaway statement of fact, with no details or elaboration and usually little or no context
- Use of euphemisms to refer to the enslaved and slavery, most commonly *servants* and *servitude*
- Use of the passive voice and neutral pronouns to discuss enslaved people's labor and achievements

- Universalizing and ahistorical statements that clearly refer only to (elite) white experience

These multiple devices are all included under the concept of symbolic annihilation, since they all work to erase or marginalize any consideration of the institution or experience of slavery. Our concern is not that any specific individuals or sites are acting with malice or the intent to symbolically annihilate this experience, but rather that there is such a powerful pattern of erasure that the pattern must be addressed.

An Overview of Exclusion and Symbolic Annihilation at Plantation Museum Sites

Approximately 25 percent of all the sites across the three states failed to mention slavery or the enslaved in *any way* whatsoever. Sites that mention slavery *one to three times* constitute approximately 30 percent of all plantation sites we visited. All together, sites that engage in symbolic annihilation as their primary strategy make up 55.7 percent of all sites. At these sites slavery is mentioned in relation to the number of enslaved people owned on a specific site, or used in reference to a specific building ("There is a slave cabin outside") or to a specific task. These references serve to marginalize those enslaved since they are provided without any contextualizing discussion of slavery, either at the specific site or in the region as a whole. Our argument is that this type of framing does not contribute to an understanding of the institution of slavery or the lives of those enslaved.

At this point we'd like to be clear that *nearly 83 percent of all plantation sites in this study have symbolic annihilation as one of their primary strategies in relation to slavery.* In our discussion we have separated out 27.0 percent of these sites and included them under the category of trivialization and deflection (discussed in chapter 5) because they employ this strategy *in addition* to symbolic annihilation. In this chapter, however, we will only be providing examples from the 55.7 percent of sites that engage in symbolic annihilation without also employing trivializing practices. The fact that such a high proportion of the sites principally engage in symbolic annihilation is somewhat astounding, particularly given the development of scholarly work that explores plantation architecture, life behind the big house, and the experience of various enslaved persons. Our research suggests that symbolic annihilation occurs even at sites that have published books about the institution of slavery on that specific site. For example, a summer 2000 tour at Poplar Forest in Virginia yielded no mention of slavery or enslaved people. At the end of the tour Professor Eichstedt asked if anything was known about slavery at the site. She was directed to a slave cabin that sat at the edge of the property; no further information was provided. Yet Poplar Forest published *Hidden Lives: The Archaeology of Slave Life at Thomas Jefferson's Poplar Forest* in 1999. So while there is some knowledge available about the lives of enslaved persons at Poplar Forest, it was not provided on the two different tours attended at the site. This is also the case with Nottoway Plantation in Louisiana and the Antebellum Plantation in Georgia. Books are available that offer general details of slavery and mention the individual plantation (or the various plantations, in the case of the Antebellum Plantation) around which the tours are currently organized. However, virtually none of this information is shared on the tours. This is an example of symbolic annihilation.

As we explained in chapter 1, white-centric tours are those that normalize and valorize white ways of organizing the world, including the world of labor and enslavement. Such a term also suggests that anything but whiteness and white ways is considered superfluous, anomalous, and marginal. Symbolic annihilation clearly is a white-centric practice in that whiteness is at the center of the discourse and is generally unquestioned and unnamed. This is characteristic of the typical site in the contemporary South. The foci at these sites, as laid out in the previous chapter, are the buildings' interiors and exteriors, the grandeur and wealth of enslaving families, and the upper-class status and fame of their friends or visitors. Clearly, talking about furniture, architecture, and the rest is not inherently bad. Our argument is that these comprise the primary foci of tours and are presented in such a way that excludes acknowledgment or discussion of how the system of enslavement provided the foundation for this wealth and lifestyle. Consider the following comparison. The number of references to furniture averaged 50 per site (ranging from 20 to 100). Among the sixty-five sites that use symbolic annihilation as their primary strategy, then, there are approximately 3,250 mentions of furniture. In contrast, sites that mention slavery three or fewer times contributed 53 mentions for the state of Virginia, with similar numbers for Louisiana and Georgia—a total of 103 mentions. *That translates to thirty-one times as many mentions of furniture at these sites than of slavery or those enslaved.* Similar figures hold for the other categories, such as architecture. The overwhelming presence of these objects and relationships constructs a discursive formation that has no room for the discussion of something as untoward and unpleasant as enslaving other human beings.

In the following pages we provide mini-tours of three sites: Berkeley Plantation in Virginia, Nottoway Plantation in Louisiana, and the Antebellum Plantation at Stone Mountain in Georgia. Each site demonstrates the practices of symbolic annihilation and also provides a window into some of the narrative styles deployed in the specific sites.

Berkeley Plantation: Tidewater Region, Virginia

Berkeley Plantation is a privately owned and run plantation located along the James River in Virginia. It is described in the 1997 "James River Plantations in Historic Charles City County" tourism brochure as

> the site of the first official Thanksgiving in 1619; it is also the birthplace of Benjamin Harrison, signer of the Declaration of Independence, and William Henry Harrison, 9th president of the U.S., as well as the ancestral home of the 23rd U.S. president, Benjamin Harrison. *Taps* was composed here in 1862. It remains in its traditional state, furnished with authentic antiques and surrounded by terraced boxwood gardens.

As is true of most Virginia sites, there is a strong emphasis on the famous inhabitants of and visitors to the plantation. A great deal of the guided tour's emphasis in on events that occurred at the site, the architecture, and the home's furnishings. The introductory video and the docents both emphasize the importance of the visitors and inhabitants of Berkeley. Both state that the "first ten presidents" of the United States "enjoyed Berkeley's hospitality." Both tell us that Benjamin Harrison V signed the Declaration of Independence and served in the House of Burgesses, where he oversaw debates for independence. He also served as the governor of Virginia and in 1774 was elected to the first U.S. Congress.

Both the ten-minute video and docents assert that Berkeley is truly the site of the first Thanksgiving because it was here that thirty-eight colonists landed on December 19, 1619, and gave thanks for surviving their arduous three-month journey at sea. Berkeley stresses that this is before the *later* Thanksgiving held at Plymouth, Massachusetts. The tour and video discuss the Indians who "massacred" and "slaughtered" about one-quarter of the inhabitants of the settlement in the early 1600s. One of the paintings that depicts Thanksgiving shows white men kneeling in prayer on the banks of the river while painted Indian men scowl at them from behind the trees, foreshadowing the massacre to come. (In none of this are the actions that distressed the Indians prior to their move against the colonists.) Information provided at Berkeley in the video and a brochure also indicates that it is the location where "Taps" was composed during the Civil War, and where "Master George Thorpe, an Anglican, developed Bourbon Whiskey."

After touring the gardens and grounds, which included a wooden two-dimensional replica of the ship that the colonists arrived in, Professor Eichstedt attended the ten-minute introductory video. This provides an overview of the main events in the history of the area and the famous white people who inhabited it. The voice-over explains the "First Thanksgiving," discusses the "web of kinship" that was an "integral part of Virginia's ruling class," and details the political lives of various Harrison men. It also notes that Benjamin Harrison V was a "good-humored, gregarious man, who liked a good fox hunt," that George Washington often visited, that William Henry Harrison was elected the ninth president of the United States but died within several days of his inauguration, and that the twenty-third president was also named Benjamin Harrison and was a member of the family. After a burst of ominous music, we learn that during and after the Civil War Berkeley experienced financial troubles and occupation by 140,000 federal troops. General McClellan was here as part of the occupying force, and Lincoln was here twice. Happier music signals that while Berkeley lapsed into disrepair after the Civil War, it was purchased by John Jameson of Scotland, whose son Malcolm inherited Berkeley in 1927 and restored it to its former glory. The video instructs us that the window frames, floor, and roof are original to the house, while the furniture is from Westover Plantation. The brick terraces, visitors hear, were built by hand, with the assistance of oxen. Bringing us into the present, the video concludes, "Today, five hundred of more than one thousand acres are still a working plantation" where crops are harvested with mostly modern technology.

Our period-attired tour guide met us when the lights came on. This fortyish white man provided further details about the plantation, focusing on the details of construction, furniture, and family history. For instance, as we entered the main house, he explained that when Benjamin Harrison IV wanted to build the house, he bought Rob Wilson out of Williamsburg's debtor's prison. Wilson served as his master builder, who, with the labor of a hundred slaves, built the house using plantation resources. Our guide explained that the exterior walls are thirty-six inches thick from floor to roof, while the interior walls are eighteen inches thick. The house was built in the Georgian style, with its symmetrical and balanced appearance. The hallway was used as a dance hall; we were told that dances such as the minuet and the Virginia reel were developed for narrow halls such as these. The guide informed us that we came in through the carriage entrance, though white visitors would likely not have done so in the 1700s; they preferred to travel on the river, since "inland paths were mainly Indian trails, and travelers were apt to be attacked by Indians or highwaymen." In a later room we were told of the changes made to the woodwork in 1790 by Benjamin Harrison VI. Harrison had been a friend of Thomas Jefferson; he visited Monticello and was amazed at its interior. So Harrison took down all the pine paneling in Berkeley and had new woodwork, called "Adam's woodwork," built in the house.

In the parlor we received the information that Berkeley Plantation is currently occupied by Malcolm Jameson and his wife, Grace. Malcolm Jameson, nineteen when he moved here in 1927, was responsible for restoring the building and grounds. Grace Jameson restored the interior and purchased the antiques at an auction in New York. In this room and the following one the docent described the pieces of furniture (some of which are 250 years old) and the various accoutrements found throughout the house (such as vases, portraits, and a Waterford crystal chandelier). Here we were provided with the second and final mention of slaves on the tour; with a note of concern, visitors were told that in January 1781 Benedict Arnold and the British infantry took all the furniture out of the house and burned it, shot the cattle, and took forty slaves.

In the formal dining room the docent pointed out that the dependency outside was a kitchen. The docent noted that "it [food] came" into the house here, without mentioning who brought it, and later said that "they would" bring the food in from outside. He said that pathway was called a "whistling pathway" because "they were required to whistle so they couldn't taste the food as they carried it." Most people on the tour laughed at this statement.

While standing in the owner's bedroom, we were told that it served as the plantation's "operations center." The docent pointed out a door that opened directly outside and noted that it allowed the owner, who did a lot of traveling, to leave easily, and it also allowed the overseer to come in without disturbing the rest of the home. Our attention was directed to a bed with a "tobacco canopy," embroidered with a tobacco-leaf motif; tobacco was the central crop at this plantation and all along the James River. Wealth came from tobacco, which even served as currency in the early days of settlement. As at a number of other sites, we learned here that the phrase "sleep tight" comes from the ability to tighten the ropes supporting the mattress on the bed frame. The room also contained what the docent called a "master's desk"; this particular specimen was built in Virginia over two hundred years ago. There also is a small desk that was built in the 1690s in England. The docent pointed to initials carved into the door frame, suggested they could have been those of the owners, then smiled at us and said, "So, as you can see, since 1690, Virginia has been for lovers." This last statement references the larger romantic framing of Virginia through the official state promotional phase "Virginia is for lovers."

Thus in the short tour and video, the focus on the famous white men who lived at the site, the architecture, and the furnishings, along with the minor themes of romance and war, serves to exclude any meaningful discussion of the institution of slavery.

Nottoway Plantation: The White Castle, River Road, Louisiana

A prime example of symbolic annihilation in a plantation site in Louisiana can be found in Nottoway Castle, advertised as the biggest plantation house in the South. The video *Nottoway Memories*, available for purchase in the gift shop, invites visitors to "experience and savor the aristocratic splendor that was the old South. Nottoway is the ultimate in southern grandeur; southern hospitality at its finest." To Professor Small, who visited this location in 1997, and Professor Eichstedt, who visited with accompanying graduate students in 2000, the massive white building with six major columns and huge extensions on either side of the main structure seemed more like an imitation English castle than a plantation; it is not surprising that its nickname is "The White Castle." (However, the majesty of the scenery at the house is strangely juxtaposed with the enormous, smoke-belching oil refineries that punctuate the rural landscape as one approaches via the main road.)

An excellent example of commercial planning, this plantation complex leaves nothing to chance. Upon arriving at the site, visitors must pass through the gift shop in order to get to the plantation house. Plantation memorabilia—dolls, books, pictures, and a sundry array of souvenirs—surrounds the guests; all the items for sale serve to maintain the construction of a genteel preemancipation South. This commercial enterprise also invites interested visitors to stay overnight as bed-and-breakfast guests. There

Sign for Nottoway Plantation on the River Road, Louisiana.

are ten rooms and three suites available to rent at rates that in 2000 ranged from $105 to $250 per night.

The tour that Professor Small completed had twenty-four people on it. All except for him were white; eleven were women, including one carrying a small baby in her arms. The tour guide was a white woman who appeared to be in her late fifties or early sixties. This tour was organized a little differently from others Professor Small had taken at other sites. As Professor Small entered the front door, he encountered three staffers, all white women over the age of fifty. One approached him and explained in a deep southern accent that tours were continuous and that he should go up the stairs to the music room and join the tour that had just started. After he joined the group, it became clear that the start of the tour was actually downstairs, and so when his group arrived downstairs, they were joined by a new tour guide. This reconstituted group then continued on through several more rooms until they arrived back at the music room. As the tour continued, people would join or leave it, depending on what room they had begun in.

When Small joined the group, a white woman docent, also in her late fifties or early sixties, was finishing a detailed description of a harp and three pianos. The group then passed into the Ancestral Hall, where the guide described the Louis XIV furniture and said, "You may notice that the furniture is very short—this is because the people in those days were much shorter than people are today." (This was a statement that both Small and Eichstedt heard repeatedly on various tours.) The tour continued out onto a porch, and the guide said admiringly, "Here you can see the mighty Mississippi." She informed us that while the river appears quite close now, it was originally further away; over the last century the river changed course and moved closer to the house. We then passed through a room described as the "overnight guest room/morning sitting room," where the bed-and-breakfast options were described. According to the guide, the furniture in this room is not original.

Next was the Wicker Room—stocked with wicker chairs and wardrobes—and on to the master bedroom, to which the nursery is connected. The rosewood bed was described in detail, as was the thread Mrs Randolph used for embroidery—"it cost a dollar twenty-five per yard," said the guide. She then added, "We have a lot of Civil War artifacts downstairs [in the basement], and you can see them when the tour finishes." Next we entered Cornelia's room, and the guide talked as if everyone knew who Cornelia was; it became clear to Professor Small that she had discussed Cornelia

Known as the "White Castle," Nottoway is the largest plantation house in the South, with 365 doors and windows—one opening for each day of the year. As a plantation museum, it also engages in symbolic annihilation.

earlier on in the tour, prior to his arrival, and thus assumed everyone knew who she was. From Cornelia's room a door leads to Sarah's bedroom. After describing Sarah's room, the guide announced that the tour was over and said that if there were people who had not yet completed the whole tour, they should wait under the chandelier in the hall downstairs and continue with another group. Professor Small did so and completed the rest of the tour. About ten people from the previous tour continued with him, and the group was joined by a different guide, who introduced herself as Louise. A white woman with a southern accent, she was at least in her early sixties.

Louise began by describing nearly everything in the hall—with the notable exception of two statues of Black servants. She pointed to a life-size portrait of a white family and told us that the original owners, pictured in the painting, were the Randolphs, who moved to the house with "a large dowry" and "twenty household servants." Over time they "acquired three hundred slaves and fifty-seven household servants." She said that construction on the house was begun in 1849 and finished in 1859, and that it cost $80,000 at the time. Mr. Randolph was extremely rich and spared no expense to build and furnish the house. For example, we were told that the closets were taxed as separate rooms, but this did not concern him—he was wealthy enough to afford it. The building boasts 200 windows and 165 doors—one opening, we were told, "for every day of the year." Furthermore, special arrangements had been made to build an entire wing for the family's six girls, who, it was explained, had to be kept separate from the boys.

We then entered Mr. Randolph's private room, where his ingenuity was described, as was the black marble fireplace. Louise said that lots of food was stored in the basement floor, where the earth kept it cool. There was one crop a year, so the Randolphs had to plan ahead to feed the family and servants. She said that the basement windows had bars on them to prevent animals, particularly cattle, from getting food.

Next was the ballroom, which has a white floor, ceiling, and walls; the white was designed to enhance the ladies' dresses of the time, said Louise. The piano (made in London in 1840), mirror, marble fireplace, and chandelier were described, and we were told that the columns in the middle of the ballroom make it seem like two rooms. The guide said that the room is still used—"in fact, we have a wedding here tonight at six P.M." Next we toured the dining room, and then Cornelia's room. Here we were told that Cornelia, at the age of seven, kept a diary. "She was a bit of a rebel," said Louise, "and we have to admire her for that. She wrote down things not acceptable in the day. But at least we have her diary to tell us about them." The docent presented this as significant; stating that, unlike many other things written at the time by adults, this diary was not subject to the biases of adults and so offered authentic insights into the period. On all tours, visitors are told that Cornelia's diary is available for purchase in the gift shop.

In Sarah's room, the guide described the half-tester bed and reminded us once more that "these rooms are all rentable." We continued out onto the back gallery, from which we could see a beautiful garden. We saw a swimming pool, installed in the 1980s. Louise pointed to Randolph Hall across the way, a restaurant that is open for lunch and dinner. After Louise's group entered the music room, Professor Small exited the tour and went to the basement to view the Civil War artifacts, which included furniture and a range of photographs.

During the guided tour Randolph's business prowess, meticulous record keeping, and ingenuity were centrally featured. Visitors were told that he was able to build up his fortune by dividing the plantation into four plots and borrowing money against the different sections. Additionally, at the time of the Civil War, before the Union Army arrived, Mr. Randolph took those he enslaved to Brownsville, Texas, where he continued to work them in the cotton fields of Texas throughout the conflict; therefore the Randolphs did not suffer great economic deprivation like many of their neighbors. Another example of the Randolphs' cleverness is that Mrs. Randolph kept her jewelry from being stolen by hiding it in the columns of the four-poster bed, originally designed by Mr. Randolph to keep mosquito nets tidy during the night. Ingenuity is also reflected in the advanced plumbing system used in the house; rainwater was collected on the roof in copper tanks and fed into the house. According to our guide, Randolph "was always ahead of his time," and "all of the details we use on our tours today" come from the "meticulous record keeping of Mr. Randolph." He left thirteen hundred pages of original documents that are now stored at Louisiana State University for safekeeping.

In addition to knowledge of the business dealings of the Randolphs and the physical details of Nottoway, the docent provided numerous details regarding the successive owners that Nottoway has known. We learned family members' names and ages, and heard of their personal growth and development, education, social activities, marriages, and other important events in their lives, as well as their idiosyncrasies. For instance, as was common for elite white families during that era, daughters were taught to play music, and the family held spectacular balls. These details are nested within tones of admiration, amazement, humor, and empathy.

The human aspect of the elite whites on the plantation is a central theme throughout the tour. For example, only the last of Mr. Randolph's children was born in this house; the other ten were born in a four-room cottage. The smiling docent stated, "You can imagine, coming from four rooms to sixty-four rooms, the kids really had a ball."

While the master-enslaver and his family were described with awe and admiration, this meticulous attention didn't extend to Blacks. To begin with, Blacks are absent from the images that adorn Nottoway's rooms and hallways except for two large statues of Black servants that were located in the main downstairs hall (mentioned briefly above). At about eight and a half feet tall and with candelabras on their heads, the statues were hard to ignore, but there was no mention of them by the docent, though virtually every other item in the main hall was described.

On the tour the words *slaves* and *servants* were mentioned several times, each time in a way that achieved symbolic annihilation. For instance, while the docent said that the original family arrived with "twenty household servants," she noted that over the course of developing the plantation they "acquired three hundred slaves and fifty-seven household servants"; no more information is explicitly provided about the enslaved. Instead of discussing "slaves," we are provided with information about "servants"—a common rhetorical device in symbolic annihilation. The term *servant* is used five times, first in the guide's mention of the crops "used to feed the family and servants," and second as she pointed out the window to where the "servants' quarters" were located. The third use occurred as the guide noted that each room had a bell, and when the bell rang, the servants were required to come to that room. The tour guide smiled as she explained that coming to the right room was a pretty good skill given that there were so many rooms; she added that the bell idea was an example of Mr. Randolph's ingenuity. The fourth use of the word was when the tour guide said that house guests always had a servant with them day and night, to take care of their every need. The final and fifth use occurred in Sarah's room, where the docent explained that "there is a little bed in the room for the servants." Immediately after this notation of where a servant would have slept, the guide again commented on the plantation's bed-and-breakfast angle and said, "These rooms are all rentable."

Slaves and *servants* are also implied a couple of times, by use of the passive voice. For example, the docent said, "The lawn was mowed in those days." In the dining room, she said that when the food was ready, "they" would bring it to the butler's pantry, the butler would bring it in to the dining room, and "they" would serve it to the guests.

When Professor Small left the house, he saw a brown barn-type building. He asked two Black women who were carrying linen what it was, and they informed him that it was "just an old building . . . an old slave building" and that he could go look at it. The building was covered with large shrubs and bushes, some over fifteen feet high. One of the doors was missing its bottom half, and the interior was piled almost to the top with junk, including pipes, wood, tables, glass panes, and other cast-off material. There was no apparent access into the building, and it was obviously not a building that organizers expected anyone to tour. This neglected building and its lack of interpretation stand in stark contrast to not only the house and its belongings but also the immaculate lawns, ponds, and gardens. Such lack of care and interpretive focus is an example of symbolic annihilation; the allowed deterioration of physical structures where the enslaved either lived or worked mirrors the lack of verbal and intellectual attention paid to slavery in the rest of the site.

This symbolic annihilation is continued in the video *Nottoway Memories* (not shown during the tour but available for purchase at the gift shop). The video, narrated by a white southern woman, Cheri Aucoin, takes us on a guided tour of the main rooms of the house and describes Nottoway's successive owners, including the current owner, who restored the big house. The video mentions slavery three times, twice in perfunctory ways (we are told the number of enslaved persons). The third mention of slavery occurs in the last moments of the video, when visitors learn how the plantation got its name. Apparently the original owner of the house, Randolph, moved to Louisiana from Virginia, where he had lived next to the Nottaway River. One day an enslaved person who was chopping some wood kept shouting, "Knot away, knot away," because the wood had to have the knots chopped out of it. Mr. Randolph, who had forgotten the name of the Nottaway River, was nostalgically reminded of it and immediately adopted the name for the plantation (spelling it somewhat differently). Thus one of the enslaved, naively and unknowingly, helped him to remember a longed-for place. In this story, the frivolity, silliness, and joyful working attitude of an enslaved person are used to give character to the name of the house. The framing of the story not only provides a stereotypical image of a happy slave working but also notes the nostalgia of the plantation owner. This video framing is in line with that found throughout the guided tours and continues the theme of symbolic annihilation.

The Antebellum Plantation at Stone Mountain, Georgia

Located just outside of Atlanta, Georgia, is Stone Mountain Park, a large complex of outdoor and indoor venues that includes parks, laser shows, and a large carving in Stone Mountain of the Confederate heroes Jefferson Davis, Robert E. Lee, and Thomas "Stonewall" Jackson. One of the attractions at the park is the Antebellum Plantation complex. In the mid-1990s visitors could also go to the Road to Tara Museum, which is now defunct. There is an entrance fee for the park, and separate entrance fees for the Antebellum Plantation complex and (when it was in existence) the Road to Tara Museum. When Professor Small visited it in 1996 and 1997, there was a docent-guided tour of the complex and a separate tour of the Dickey House. When Professor Eichstedt visited it in 2001, there was no longer a guided tour operating in either the complex or the Dickey House, nor was the Road to Tara Museum still in operation. During the 1997 tour undertaken by Professor Small, the docent drew visitors' attention to various aspects of the buildings, particularly exteriors and interiors, and occasionally mentioned people who used to live in them, sometimes by name. A significant number of the detailed comments provided by the docent appear verbatim in the complex's leaflet or in a book by Norman Shavin and Robert Peters (1985), both of which were available at the kiosk at the start of the tour. Shavin and Peters write that "THE ANTEBELLUM PLANTATION is as genuine a reproduction of a pre–Civil War Georgia plantation as research can make it" and "We hope that when you enter these gates you will enjoy the feeling of plantation hospitality and tradition" (ibid.: 7).

In response to the many visitors to Georgia who came there expecting to find *Gone with the Wind*'s Tara, the Stone Mountain Memorial Association enlisted an authority on antiques, Christie McWhorter, to locate appropriate buildings and "to develop a plantation complex to illustrate generally how a well-to-do family lived in the period between 1820 and 1860, on the eve of the devastating war" (ibid.: 5). The complex was opened in 1963, and in 1974 the Stone Mountain Memorial Association acquired the contract to run it. In the leaflet that visitors obtain at the complex's kiosk, the Antebellum Plantation Complex is described thus:

The Antebellum Plantation at Georgia's Stone Mountain Park is a collection of original buildings, built between 1790 and 1845, which represent a pre–Civil War Georgia plantation. After years of research and planning, buildings around Georgia were chosen because of their authenticity and historical value and moved from their original sites. These buildings were then carefully restored at Georgia's Stone Mountain Park. A strolling tour through the scenic complex provides a realistic view of the lifestyle of antebellum Georgians.

When Small toured the Antebellum Plantation in 1997, there were seven white visitors along on the tour with him; they included three young children and an elderly man and woman. The female docent took visitors to several of the buildings in the complex, offering commentary on the construction and architecture of the buildings, on items in the rooms, or about the lives of the people who had once lived in them. While information was provided for most of the buildings on the tour—for instance, the Kingston House (the overseer's house) and the doctor's cabin—we focus discussion here on the Dickey House and briefly note comments made in the doctor's cabin and the slave cabins.

In the doctor's cabin a plaque on the outside wall at the front informs visitors that Dr. Chapman Powell "often gave medical aid to Cherokee Indians" and that he built a log cabin in 1826. The docent said, "The doctor's cabin represents Mammy's cabin," and told us, "Mammy was one of the most important persons on the plantation, having supervision over household servants, cooking, sewing, housekeeping, and care of the master's children." This is the first reference to the presence and labor of enslaved people, though it is not explicitly stated that Mammy was enslaved.

The two slave cabins on display were from the Graves Plantation, near Covington, Georgia; we were told that they were for house "servants," who lived near the big house. "Slave quarters" were for field hands and were located near the fields. In the second cabin the docent said, "This cabin would have been for a small family, or perhaps a single slave." She added, "It is very inferior to the [big] house, but still is spacious lodging."

The rooms in the Dickey House are numbered, and in room 300 we were told by the docent, "This is a delightfully feminine room for the eldest daughter" and "It has a lovely portrait of a little girl." In the formal dining room the guide said, "Guests dined in quiet dignity in this room." When we got to the basement the second reference to Blacks occurred. The docent, in describing the children's dining room, said: "Under the guidance of Mammy, the children ate here until they 'learned their manners'"; an almost identical phrase is found in the Shavin and Peters book (ibid.: 42). The tour ended in the garden area, where the visitors were informed that "the Antebellum Plantation is complete in every detail, from the century-old wrought-iron gate you enter to the gazebo in the garden. It recalls upper-class rural Georgia of a century past and reveals much of the richness, self-sufficiency, and the charm of a bygone day."

During the tour the docent noted details of the various buildings as we passed through them: when buildings had been built, what materials had been used, what style of architecture could be seen, what changes had been made, and so on. Especially in the Dickey House, our attention was directed to numerous pieces of furniture. The tour guide described in immaculate detail the various antiques in the different rooms and conjured up the air of gentility, nobility, ease, and comfort that characterized the lives of the white family that occupied the house. Rooms that were elegant, cozy, warm, and inviting were occupied by whites; no mention was made of who provided the labor to make the rooms so comfortable.

In the kitchen, as at most other kitchen sites across the South, the focus was on the utensils and not on the people who performed the work. During Professor Small's tour various items such as an English steam pudding mold, rolling pin, pewter pitcher, and cherrywood dough tray were noted. When Professor Eichstedt visited in 2001 there was a costumed white woman in the kitchen who asserted that while normally she would have been doing a cooking demonstration, it was impossible to cook that day since the firewood was wet. While at many sites the kitchen is the only place where the enslaved are mentioned, at this site no mention of those enslaved occurred.

Overall, Blacks are mentioned in very perfunctory ways; these mentions are limited to comments regarding Mammy and the slave cabins. The intricate details deployed to describe the artifacts of the white homes and the lifestyles of the white occupants are absent from discussion of those enslaved. Instead it is short, sharp, and to the point. No attempt is made to conjure up the life of brutality, misery, labor, toil, and suffering that was more likely to be their experience. While whites have names, identities, individuality, feelings, and emotions, Blacks have nothing. Additionally, the presentation of the one figure who is discussed, Mammy, is ahistorical and caricatured; any information provided is sparse and uneventful. Interestingly, when Professor Small visited the complex in 1996 and 1997, there was a "Mammy's cabin" in the complex; when Professor Eichstedt visited in 2001, none of the buildings was labeled this way, nor was it obvious what building used to be so labeled.

The leaflet and Shavin and Peters's book about the plantation (which was no longer sold at the complex in 2001) complete the tenor and emphasis of the tour. The book focuses almost exclusively on the genteel lives of those whites who occupied the houses and the tireless efforts of those involved in the reconstruction of the site, perfunctorily describing the slave cabins and Mammy's cabin. Shavin and Peters also spend one page discussing the "myths" of plantation life; for instance, they counter the idea of "happy-go-lucky, deferential" slaves and also the idea that many, or even most, white southerners were slaveholders. However, this section of the book is quite short and without much of the interest, emotion, passion, and nostalgia that are evident when the authors describe the lives of the upper class

Finally, reflecting the local flavor of many tours in Georgia, the book makes a number of references to *Gone with the Wind*. First of all, it tells us, "All plantations were not created in the image of Tara, the splendid but fictional mansion of 'Gone with the Wind'" (Shavin and Peters 1985: 3–4). Later we are told that "this manor was chosen to typify a cotton planter who owned about 100 slaves and, obviously, lived well. It is, therefore, more modest than the grand Tara mansion which producer David O. Selznick conceived for 'Gone with the Wind.' Indeed, Selznick's concept was far more elegant than Atlanta author Margaret Mitchell described in her Pulitzer Prize[–]winning book" (ibid.: 30). The book continues: "Unlike fictional Tara's pristine white walls the Dickey house is painted yellow-buff, trimmed with dark green doors and shutters. Tradition has it that a slave accidentally discovered an off-white color by dropping his white paint brush in Georgia clay. His mistress liked it so well that she ordered him to keep 'muddying it up'" (p. 31).

The movie *Gone with the Wind* plays an important role beyond being a reference and framing point at the Antebellum Plantation; it is the premise for to the Road to Tara Museum, housed in a small building just outside the plantation but within the Stone Mountain Park complex. When the Road to Tara Museum was still in operation, a small blue leaflet handed out at the kiosk informed visitors: "The Road to Tara Museum has an intriguing collection of *Gone With The Wind* and Margaret Mitchell memorabilia. Newly relocated to the beautiful Stone Mountain Park. Discover one of the

The Road to Tara Museum at the Antebellum Plantation, Stone Mountain, Georgia, demonstrates the centrality of the film *Gone with the Wind* in representations of the genteel South in Georgia plantation museums today.

largest permanent collections of GWTW in the world." The museum was in a small house originally built in the 1840s in Alabama and subsequently transported to this site. (Before the museum was transferred to the Stone Mountain complex, it was open to the public in Atlanta.) Toward the back of the house there was a gift shop selling memorabilia such as postcards, posters, books, and dolls. There were glass cabinets filled with Scarlett O'Hara dolls of different sizes, copies of dresses and clothes worn in the film, original books published about Margaret Mitchell, copies of newspaper articles, Margaret Mitchell's typewriter and huge posters, and black-and-white stills from the film. One huge poster showed Rhett kissing Scarlett. Two almost life-size black-and-white cardboard cutouts had the two characters looking at each other with a smile. One black-and-white photo showed Rhett Butler pouring a drink into Mammy's glass, with her smiling at him. Underneath the photo a placard provided a brief biography of Hattie McDaniel, the actress who played Mammy in the movie, with her dates of birth and death, and reminded us that "she was the first black to win an Academy Award, it was for the role of Mammy." While the Road to Tara Museum is no longer at Stone Mountain Park, *Gone with the Wind* still exerts a presence. In 2001 there was an exhibit of the Shaw-Tumblin collection of *Gone with the Wind* memorabilia in the park's Memorial Hall. Visitors to the park could not only see the exhibit but also get a "Scarlett special" at the hotel and attend a *Gone with the Wind* ball.

Specific Techniques of Symbolic Annihilation

Each of the plantations provides representative examples of the practices of symbolic annihilation. In all three sites the extensive focus is on the activities of the wealthy plantocracy and their families, politics, and material achievements.

Perfunctory Inclusion of Information on Slavery

The fact that enslaved people provided the vast bulk of the labor that created the enslavers' wealth is erased; there are few mentions of the institution of slavery or those who were enslaved at all. Even when slavery or the enslaved are mentioned, it is done in a fleeting or perfunctory manner, and in a way that aggrandizes the master-enslavers.

While sites used the framing of romance, the focus on furniture, architecture, and family life and, as we'll discuss in the next section, the use of euphemisms to avoid naming slavery, approximately 75 percent of all sites occasionally did use the word *slave* or *slavery*. These sites used such terms from one to three times during a tour that lasted forty minutes on average. None of the sites included in this section provided a context for understanding the institution of slavery or the experience of enslavement for specific people on the plantations under discussion. Instead, information was presented in disconnected ways—if the word *slave* was mentioned, there was no context provided, nor information about a particular enslaved person.

Many sites at which there was minimal mention of slavery and those enslaved provided three basic sorts of information about those enslaved: numerical information about how many enslaved persons lived on the property, information about housing for those enslaved, and a brief statement of a task that an enslaved person would have performed. Sometimes the number of those enslaved was included at the beginning of the tour—usually in relation to the number of acres that comprised the plantation. In some cases, the provision of this information is through the use of lists. A striking example from Virginia is that found at Red Hill, a national monument dedicated to Patrick Henry. Visitors take self-guided tours of the property

Cabins that formerly housed enslaved people, such as these at Laura Plantation, were often left uninterpreted at a variety of sites.

after watching a film that does not mention slavery at all; on the tour, there is a text plaque that states:

> Red Hill is so named because of its soil and its location overlooking the Staunton River. Patrick Henry spent the last five years of his life here. His initial purchase was 700 acres; additional acquisitions brought the total acreage of the plantation to 2,920. Tobacco was Henry's chief crop; corn and wheat were also grown. He owned 66 plantation slaves, 21 horses, 167 cattle, 155 hogs and 60 sheep. Patrick Henry called Red Hill "one of the garden spots of Virginia." Although he was in failing health, his final years were apparently happy ones.

In this case the ownership of humans is put in the same context as the ownership of hogs, sheep, and cattle. While Henry was an important proponent of liberty and freedom in the new republic, no mention is made of the apparent contradiction in this American hero being an enslaver.

Another representative example comes from Louisiana's Oakley Plantation. As we entered the smoking room in the Oakley Plantation, we saw a large bookcase with original books in it and some large original maps of Louisiana that indicated plantations' locations. The tour guide waved her arm toward

A prime example of symbolic annihilation is found at the Hofwyl-Broadfield plantation in Georgia, where quarters for enslaved people have been transformed into rest rooms.

the map and said, "Three thousand acres and fifty slaves got you on this map." She said nothing more, and then the tour continued into the following room.

In addition to the number of enslaved persons being a piece of information frequently provided for the plantations under consideration here, the mention of "slave cabins" or "slave quarters" was common. As we noted in the previous chapter, the presence of cabins at a site does not ensure that either the cabin or slavery will be discussed; at a number of sites, former slave quarters are simply abandoned. As we described earlier, at Nottoway Plantation a large slave cabin stands at the side of the house, used for the storage of what looked like junk. The docent fleetingly mentioned the cabin and pointed to it through a window as she conducted the tour. We visited several sites in Georgia in which slave cabins made of tabby are open to the public and have an official marker or signpost but are not part of any organized tour. One example of this kind is the ruins of the slave hospital from Retreat Plantation, which is located on grounds that are now part of the Sea Island Golf Course on St. Simon's Island. This site has an official marker and a brief description of the hospital. Several other slave cabins located on the island were originally part of Hampton Plantation. A notable example of the disrespect with which the former homes of the enslaved are now

Bed-and-breakfast units at Tezcuco Plantation in Louisiana, based on what the site's brochure calls "slave cabin designs."

regarded can be found at the Hofwyl-Broadfield site near Darien, Georgia, where the building is now being used as a rest room. At other sites slave cabins are used as storage sheds, housing for contemporary workers, or bed-and-breakfast units.

The use of slave cabins for bed-and-breakfast units is particularly noteworthy. First, bed-and-breakfasts that market themselves as plantations are explicitly making their connection to an era framed by this industry as romantic. This labeling occurs even though the term *plantation* wasn't commonly applied to such sites, at least in Virginia, until the 1930s. Plantations go a step further in romanticizing this period by using former slave quarters for guest housing. At several sites in Louisiana, bed-and-breakfast accommodations were constructed out of such cabins or, in one case, the building that held the plantation kitchen and sleeping quarters for the enslaved cook. At this site we were told that there is a ghost that has been known to frequent that cabin and to shake the bed of the guests staying there. At Tezcuco, a large bed-and-breakfast site that also does tours for day visitors, they note in their advertising that the bed-and-breakfast cabins are based on a "slave quarter design." At two other sites in Louisiana docents indicated that they wished the site had slave cabins; as one docent put it, "I

At Madewood Plantation, Louisiana, a former slave cabin is used as a bed-and-breakfast unit that guests pay over $100 a night to stay in.

wish we had some [slave cabins]; they would make pretty little bed-and-breakfast rooms."

One other site in Louisiana is worth mentioning: The Cabin, an eating establishment that is constructed out of slave cabins. On the restaurant's combination menu and brochure, visitors are told:

> The Cabin Restaurant is unique in all the world. It began as one of the ten original slave dwellings of the Monroe Plantation. It is approximately 150 years old.
>
> As one looks around upon entering, the Cabin gives off an aura of authenticity and realism. The original cypress roof is still visible from inside, and even the spider webs of 100 years ago are still clinging to the ceiling. The walls are papered with ancient newspaper fixed to the wall with a mixture of flour and water. This was the way the slaves insulated the walls of the original slave dwelling.

Beyond this, there is no discussion of the lives of those who were enslaved. At the end of the text, the author/owner writes: "Our goal is to preserve some of the local farming history; serve meals typical of the River Road tradition, and make your visit a relaxed and memorable one." We consider such use of these structures to be examples of "plantation chic"—a framing that stresses romance and relaxation and turns sites of Black suffering into locations for white consumers' pleasure.

The final perfunctory way that sites mentioned those who had been enslaved was through mentions of specific tasks that were performed. In these cases, docents might mention a task that was performed, but without providing a context. For instance, at Chretien Point Plantation, also in Louisiana, when we entered one of the downstairs room, the guide pointed to a bottle holder on the wall as she passed it and mentioned, "The slaves made this." A couple of times throughout the tour the term *servants* was also used to refer to those who had been enslaved and the work they performed.

Euphemisms

As we pointed out earlier, one way of symbolically annihilating both the system of slavery itself and those who were enslaved is to use words other than *enslavement* to describe the situation that existed. Euphemisms for this are found in the tours across the various states. There are particular aspects to note. The first is when the word *slavery* is omitted and another word, such as *employment* or *service*, is used in its place. At Chatham Manor, a National Park Service site in Virginia, the main textual display visitors encountered is found in the parking lot. It states:

> This expansive estate and its impressive Georgian dwelling have dominated Stafford Heights overlooking Fredericksburg for two centuries. William Fitzhugh, a wealthy landowner from Virginia's Northern Neck, completed construction of a new residence in 1771 and named it in honor of William Pitt, Earl of Chatham. Fitzhugh and subsequent ante-bellum owners of Chatham managed a large plantation employing as many as one hundred slaves.

Here the word *employing* stands in for *enslaving*. A similar elision happens at another site, where a plaque states that "83 African Americans lived and worked here." The words *slavery* and *enslavement* are not used to label their experience, which is thereby erased. At other sites the language of servitude stands in for the forced labor of enslavement. For instance, at Stratford Hall, a Virginia site run by a private foundation, there is a "memorial cabin" dedicated to a longtime employee of the property. The cabin is a very small one-room wooden building with an empty bed frame in it, a very low ceiling, a rough wooden table, and a bench. The man this cabin is dedicated

A stone marker at Stratford Hall in Virginia pays tribute
to a "faithful servant" whose family had "served the Lee
family for several generations."

to was born after the Civil War was over, so he was never enslaved; however, the quote on a plaque at this cabin is interesting. It reads:

In memory of William Wesley Payne (Uncle Wes). Whose Family has served the
[Stratford] Plantation since the time of Thomas Lee. Born Stratford January 6,
1877, Died Stratford February 27, 1954. Given with respect and affection by the
Board of Directors of the Robert E. Lee Memorial Foundation.

At Red Hill, the Patrick Henry National Memorial, a plaque outside the
slave cabin says it was the "home of Harrison and his wife Milly, longtime

servants of the Henry family. Harrison, when a small boy, is believed to have been Patrick Henry's slave and later, coachman for his son Jon." In the museum there is a picture from the 1800s of "Uncle Harrison and Aunt Milly, Coachman and Housemaid for the Henry family. Served two generations." The use of the kinship terms *uncle* and *aunt*, both in this example and the previous one, are in keeping with the practice of speech employed by those who were master-enslavers and those who, in the Jim Crow era, continued their exploitive relationships with African Americans. The use of this language positions these individuals as members of the white family, and the use of the word *served* masks an oppressive relationship.

Another example of the use of such euphemisms occurred at Kent and Oakley Plantations in Louisiana. Professor Small completed a tour of the Kent House in Alexandria, Louisiana, in July 1997, accompanied by two African American friends who live in Alexandria. The Kent House is a composite plantation complex that includes slave cabins and a main house as well as several other buildings. The guided tour was in two parts. The first section of the tour lasted an hour and a half and was conducted by a white man in his forties with a southern accent. The second part was of the main house and was conducted by a white woman in her fifties, also with a southern accent.

The male guide often appeared uncomfortable. Part of this may have been due to the midday sun, as it was indeed hot, but he also hesitated much more often when discussing subjects that involved enslaved people than topics that did not. He kept referring to the enslaved persons as "workers," another euphemism for enslaved persons. He told us that the buildings, all dating back to the early 1800s, were not original to the site but had been brought from surrounding locations in central Louisiana. He explained that this was a cotton and sugar plantation, and when he was asked by one of Small's friends who did the work on the plantation, he replied, "The workers." As we passed through the grounds, adjacent to the sugar mill was a huge pole that the guide said was the "sugarcane masher, used by an animal and a worker."

The docent then proceeded to what he called "the workers' cabins," which were clearly slave cabins. The first cabin had two rooms, and one of Professor Small's friends asked how many people lived in the cabin. The guide said he thought about fifteen workers in one room and another fifteen in the adjacent room, adding that the workers made cigars.

The male guide's studious avoidance of the word *slave* (in addition to using the term *worker,* the guide frequently used the passive voice, saying that "the work was done," "the food was cooked," "the tools were used," and so on) was highlighted by the fact that the second guide used the term *slaves* several times and did so without apparent discomfort (details of this section of the tour can be found in the next chapter).

During Professor Small's tour of Oakley Plantation in 1999, his group went upstairs and entered Eliza's room, where the docent described the bed, the mosquito net, and the armoire (the last being original to the house). The docent mentioned that the armoire had been found in the barn, where it had been used as a tool box, and she added, "It can be completely disassembled." Then she pointed to a chamber pot, described its discreet location inside the nightstand, and added, "The maids would empty it in the morning." At Callaway Plantation, in Wilkes County, Georgia, enslaved persons were called "hands," and we were told that "servants" made the coffins on the plantation.

The most consistent euphemism employed that symbolically annihilates those who were enslaved and erases the reality of their experience is the term *servants*. For instance, at several sites docents said that "servants" would bring food into the dining room. At a few sites staff or text plaques pointed out that *servants* was enslavers' preferred word. As one white woman guide noted, "We use the word *servant* because that was the word they used. Saying the word *slave* was considered impolite, so they used the term *servant* instead." The choice to use the word *servant* can be understood as an attempt to be historically accurate, but the euphemism was used in the past because the reality of the situation was too ugly to be directly faced; this does not seem like a good reason to continue its use today. One Virginia docent who used the word *servant* continuously throughout her tour seemed to be suggesting that contemporary African Americans' dislike of the word *slave* prevented her from using the term. She said, "They really don't like that word, so it's not clear what we're supposed to say anymore. It really is a shame because they really could learn a lot too, like about the huge number of blacks that owned slaves. But we can't talk about that either." Here the white guide was arguing that African Americans control the use of the word *slave* and suggesting that they are misguided. Her framing does not suggest that whites in the past or today control language or the interpretation of the lives of African Americans. Her notion that there were "huge numbers of blacks that owned slaves" also displaces responsibility for the system of slavery from elite whites; blacks are seen as equally culpable.

The use of *servant* is widespread throughout the sites. Sites that never used *slave* or *slavery* might use *servant* twenty times, along with the ever-present passive voice (described below). *Servant* was often used when a specific piece of furniture or tool, such as a kitchen utensil, bell system, or punkah, was being discussed. The term *punkah* refers to a large fan suspended above the dining room table by a hinge-and-pulley system. Discourse around this object was sometimes awkward, since to explain its workings the guide had to note that someone would have to operate the pulley in order for the fan to move. At two sites the tour guide said that a "servant" operated the punkah. At Chelsea Plantation, a privately owned Virginia site, the tour guide (who was also the owner) said that a "colored mammy used to sit in the corner and work the pulley." At Beaufort Plantation in Louisiana the tour guide said that a "young boy would operate the pulley and say 'Shoo fly, shoo fly.'" In Professor Small's 1998 visit to Oakley Plantation at the Audubon State Commemorative Park, the tour guide, after telling visitors that only three pieces of furniture were original to the house, described the punkah in the dining room as one of them. She pointed out what looked like a flat piece of wood, about eighteen by twenty-four inches, hanging by a piece of rope above the table, and demonstrated how the device operated. She added, "The rope would be pulled all through dinner, giving a cool breeze, and it would keep the flies off your dinner." On a later visit to the same site by Professor Eichstedt, an enslaved person (specifically a child) was identified as the person who would provide the labor.

In addition to using words such as *servant* to obscure the workers' enslaved status, pronouns, particularly *they,* and neutral-sounding nouns were used to reference those who must have been enslaved—for example, "They would have several fires, and would regulate the temperature" by raising or lowering the cooking pots, and "Keeping enough meat throughout the year to feed his many people was one of the problems of the plantation owner" (Shavin and Peters 1985: 22). Such strategies "work to mask the facts of domination" (Moon 1999: 188; see also Scott 1990). Moon goes on to say that "euphemisms cloak racist expression with a veneer of 'bourgeois civility/gentility,' while enabling white people freely to express racism—in coded ways—as a signal of white solidarity" (ibid.).

Use of the Passive Voice

Another common rhetorical strategy identified by Moon is the passive voice, which "allows white people to recognize historical events (and

A punkah at a Louisiana plantation. At mealtimes enslaved people would pull the cord leading to the punkah, to keep the white family cool and to keep flies away from the food.

thereby demonstrate their tolerance and empathy for racial others), while repressing any connection to them" (1999: 189). Like the use of euphemisms, the passive voice allows speakers to avoid identifying injustice or to avoid laying or accepting blame.

Use of the passive voice occurred at every white-centric site we visited. While some sites did a better job of discussing the institution of slavery and the lives of those enslaved, all staff at some point lapsed into passive voice. This is as true of Black-centric sites as of white-centric ones, since use of the passive voice is quite common in the English language. However, it was used much more at white-centric sites in situations where the docents otherwise would have had to mention the term *slave*, and it was used in those situations for ideological reasons. When the passive voice is used, no one is actually identified as having carried out specific labor; things just happened. For example: "Night dirt [which refers to the chamber pots] and linens would have been taken down out of sight of the guests." "Meat was prepared here." "Fruits and vegetables were grown." "Food came in through that door." "Crops were planted in the spring and harvested throughout the summer and fall." "Furniture would be moved to the edges of the room to make room for dancing." Like the invisible hand of the capitalist market, working for the good of everyone in the market, unknown hands worked for the benefit of the master-enslaver and his family Extensive examples can also be found in the literature available about the Stone Mountain complex in Georgia, such as Shavin and Peters's book. About the dining room in the Kingston House, we are told that "food was brought from the kitchen downstairs via the outside stairway" (1985: 10), and that "in the winter food would be 'kept' warm in the 'keeping' Room before it was served to guests upstairs" (13). In the Thornton House, "meals prepared in an outside cookhouse were passed through a door between the twin chimneys and placed on a shelf" (18). In the barn complex "cows were milked and other animals kept" (22). "The hogs were slaughtered, plunged into a barrel of hot water, scraped and eviscerated. The meat was cut up and laid aside to cool" (22). Of the cookhouse, we are told, "All the cooking for the plantation owner's family and the manor and barn servants was done over the open fire, and then taken to the manor warming kitchen where it was kept until served" (26). At Madewood Plantation in Louisiana, the docent explained that "over six thousand bricks were made on the plantation."

A final example of the use of passive voice comes from a 1998 tour of Kenmore Plantation in Virginia. A young white woman dressed in period garb was interpreting cooking in the plantation kitchen for the visitors in attendance. She spoke about the various implements on display and then moved to discussing a small oven built into the brick fireplace's wall. She told us that coals would be placed in the oven to heat it and that "they" knew when the oven was at the correct temperature because "an arm would be put into the oven and you would count till twenty. If you could only make it to fifteen or so, then it was hot enough for baking." It should be perfectly clear that the arm going into the fire would almost invariably be an African American arm. The use of "you" is interesting since it locates the visitor as a person who might be sticking his or her arm into the oven, or at least doing the counting, and it's used in conjunction with the phrase "an arm," which apparently isn't attached to a specific person—but like the examples of passive voice and euphemism cited earlier, it serves to erase the presence of the actual enslaved people who carried out these tasks. This practice, we should note, was identified in 1975 by Thomas Greenfield; very little has changed today (see Greenfield 1975; Horton and Crew 1989).

Universalizing and Ahistorical Statements

On many of the tours guides made statements that seemed to refer to all people present in the period that was being described. It did not take much reflection to realize that such statements actually referred to a small and narrowly defined group—elite whites or elite white men. For instance, at a significant number of sites across the three states, docents describing the hospitality of the plantation would say that "everyone was welcome here; no one would be turned away." Clearly this was not true; African Americans, even those who were legally free, and poor whites would not be welcome as guests. The "everyone" that was spoken of repeatedly at these sites really referred only to members of the white elite. Such universalizing occurred in all three states.

At the Antebellum Plantation, when Professor Small's tour group entered one of the bedrooms, the guide said: "The mellow plantation-made brick and hand-hewn overhead heart-pine beams give this room a warm feeling, one to be lived in and enjoyed" (but only by white folks, a distinction that is not made). At Rosedown Plantation in Louisiana, visitors were told, "Our house is filled with the joys of family and the laughter of children" (that is, elite white children). At Shadows on the Teche in Louisiana, the guide told us that "anyone who want to be a planter could do it" (that is, anyone white) and that after the Civil War many women remained unmarried (that is, white women) because "there was no one to marry, they were all killed in the Civil War" (that is, the white men). In all these statements, white people's experiences are represented as being those of all people.

A tourist booklet promoting Washington-Wilkes County, Georgia, says, "You can feel the patriotism, as you walk on the streets of Washington," "Wilkes County stood at the forefront of this country's budding, burning desire for freedom," and, talking of the founding of the colony, "This was a time of leaders who risked their lives and fortunes to forge a civilization out of the wilderness." It is clear that it is white people being referred to, erasing not just the Black inhabitants of the area but also the thousands of Native Americans present at the time the colony was founded. These examples are typical of the larger, more common problem of universalism and the refusal to acknowledge whiteness, a pattern that is common across the South and indeed across the nation (see Gabriel 1998 for examples).

Interestingly, the tendency to use universalizing statements was also evident in tour guides' attempts to locate visitors in relation to the site. However, we should note that this happened only to Professor Eichstedt, who is a white American, and not to Professor Small, who is Black British. On tours that Professor Eichstedt undertook, she and her fellow white tourists were told, "If you came to visit, this is where you would sleep" or "If you were a guest, this is what you would eat along with the family." The "you" is clearly a person socially defined as white.

Additionally, some sites used framing that is ahistorical as well as universalizing. Such a voice decontextualizes people and practices, removing them from concrete historical moments, dynamics, and politics. Instead, practices and characters are presented as if they extended across the whole South or across an unspecified period of time. For instance, at the Antebellum Plantation in Georgia, the docent leading tours of "Mammy's cabin" described the figure of Mammy in an ahistorical manner, and the site's booklet continues this deployment, explaining that Mammy was an important figure on the plantation, as she did the cooking and cleaning in the big house and supervised other slaves. Additionally, the construction of Mammy is presented as if it existed across all plantations, a fact that is not true. This reduces the enslaved to stereotypical roles and identities rather than treating them as real individuals who lived in specific times and places. This is all the more striking because while some enslaved African American women fulfilled the role associated with this stereotype during the antebellum period, the image of Mammy is primarily a post–Civil War invention (Clinton 1982; Guerrero 1993). Also, it is important to note that many African Americans recognize the image of Mammy as a white construction designed both to deflect attention away from the sexual exploitation of enslaved Black women and to present a Black woman who was more interested in the happiness of white people than that of her own family (Turner 1994: 24–25). In its typical portrayal, the image of Mammy is one that emphasizes her devotion to whites and her willingness to sacrifice everything for them.

This reduction of enslaved people to stereotypes is carried out, as we noted before, in the gift shops as well. If images of Blacks exist here, they are usually stereotypical renditions of Mammy, the pickaninny, and the uncle (see Bogle 1973 for descriptions). Whites are thus urged not only to reduce Blacks to these stereotypes but to consume these images and present them in their homes.

It is also important to note—as we mentioned in chapter 1—that the vast majority of the sites themselves, and in particular their physical structures, are anachronisms. That is, they are constituted by a number of sections built, rebuilt, or modified in different time periods. When docents describe various parts of the exteriors or interiors or mention various artifacts, they are covering an extensive sweep of time. In addition, we often hear stories at these sites about different families that occupied them over a period of decades and even centuries. For example, a tour of the Hay House (whose formal name is the Johnston-Felton-Hay House) in Macon, Georgia, is a tour across the lives and changes of the building over 140-odd years. The house was designed in 1855 by the New York architectural firm of T. Thomas and Son and built for William Butler Johnston, who was born in 1809 on his father's plantation near Eatonton, Georgia. He married Anne Clark Tracy in 1851, and they moved into the house in 1860. William Johnston died in 1887; his wife survived him until 1896. The second owners of the house were William Hamilton Felton, a superior-court judge, and his wife, Mary Ellen Johnston Felton, who was the daughter of William Butler Johnston and inherited part of the house. The Feltons undertook a major renovation of the house at the turn of the century and in 1912 had the house wired for electricity. They had control of the house until 1926, when both Mary Ellen Johnston and William Felton died. Their son, William H. Felton Jr., sold the house that same year to Parks Lee Hay, a banker, and his wife, Maude Hay. Parks Hay died in 1957, and Maude Hay died in 1962; shortly afterward the Hay family opened the house as a museum. In 1977 the family decided to convey the house and contents to the Georgia Trust for Historic Preservation, which has had the house open to the public since 1978. With this series of owners, each of whom decorated the house in his or her own way and each of whom had a distinct life story, a tour through the Hay House can confuse visitors as they try to understand which owner created specific features of the house.

Another example comes from the Kent House in Alexandria, Louisiana. While the guides here strove to be historically accurate, telling us where items came from and when, and which are originals and which replicas, once again they often compress the history of the house into one event, period, or occurrence. For example, one guide moved back and forth between two sets of owners, the Baillos (largely of the 1700s) and the Hynsons (largely of the 1800s), and after describing key items from the 1800s said that the slaves were looked after very well and had a doctor to visit them because this was the policy of the Spanish. In fact, the Spanish had ceased to control Louisiana long before the nineteenth century began.

Not only is time collapsed in these tours, but so too is space. The Antebellum Plantation at the Stone Mountain Complex appears as a spatial anachronism, although all the buildings are from the antebellum period. The complex is made up of buildings from several different sections of the state—the overseer's house from Allen Plantation in Kingston, the log cabin from DeKalb County, the Thornton House from Green County, cabins for enslaved people from Graves Plantation in Covington, the necessary house from Talbotton, and the manor house from Dickey, Georgia—and several states. When we arrived at the Thornton House, we were told, "This house is some fifty years older and is not a part of the Antebellum Plantation but is part of the tour for your pleasure."

Overall, the compression of time (and space) into a forty-minute tour or a leaflet not only is confusing but also makes it difficult to treat the topic of enslavement with respect, as the number of people who were enslaved varied greatly at a specific site over time and also between different sites, as did the crops raised and the attendant labor practices.

Narratives of Whiteness

All the strategic rhetorics described above work to erase the institution and experience of enslavement and the presence of African American people. Visitors who experience these rhetorics are thus encouraged to continue an inaccurate and mystified understanding of the importance of the institution of slavery and the experiences of enslaved African Americans for specific master-enslavers, for particular states, and for the whole United States. The lives and experiences of those who were enslaved and their contributions to the South's economy and to the impressive architectural legacy that has survived the institution of slavery are clearly not thought to be worth considering. What is believed to be worthy of consideration, however, are the white enslavers.

So far we have detailed the symbolic annihilation of African Americans and the institution of slavery as a whole. At sites that employ this strategy, a visitor could never be confronted with the fact that enslavement existed. What one cannot avoid at these sites is a certain kind of representation of the white master-enslavers—narratives of whiteness that symbolically annihilate the institution of slavery and African Americans.

In general, the bulk of white-centric sites that we visited were interested in demonstrating, or at least asserting, the generosity, hospitality, morality, and democratic nature of the master-enslavers. This is in line with a presentation of plantation society as genteel and honorable. (We also would argue that such assertions are in fact necessary when sites are repressing the reality of slavery.) Even most sites that did discuss slavery in more than a minimal way worked to construct the master-enslavers who lived there as honorable, moral, and generous people. Some sites also endeavored to demonstrate that the master-enslavers who lived there were very ingenious and to point out when they could properly be understood as inventors. The ways that these categories are constructed are fleshed out below.

Whites as Hospitable and Generous

Approximately 85 percent of all white-centric sites and almost 100 percent of sites that engage in symbolic annihilation had tour guides and text that positioned the master-enslavers as hospitable, genteel, and generous people. The general framing of this was accomplished through statements made by staff on tours. For example, at several sites in Virginia docents used the physical marker of the pineapple motif in pediments, carvings on columns, and moldings to talk about hospitality. They noted that the pineapple was meant to denote hospitality and that when visitors saw this symbol they knew they were in a particularly generous and welcoming home. A number of sites explicitly used the phrase "no one was turned away" to reference the generosity and care provided by the master-enslavers. Several sites in Virginia were described as being "a center of hospitality and gracious living" or a place where "hospitality reigned supreme." At one publicly owned site, a staff member asserted, "Everybody was very, very friendly; no person would go hungry."

The hospitality of specific sites was also noted to explain why certain sites had not been destroyed during the Civil War. For instance, at Shirley Plantation, a privately owned and run plantation in Virginia, guests are told that during the Civil War there were four hundred Union soldiers in the yard. "The folks left [women] didn't want to help Yankees but knew that they had to help them. They didn't have lots of servants—slaves—by this point, so they had to cook themselves." Because of their "good deeds," we are told, General McClellan of the Union army worked to save this plantation after General Butler wrote and said that he wanted to put it to the torch. McClellan sent soldiers back to protect Shirley because "the women had been so gracious."

At places where guides or texts didn't explicitly use the language of hospitality, gentility, or generosity, there was much discussion of the balls that were held. It was also noted that since it was difficult to travel, when guests did come they often stayed for months at a time. The presence of guests for such extended periods of time could become both financially and emotionally tiring. At one site the docent said that when a visitor was no longer welcome to stay, his or her bed might not be heated at night, or the soup in the person's bowl might be cold. Through these signals, rather than through direct speech, a visitor would learn that the hospitality of the hosts was coming to an end.

Whites as Moral, Democratic Leaders

Whites at most sites are constructed as highly moral and, particularly in the case of Virginia, as very democratically oriented. In Virginia, whose larger state theme, as we mentioned earlier, is that it was the "birthplace of democracy," many sites work to demonstrate how the particular master-enslavers whose lives they interpret were involved in the development of democracy in the United States. Very rarely (and never at sites that don't explicitly discuss slavery) is the contradiction between owning enslaved persons and advocating for democracy discussed. Instead, in many sites the visitor will find an artifact that speaks to the presence of those considered slaves (kitchenware used by enslaved persons, a chair returned by a former slave, and so on) near a text plaque that emphasizes the master-enslaver's love of freedom. The incongruity in this juxtaposition is not highlighted in any way.

That the morality of master-enslavers is referenced or constructed through very gendered discourse should not be surprising given the ways that, historically and today, white supremacist discourse relies on the construction of "pure" white womanhood (Ware 1992; Ferber 1998). We would argue that, like white supremacist discourses elaborated elsewhere, at these sites the elaboration of the ways that white women were different from (and subordinate to) white men works to delineate and establish a racialized hierarchy.

At the sites we visited there was often a highly gendered discussion of not only the tasks that white women performed (which are discussed in detail in the following chapter) but also the leisure pursuits of white women as opposed to white men, and comments about how this white elite society ensured the purity of white women. The elaboration of purity and the steps taken to ensure it, we believe, is a way that white women are used to demonstrate the morality of plantation society's enslaving class.

At Smithfield Plantation in Virginia the tour guide asked visitors to note that the stairs that led up to what was the girl's room got narrower and shallower as they came closer to the top. The story goes, he said, that the owner built them this way to ensure that if anyone tried to sneak into the girl's room, he would trip and be found out. At another site in Virginia where the staff regularly pointed out the multiple pineapple designs throughout the house, a docent said that one particular bedroom could not have belonged to the woman of the house since there was a pineapple motif above the door: "No self-respecting woman would ever have a pineapple above her door since the pineapple signals welcome, and that would suggest she welcomed people into her bedroom." At several sites in Louisiana we toured the garçonnaire, where boys would live after they reached a certain age. One tour guide told us that boys moved to the garçonnaire "after the age of fourteen since it would be improper for them to live in the same house with their [unmarried] sisters."

At other locations the docent explicitly said that the chastity of girls was very important in society and that girls were often considered old enough to marry at the age of twelve or thirteen. As one white female staff member at a very large, private bed-and-breakfast plantation in Louisiana said, "Girls were not little girls for long. They married at thirteen or fourteen; their husbands were thirty to forty years of age." She went on to recount that one of the daughters of the family didn't want to be married to an older cousin who had gray hair. Her father forced her to marry him, and it "turned out to be the love story of the century." With a wink she concluded, "Maybe fathers should still be allowed to pick husbands for us."

Other sites suggested the decorum of the era they interpreted and the chastity of the women by discussing courtship rituals. Ten percent of the sites in Louisiana explicitly discussed "chaperone mirrors." These are convex mirrors that usually hung above the mantel and provided a reflection of the courting couple, who would be sitting on the couch in front of the fireplace. This allowed a chaperone to watch the couple from many locations, even from outside the room where the couple was sitting, and "know that they weren't doing anything." At several sites we were also told about petticoat mirrors, which were placed on the ground to allow women to check their skirts and hoops and make sure that their ankles were not showing. At one site the guide said that it was "improper for ladies to show their ankles. If a young man saw a lady's ankles, then she had to marry him." Showing one's ankles was linked to sexual access to a woman and was therefore frowned upon. Even within marriage, we were told, a man was "very lucky if he saw his wife's ankles five times during their whole marriage."

Throughout the sites personal morality was expressed through gendered discourses. In these sites the trope of the pure white southern mistress or femininity was used to demonstrate the propriety of southern slave-owning society. Other discourses—of service to the community, and the quest for democracy—were also employed to anchor southern master-enslavers' claims of justness.

The link of whites to democratic ideals is strongest in Virginia, as noted earlier. In this state there is great emphasis put on the involvement of various master-enslavers with the development of the new nation and in particular democracy. At sites that were the homes of various Founding Fathers, long lists of these individuals' accomplishments are provided, both by staff and in various texts, and we are told of their explicit contributions to the ideas of democracy. At only a few sites (which will be discussed in chapter 7) do either the tour guides or written text provide a discussion of the contradictions of advocating for individual human rights while also owning human beings. Instead, at most sites, the individuals' contributions are presented as if the democracy they promoted extended to all Americans, rather than to an exclusive group—whites. One way this is done is through comments made by docents, text, and video voiceovers that "this corner of Virginia" is the birthplace of democracy, or that a particular plantation "is a sacred place for all Americans," or that "all Americans can be renewed and restored" by visiting a particular publicly run plantation site. These comments further the erasure of meaningful class distinctions among whites and exclude the experiences of African Americans and American Indians altogether. That these sites might not be sites of renewal and restoration for all Americans is not considered.

The framing of whites as democratic, hospitable, generous, and moral is found across all three states. For instance, in Georgia, at the Alexander H. Stephens site, information is provided on the tour and in pamphlets that speaks to his generosity and integrity. On the front of the pamphlet is a photo of a statue of Stephens, with this quotation underneath the picture: "I am afraid of nothing on earth, or above the earth, except to do wrong—the path of duty I shall ever endeavor to travel, fearing no evil and dreading no consequences." The leaflet continues: "It is said that Liberty Hall was given its name because Stephens did as he pleased there, and he wanted his friends to do like-wise. Most of the rooms were neatly but plainly furnished; several bedrooms were always kept for guests, who often came and were always made to feel at home. Any stranger, passing, was 'at liberty' to stay the night—thus the name." Overall this leaflet is designed to show that Stephens was a man of integrity, decency, moral strength, warmth, and liberty, but it is all racialized. There is not a mention of the fact that he enslaved people, that he ardently defended such enslavement, or that his invitation to guests to stay at Liberty Hall excluded Blacks, legally free and enslaved.

Conclusions

We have shown how the sites described in this chapter focused in detail on exteriors (the construction and architecture of houses and gardens), on interiors (decor and furnishings), and on creating a rich and impressive tapestry of the lifestyles and character of the white elites who lived on these plantations. We have demonstrated how the display of images (such as paintings, portraits, and artifacts) and the particular range of topics raised and discussed by tour guides serve to circumvent any discussion of slavery, of the enslaved, or of African Americans. There are numerous occasions on which the fact of slavery is acknowledged or mentioned, but at these sites it is done in a perfunctory and fleeting way.

The overall effect of the discursive framework, rhetorical devices, and narrative styles described here is to symbolically annihilate the presence of African Americans and their importance in the amassing of wealth, the construction and maintenance of massive plantation mansions, and the development of cultural institutions across the antebellum South. Narratives that focus on grandeur, glory, and gentility and aggrandize southern white elites also erase or symbolically annihilate the fact of enslavement and the horror and cruelty that lay at the center of plantations. That these types of narratives of whiteness are coupled with the erasure of enslavement is not surprising. The fact of slavery is present at these sites; that those who lived there enslaved other people is inescapable, even while it appears unmentionable. We would argue that the repression of reality requires that whites construct stories about white history that emphasize goodness, democracy, and gentility. These spoken narratives counter the one that hangs unspoken in the air—they talk back to the voices that are unacknowledged. In cases where sites have chosen to talk about enslavement and those who were enslaved, it is generally not enough just to present stories about the general goodness and morality of whites. At these sites, docents and texts often tell of the loyalty or faithfulness of enslaved people, of happy or grateful slaves, and of the generosity and care that white enslavers extended to those they enslaved. It is to a consideration of these methods of trivializing slavery and deflecting attention away from its unpalatable aspects that we turn in the next chapters.

5 || Trivializing and Deflecting the Experience of Enslavement

In the last chapter we explored aspects of the strategy of symbolic annihilation, where slavery either was not acknowledged or was mentioned in minimal and perfunctory ways. In this chapter we consider the second rhetorical strategy used to manage discussions of slavery and those who were enslaved: trivialization and deflection. This strategy mentions the institution of slavery and those enslaved, but in ways that serve to trivialize the significance and experience of slavery. This is often done through humor or mockery. While the fact that these sites mention slavery appears to be an improvement over locations that symbolically annihilate it, the inclusion is framed so that it continues a demeaning, distorted, and trivialized understanding of slavery.

This belittlement is accomplished through a number of rhetorical devices, organized through two broad categories. The first category involves explicit talk about Blacks and the institution of slavery, including both representing slavery as a possibly benevolent institution and using the trope of the happy or grateful slave (in which details of individual enslaved persons are provided to show that they received favors and rewards from the master-enslaver and that they expressed contentment in slavery). The second category involves a focus on whiteness and whites, rather than Blacks and enslavement. One way this strategy operates is by valorizing whiteness through references to good owners or owners' good intentions. Alternatively, by using the narrative of whites as hard workers, it emphasizes their labor and erases that of Blacks by appropriating it.

We want to make it clear that these particular strategies are not necessarily the dominant narrative through which any individual tour may be organized; in the majority of tours they are not. As we've detailed before, only 17 percent of all sites we visited mentioned the word *slave* or *slavery* more than three times in the tour. Our experience is that some of the sites that mentioned slavery between one and three times employed both symbolic annihilation and trivialization in their framing. We also find trivialization in sites that mentioned slavery and those enslaved more than three times. The point is that the rhetorical devices that position African Americans as comfortable with or civilized by slavery occurred in multiple sites.

We also are not suggesting that tour guides and white visitors seek to minimize the experience of slavery or the suffering of enslaved people in any conscious way. We do not have the evidence to suggest that this was the case. However, we would argue that this is not the point. Along with the particular information provided, it is the larger social and political context and the emphasis of the tour guide that create the overall feel of the tours. In the absence of substantive discussions of some of the harsh realities of life experienced by the enslaved, the comments and framing of the kind we discuss below are likely to have an invalidating and demeaning effect. This strategy, in addition to symbolic annihilation, is employed at 27.0 percent of all sites. Another 16 percent of sites in other categories (segregation, in-between, or relative incorporation) use tropes and representations that are trivializing and demeaning to the experience of enslaved African Americans.

Trivialization works, we believe, because it draws on contemporary and historical framings of both Blackness and whiteness and because it perpetuates stereotypes. These stereotypes may be untrue, but there is considerable research suggesting that a substantial portion of the white population adheres to the ideas that underlie them. For instance, in 1992 a nationwide random-sample survey by the Anti-Defamation League found that 76 percent of white respondents agreed with one or more anti-Black stereotypes, such as that Black Americans "prefer to accept welfare," are "less ambitious" and "more prone to violence," and have "less native intelligence" than whites. Fifty-five percent agreed with two or more stereotypes, and 30 percent agreed with four or more (Anti-Defamation League 1993: 10). These nationally operating white fictions are linked with the rhetorical and representational strategies employed at plantation museum sites; the relationship is dialectical in that the larger white fictions underlie the viability and acceptance of imagery used at plantation museums and at the same time are simultaneously renewed by them. Note that in many ways, the strategies discussed in this chapter resonate with racialized strategies in other realms of representation and public life. We will return to the connections between strategies discussed here and larger racialized ways of knowing in the chapter's conclusion.

Representing Blacks and the Institution of Slavery

The devices discussed in what follows are not presented by the docents within a context of critical reflection. Indeed, they often provide the bulk of information that is presented about those who were enslaved and the institution of slavery itself. These deflective devices move the visitor's gaze to other issues of various kinds, such as the nature or characteristics of Blacks, or owners' good intentions. The stories recounted below also highlight the power and influence of individual docents in framing the entire context of slavery during the tour.

Slavery as a Benevolent Institution

The first example of a rhetorical tactic that we characterize as trivialization and deflection is one that suggests slavery was not so bad or was a benevolent institution. While the norm across plantation museums is generally to erase the significance of slavery through silence, there are a few sites where either the staff explain that the plantation owner believed that those he or she enslaved were better off (economically, psychologically, or morally) than poor whites of the same era or the docents themselves assert that those who were enslaved were better off than poor whites.

The first example of this comes from Virginia. At Sherwood Forest, the home of the Harrisons and the Tylers, the white male tour guide described how Julia Gardiner Tyler, the northern-born wife of President John Tyler, said that "slaves were treated much better than poor people in England that she had seen" and how after her husband died, she went back to New York and continued to espouse white southern ideals regarding slavery. At the end of the tour, the docent again brought up Julia Gardiner Tyler's feelings about slavery when white visitors asked him to explain the geographic boundaries of the Confederacy. After ruminating about the number of states that seceded, he said, "It [life in the South] was an agrarian way of life. The North was more industrialized, it was based on different ways of life. It [the

South] depended on slave labor." He went on to assert that "of course, some people [such as Julia Gardiner Tyler] in the North became sympathizers" and that "Julia thought that slaves were better off here." The two white British people on the tour then remarked, "Yes, that was the beginning of the Industrial Revolution, things were pretty miserable."

At Mount Vernon, home of George Washington, we learned on the segregated "slave life" tour (see chapter 6) that Washington believed slavery to be an economic drain on master-enslavers, as they "often had more slaves who they took care of than who were productively working on the plantation." Enslaved people here are presented as being cared for in ways that cost more than the value of the labor they provided to the enslavers. The docent asserted that Washington believed slavery would die out on its own because it was an economic failure, and he was distraught when the cotton gin was invented, as it led to the intensification of an already bad situation.

In Georgia, at the Robert Toombs House, a text plaque for a display called "Life on a Plantation" features a quote about Toombs, attributed to Alexander H. Stephens, suggesting that he not only was a very hands-on owner but also made decisions that benefited those he enslaved:

> Notwithstanding his engagements in law and politics and the fact that his plantation was two hundred miles from his domicile, he held management under complete control, planned all the crops, and by correspondence kept informed just how matters were going on, and gave directions. His system and its success was wonderful. He would have as overseers only men of sobriety, good sense, and humanity.

While it may be true that some enslavers did believe that enslaved persons were better off than poor whites, or that Blacks would be lost without the "protection" that slavery offered them, these beliefs are largely presented free of any critical context that might call this view into question. Our experience with the majority of docents at sites across all three states suggests that most docents did not have any formal or extensive training or research experience in the topic of slavery and are not likely to have at hand the facts about the relative treatment of enslaved persons across plantations, let alone across the South as a whole. Nothing, in our experience, was ever said to contradict the views that the master-enslavers espoused and which the docents appear to be stating as fact. This creates the impression that what they are reporting (the views of the enslavers) is in fact true—that enslaved people were better off than those who were free and poor, either Black or white.

The Happy or Grateful Slave

A disturbingly common narrative used to talk about those who were enslaved falls into what we call the trope of the happy or grateful slave. This narrative is best understood as an extension of the Sambo myth constructed by many powerful whites about Blacks (Elkins 1976; Guerrero 1993; Turner 1994). In this construction, people of African descent are seen as childlike, simple, and unable to care for themselves; it insists that the enslaved were happy within their enslavement and grateful for the leadership or care provided by their master-enslavers. Rather than being unhappy or rebellious, the enslaved felt affection for and loyalty to their master-enslavers.

These stories are significant not only because they show up at 19 percent of sites but also because of their resonance with larger derogatory racialized discourses about Blacks that suggest that people of African descent are incapable of self-control and self-rule. The rhetorical device takes on slightly different variations that include explicitly highlighting the loyalty of the enslaved, suggesting their faithfulness through recounting how some enslaved persons betrayed potential revolts, and noting that a percentage of enslaved persons remained on the plantation after legal emancipation. Each of these variations is presented without a context—that is, there is no discussion of punishment of enslaved people nor of the economic and political restraints faced by those legally freed at the end of the Civil War. Instead, acts undertaken by some enslaved people are referenced without the larger context of horror, brutality, and dehumanization that was an intimate part of the institution of slavery.

One example of a speech act that represents the happy or grateful slave story in Virginia include a reference on a text plaque, viewed during a 1997 tour of Gunston Hall, to the presence of a "faithful and humorous old servant." A striking instance of this trope comes from the textual presentation found during a 1998 tour of Chatham Manor, a National Park Service site in Fredericksburg. The site explores the various people who owned the property, the role the property played during the Civil War battles located in Fredericksburg, and the medical practices used during this time. There is also attention paid to the famous white people who volunteered to come care for wounded Union soldiers, including Walt Whitman and Clara Barton. One of the rooms seen on this tour was set up to discuss life on the plantation. A number of text displays allowed visitors to learn of the property's owners and their activities. There was also some, though minimal, information on slavery. In this room, mounted on one wall, is a copy of the will of Hannah Colter, the white woman who owned the plantation from 1838, when her husband died, to 1857. The highlighted selection of her will indicates that she wants her "faithful servant," Charles, to be freed and given funds to go wherever he wanted; the executor was to give him an annuity of $100 until his death. She manumits the rest of the slaves—she owned a total of ninety-two—and orders her executor to provide passage to Liberia (which she mentions several times) or any other state or country in which they want to live. Then it reads, "I further direct that if any of said servants shall prefer to remain in Virginia instead of accepting the foregoing provisions, it is my desire that they shall be permitted by my executors to select among my relations their respective owners."

Next to the copy of the will is a copy of a sales notice that reads:

> This fine residence and farm was sold at public auction. . . . We understand that most of the Negroes of the estate have chosen Mr. Lacy as their Master, preferring slavery, and a residence on the old plantation, to their freedom in a strange country, the will of Mrs. Coalter [sic] giving them their freedom if they chose. "Freedom-Shriekers" will please take note of this.

The text below this says: "A news account and editorial comment from the Fredericksburg *Weekly Advertiser*, November 15, 1857." The impression is that enslaved persons had the opportunity to leave and instead chose to stay. The fallacy of this representation was brought to light on a Black history tour of Fredericksburg (which was arranged through personal contacts and is not an official part of the Fredericksburg history tours sponsored by the local tourism center). What the Black docent explained (and which he provided references for) was that those enslaved at Chatham did not, in fact, have the opportunity to choose to stay or go. Relatives contested Colter's will, and the section that freed her slaves was deemed invalid on the grounds that only humans could legally make choices and that enslaved African Americans were defined in the U.S. Constitution as less than human (Feagin 2000; Lopez 1996). It is important to note that the representation at Chatham Manor has since been corrected to include this information.

Another public site in Virginia, Meadow Farm, located outside Richmond, has as one of its claims to fame that two of its slaves reported to their masters that Gabriel's Rebellion was beginning, and thereby averted a major disaster. At this site slavery was mentioned several times, primarily in relation to the number of enslaved persons owned at the site and their worth. Other themes include the struggles faced by the Sheppard family after the Civil War. One text plaque notes: "In the aftermath of the Civil War, the Sheppards experienced economic hardships. Their Confederate currency was worthless and they struggled to farm their land without slave labor. John continued his medical practice until his death in 1877." A text plaque at the entrance to the site describes the various owners of the land and includes the following: "In 1800, Sheppard family slaves thwarted plans for a well-organized slave uprising known as Gabriel's Rebellion." In a small room with a display of artifacts from the white family that settled the land, the Mosbys, the story of the suppression of the rebellion continues. A text plaque reads, "Sheppard family slaves, Tom and Pharoah, informed authorities about the intended slave uprising known as Gabriel's Rebellion. Mosby Sheppard wrote on behalf of his mother, Elizabeth, to the governor regarding the state's request to purchase Tom and grant him freedom as a reward for his loyalty." In the letter Elizabeth notes that she needs no less than $500 from the state in order to sell him. During the tour, the white southern female employee also noted that "two slaves" had told Mosby Sheppard about the uprising known as Gabriel's Rebellion, which was a "planned massacre of white families by their slaves."

From Louisiana comes a representative example that references not only the loyalty of those enslaved but that of the master-enslaver as well. At this site, the docent said, "It sounds like he [the master-enslaver] was very devoted to his slaves and they to him," and later she told us that "they [the slaves] were family."

Rosedown Plantation, located in the Feliciana area of Louisiana, provides clear examples of the narrative of the happy or grateful slave. At Rosedown, visitors tour by themselves and listen to taped narrations in various locations. The following narration is found at the site of the kitchen, and is presented in the voice of "Henrietta, the slave cook," who speaks in dialect. Throughout her discussion of the Turnbull family and her own, she makes several comments regarding the "good owner" status of the Turnbulls. At one point she says, "Miss Martha, we all love her, she is good and kind. . . . You know, once a week, Massa give each slave, men, women, girls, and boys, when they's old enough to go to the field, five pounds of good clean bacon, one quart of molasses, and as much meal for bread as they want and one pint of coffee." She continues, "Our massa and mistress was good to us when we was sick. They sends us to the doctor right off and the doctor do all he could for us. They even build a hospital for those who be seriously ill. Miss Martha, our massa even come to check and see how we feeling." The cook then goes on to detail how "the worst times we ever had were when the Yankee men come through." After detailing all the destruction that the soldiers wrought, the narration continues, "The war over now, and we free now. We ain't have no celebration after we's freed. We ain't even know we was freed until a good while after. After that, Miss Martha let all the slaves go, 'cept for me, I stayed. Miss Martha ain't got no help now, and Massa Turnbull he gone too. So I reckon she needs me, so I stayed."

This example from Rosedown is perhaps one of the clearest examples of the loyal-slave and good-master narratives rolled into one. Here, as at other sites, Black voices are used to frame whites in socially more desirable ways—they are presented as victims of northern hostility, as innocent in the eyes of those they enslaved, and as valued and loved by them.

Loyalty after Emancipation

Another way that the loyalty of enslaved people to their master enslavers is highlighted is through stories detailing how individuals who were previously enslaved stayed on the plantation and continued to work after being emancipated. Again, this speaks not only to the loyalty of those enslaved but to the goodness of those who enslaved them. At Oatlands Plantation in Virginia the docent said that at the end of the Civil War "the slaves had nowhere to go, they needed to be cared for, so they [the owners] paid them wages." This suggests that the owners were doing those newly emancipated a favor by paying them, rather than noting that paying wages was now a legal requirement. At Belle Grove Plantation, owned by the National Trust for Historic Preservation and run by a private foundation, the brochure notes that the "plantation became a haven for refugees . . . including former slaves made homeless by emancipation." At Shirley Plantation, another private, for-profit site in Virginia, the docent explained that ten Black families stayed on as tenant farmers after the war; this, she asserted, "speaks to how well they [the owners] treated their slaves."

Similar stories of enslaved persons and their descendants who stayed on the plantation or homestead of their master-enslavers come from other sites. For example, at the Hofwyl-Broadfield plantation near Darien, Georgia, we learn from the video that several Blacks and their children stayed on at the plantation after the Civil War and remained there well into the twentieth century. One who had worked on the plantation for over thirty years, Rudolph Capers, appears in the video in clips from an interview that he did in the 1970s. Specifically, we hear his voice (with subtitles appearing on the screen in case viewers cannot understand his regional dialect) as he describes in tones of admiration and praise the efforts made by the two Dent sisters—he calls them Miss Ophelia and Miss Miriam—to keep the plantation economically viable and within the family. We see what appears to be a black-and-white photograph of him, though what year the photo was taken is unclear. Another example can be found in Roswell at the Archibald Smith Plantation House, where during a visit made in 1997 we were told of an elderly Black woman, Mami Cotton, who still lives there. Another example comes from the Jarrell Plantation in Georgia, where the video told us that following the Civil War many of Jarrell's slaves remained on the plantation.

Similar stories are found in the literature that helps advertise these plantations. As part of the tourist literature and books produced about the "Golden Isles" of Georgia, we learn of the life of an African American named Liverpool Hazzard, who had been enslaved on one of the Butler's Island plantations. We see him in a black-and-white photograph standing with another African American man alongside an oxcart and a car. One of the activities that had been frequent on Butler's Island plantations, we are told, was boat racing. We are told that "Liverpool Hazzard of Butler's Island plantation was one of the last slaves who participated in the rowing regattas before the Civil War interrupted these activities" (Sullivan 1990: 18). We then hear from Hazzard himself:

> Old Marster was good to his oarsmen. For three months before the race he wouldn't let us do any work. He'd lock us up if we did, and we'd jest eat and practice and make our muscles strong. He'd sit in the stern of the boat and would keep urgin' us on—calling us by name when we would slack up. At our best we could do the mile in 6¼ minutes. Old Marster loved the races and used to bet $500 on us every time, and when we would win there was sure some celebratin' on the plantation.

We are told nothing else about Liverpool Hazard, neither what he did on the plantation when he was enslaved nor what he had been doing since. He is there to aggrandize the master-enslaver (Sullivan 1990).

Similarly, in the "African-American Heritage Highlights" leaflet produced as part of the tourist information on Brunswick and Georgia's "Golden Isles," we hear about another enslaved person, "Neptune Small, a faithful servant of the King family, onetime owners of St. Simons Retreat Plantation." The leaflet tells us that Small was born in 1831 and looked after the King children. The story of his faithfulness deserves quoting at length:

> When war broke out in 1861, Small accompanied one of the King sons, Henry Lord Page King, into service in the Confederate army as King's manservant. In December of 1862, at the battle of Fredericksburg, King volunteered to carry a dispatch to another section of the Confederate lines. King completed the mission but was killed before he could return to his unit. When none of his comrades would risk the constant rifle fire to retrieve King's body, Neptune did so. Neptune accompanied King's body back to St. Simons where it was buried at Christ Church cemetery. Neptune, who could have chosen to remain on St. Simons, instead returned to the war, serving the youngest King son, R. Cuyler King, until Confederate forces surrendered in 1865.

After the war Neptune adopted the name Small—"for his slight stature," we are told—and was given a tract of land owned by the Kings. Part of that property later became Neptune Park, which is open to the public and is the location of a house that Small built there. Small died in 1907.

Sites across the South use the trope of the happy or loyal slave and poste-mancipation stories in ways that further trivialize the experience of slavery. The implication is that if these slaves were so loyal and happy, their experience under enslavement could not have been that bad. This point is reaffirmed when people suggest that Blacks stayed on plantations after emancipation because of loyalty to their former enslavers. These narratives set up and emphasize a positive relationship between the master-enslaver and those enslaved. We are not asserting that there were never feelings of genuine caring between enslaver and enslaved; rather, we are suggesting that these relationships must be understood within the context of enslavement—that is, the enslaved person's complete lack of ability to make decisions about his or her own life. Literature on those who have been taken hostage shows that in situations of long-term capture, hostages often come to identify with their kidnappers and become emotionally bonded to them (Moorehead 1980: 213–19), but the victims' professions of loyalty do not mean they have not been kidnapped or abused. Instead, it is widely understood that the nature of the dominance, social system, and interpersonal power keeping these people in a victimized status must be recognized. Nothing less than this would be acceptable in the case of enslavement as well.

Untrustworthy Slaves

At a number of sites across the South visitors are told about how the mistress's job was to keep the keys for the plantation. "Keeping the keys" meant that the mistress-enslaver was responsible for ensuring that valuable spices, tea, and other commodities were kept under lock and key. These stories both locate the mistress-enslaver as someone with responsibilities and suggest the untrustworthiness of those enslaved. Examples of this trope are plentiful. At Oatlands Plantation in Virginia, a docent said, "The mistress didn't trust the washing of the finest pieces of silver to the slaves, so she did it herself." At another the docent commented, "The mistress kept keys to the sugars and all the things she didn't want the servants to touch locked in this closet." Other comments included "She [the mistress of the plantation] wouldn't leave it [brown sugar] out where little hands could grab it or where servants could help themselves" and "She [the mistress] had to keep track of the keys; everything here locks because they don't trust people."

The most common version of this story is that of the "whistling walk." This story, which was told across the three states, demonstrates the ways that enslavers attempted to control enslaved people. The story was always told as the visitors were either in the kitchen (generally outside and detached from the house), in the dining room, on the path between the kitchen and the house. At this point the docent would remark how enslaved people "were required to whistle so they couldn't taste the food as they carried it" from kitchen to dining room. One docent commented that the path between kitchen and house was called the "whistling pathway." At Berkeley Plantation in Virginia, where we first encountered this story, most of the white people on the tour laughed or chuckled when this story was told. We are not sure exactly what to make of this response, though we note that people laugh both as a way to express humor and as a way to manage stress in an uncomfortable situation.

In Georgia, the story was told in a similar manner. For instance, at the Antebellum Plantation at Stone Mountain, visitors now take a self-guided tour and read text plaques and handouts to learn about the various buildings and accoutrements on display. Of the text plaques positioned throughout the house, only two mention those enslaved; one of these mentions is framed through the whistling walk story. The text reads:

> From [the] window can be seen the kitchen garden, and the WHISTLE PATH from the COOK HOUSE leading into the WARMING KITCHEN downstairs. The slaves were told to whistle to let the family know food would soon be served, and too, one cannot eat and whistle at the same time!

At another Georgia site, Heritage Hall, a white male docent in his mid-fifties made an almost identical statement when he said that the "whistler's walk" went from the kitchen to the door of the dining room: "The servant had to whistle from the time they left the kitchen to when they got here so the people inside knew he wasn't tasting the food; you can't whistle with food in your mouth."

A representative example from Louisiana came from the Kent House Plantation, a composite plantation museum site in Alexandria, Louisiana. During the docent-led tour of the house, the white female docent asked the visitors if we had heard about the whistler's walk. When other visitors said they had not, she described how the servant bringing the food would have to whistle from the outside all the way to the table and could not stop whistling until he arrived in the dining room. She asked, "Do you know why he had to do that?" and upon receiving a negative reply answered, "So that the family knew that he did not taste the food. He was not allowed to taste the food." She added, "I know this sounds silly and funny, but it's true." She told the story as though it were some peculiar incident, unique to the Kent House, though essentially the same story was told at other Louisiana sites (such as the Myrtles) as well as sites in other states. Another example of the untrustworthy-slave trope comes from the Southdown Plantation House in Terrebonne Parish, Louisiana. When Professor Small toured it in August 1999, he fell into conversation with one of the persons working in the information center. As she described the house, at one point she made reference to the enslaved people who worked in the kitchen, and she added with a laugh, "They had to work with gloves to make sure they didn't touch the food."

A slightly different type of story suggests that those enslaved would fail to work hard if not constantly supervised. This was suggested in a docent's story at Bacon's Castle in Virginia about how a window was positioned so that "from this window they could see what was happening on the plantation, the could watch the garden and see who's doing their job and who's goofing off."

Other stories were framed through the lens of humor in order to tell of how the enslaved might not fulfill their duties and of the enslaver's efforts to see that they accomplished their tasks. One story was told by a young Black woman who led a 1997 tour of Oak Alley Plantation that Professor Small undertook along with twenty-seven other people (all of whom were white, and several of whom he had seen the day before on a tour of Nottoway Plantation). The guide was dressed in nineteenth-century attire and was clearly experienced at giving this tour, since she conducted the whole tour without notes. After going through a couple of the rooms downstairs, the tour group was getting ready to go upstairs but had to wait because another group was still up there. (The leaflet to the plantation points out that it receives over a hundred thousand visitors per year.) The guide passed the time by describing several upstairs rooms and then telling a story about the white children who lived in the house. The doors and windows were kept open in summertime to allow air to flow through the house, but because there was a threat from wild animals, the family had to ensure that the night nanny did not fall asleep. The family built a special chair, one in which the arms of the chair were constructed so that if she fell asleep and put too much weight on one of the arms, she would fall out of the chair and to the floor. This drew a large laugh from the crowd, to the obvious satisfaction of the guide, who smiled enthusiastically. The anecdote was told as an amusing story to make the tour pleasant and was entirely from the point of view of the family, without any concern for the circumstances of the (presumably enslaved) nanny.

Miscellaneous Tropes: Superstition and Black Owners

As well as being represented as untrustworthy, the enslaved may also be designated as superstitious in ways that cast doubts on their character. The first example of this is from the Kent House Plantation in Alexandria, Louisiana. The white male guide for a 1997 tour pointed out with a smile the "gris-gris" over the doors of the cabins "to ward off evil spirits" feared by the enslaved Blacks. He added that this practice reflected the Caribbean influence on the plantation. As we exited one of the cabins, the guide pointed to the horseshoe hanging above it, saying that the "workers" placed it there for good luck.

Finally, the horror and inhumanity of slavery was occasionally deflected by announcing that some Blacks themselves had owned enslaved persons. This was occasionally coupled with a comment about the "overly sensitive" nature of contemporary Blacks, which supposedly keeps contemporary whites from being able to discuss this issue openly. At two sites in Virginia, one a public site, another a private nonprofit foundation site, Professor Eichstedt was told that that a "tremendous number of Blacks owned slaves." At the public site this comment arose in a diatribe by the white woman docent, who argued that people such as Professor Eichstedt had no right to write about the antebellum South since "they rarely knew what they were talking about" and that it is "wrong to judge the past by present standards." Here she was referring specifically to the practice of judging slavery as wrong or bad, since "everyone" in the past had thought slavery was all right. She then noted that she had known a Black man whom she had talked to about this topic and that he had "sheepishly admitted that his family had owned slaves." The docent then explained that this man was a "very militant Black man" who had gone to the Million Man March and had been sure to take his son, though "of course he has children scattered all over the country, but that's neither here nor there." She then returned to noting that no one would talk about the fact that a "tremendous number of Blacks had owned slaves" and that this was due to "political correctness."

The other Virginia site at which this occurred was a nonprofit site where the docent was an elderly white woman. She repeatedly used the term *servants* to explain who carried out certain tasks, and at the end of the tour Professor Eichstedt asked her who the servants were. She replied that "*servants* means slaves" but "we're not supposed to use that word anymore; it causes such a to-do." Upon questioning, she indicated that she was referring to contemporary Blacks. Their disapproval, she suggested, also kept the site from discussing the fact that "some of them owned slaves, lots of them did"; not being able to discuss it was "a shame," in her opinion, because if they could talk about it, "maybe they'd learn something."

A final example of talking about Black ownership of enslaved persons to deflect attention away from white ownership occurred at Springfield Plantation in Mississippi. When Professor Small visited the site in 1999, he was led on a tour by the white owner, who served as docent. Upon learning that Professor Small was studying slavery, the guide asked him if he knew that Blacks had owned slaves too. When Small said yes, the owner produced a self-authored booklet on Black slave owners that was on sale for $3.50. The book concerned the "slave quarters" near the house, Black owners of slaves, and Native American owners of slaves in this region. "It is therefore a misconception that only white people had slaves," he said. He provided the names of a couple of plantations that had been owned by free people of color and added that there were interesting "slave quarters" out back on his property and that Small really should visit them. He then proceeded to provide anecdotes on his own sponsorship of a university student from Jamaica and the corruption of Black politicians in the local region.

Because they are not located in any kind of critical framework, the minimizing and deflecting devices discussed above move the visitor's gaze away from a consideration of the full impact of slavery and focus it on the owner's positive feelings about slavery, the loyalty of slaves to their masters, and so on. The stories we've shared above also should alert the reader to the power and influence of individual docents in framing the entire context of slavery during the tour, including producing publications for that purpose.

Representational Strategies That Valorize Whiteness

Narratives of the Good Owner

The institution of slavery was clearly complex: Its structure and texture varied across space and time, differed depending on what crops were being cultivated, and were affected by individual master-enslavers' characteristics. That is, it is clear that on an intimate level it made some difference in an enslaved person's life if the master-enslaver didn't rape the girls or women or beat, maim, or kill those enslaved. However, the context of the institution of slavery always meant that enslaved persons could not ever count on remaining with specific master-enslavers, always facing the risk of being sold. And again, the notion of "good" ownership must always be understood within the context of being owned.

Thirty-five percent of all sites, including those categorized as segregated, in-between, or engaged in relative incorporation, dealt with the moral dilemma created by the institution of slavery by presenting the master-enslavers whose lives they interpret as good owners. In this chapter we provide examples only from the sites categorized under the trivialization and deflection strategy; chapters 6 and 7 note the ways that other sites also engage in this framing of enslavement. At some sites, what a good owner was remained unspecified; it was merely asserted that the white residents there had been good owners. At other sites, as we will detail below, what constituted a good owner is spelled out in more detail. At only two sites (which fall under the category of relative incorporation, discussed at length in chapter 7) is the idea of the good owner considered in the context of the overall system of slavery. That is, while docents at these sites noted that a particular individual may have been thought of as a good owner, it was still within a context in which the people owned had no freedom. However, at the sites we discuss in this chapter, this was not the case; rather, the category of good owner is not complicated.

What exactly constituted a good owner? As we noted above, at some sites what this meant was not specified. Rather, the family under interpretation was simply defined as having been good owners. Other sites provided more texture. The docent at one private bed-and-breakfast site in Louisiana said, "Good masters would allow slaves to have a yard and grow crops. Good masters would allow them to have Saturday afternoon off and all day Sunday." Others were much more vague. At Belle Aire, owned by a private family in Virginia, the tour guide said the family who had lived there "was the last to lose their slaves in the county; they were a very fine, nice family."

At many sites that used the good-owner story, there were allusions to the fact that the master-enslaver treated those enslaved "like family." (This is the case at Mount Vernon, which we discuss in the next chapter.) This inclusion works to show the emotional relationship between those enslaved and their enslavers. At several sites we were told that the master-enslaver referred to his servants or slaves as "my people" and that he was dedicated to them.

Other sites framed what they were interpreting as a good owner by noting that the master-enslaver spent a specific amount of money tending to the medical needs of the enslaved or by pointing out the building that was used by the plantation doctor. At Ash-Lawn Highland, a site owned by the College of William and Mary, the text on the wall in the slave cabin includes a letter from Thomas Jefferson that states that the "home [that Monroe built] for house slaves was nicer than most in the area." On another wall text notes that Monroe sold slaves only if they were "agreeable" to the sale.

On a 1997 tour of the house at the Kent House Plantation, the guide described a desk located in the salon, or "ladies' room," saying that it was where the lady took care of her correspondence or "wrote a pass for a slave." A pass was necessary because any slaves found on the roads without one "would be dealt with accordingly," the docent said with a stern, matronly voice, as if the enslaved were knowingly doing something wrong and deserved punishment. She them went off into a short digression about slave owning. She said there were two very "bad slave owners" nearby but that they were the exception. Most slave owners looked after "their slaves," and if any of them was treated badly, then the master had to pay a penalty, though she did not say what that might be. "It's a sad thing to say," she said, "but after all, the slaves were an investment, and the owner did not want to harm his investment. In fact, the doctor would come to inspect the slaves regularly—it was part of the Spanish legal requirements from New Orleans—and if the doctor found a slave that had been treated badly, then the slave would be taken away from the owner." The guide then broke into a cheerful smile and said, "Okay, let's continue to the next room." Here a piece of furniture is used to segue into talking about slavery; the opportunity to continue discussing it, however, is nullified by the docent's smile and change of topic as she entered the next room.

Artifacts, such as furniture or paintings, were used as an opportunity to tell good-owner stories and to position slaves as happy or grateful in many other sites. For instance, in 1998 at Stratford Hall in Virginia, the birthplace of Robert E. Lee, a chair on display in the small museum was accompanied by a reproduction of a letter written in 1943 by the donor of the chair, Richard E. Lee of New York City:

I have a beautiful Liberty Chair formerly belong to General Lee . . . and I being a former Slaves Son, and General Lee Was allways So good to his Slaves that I brought the Chair. . . . [We] decided that you all was the ones to have the Chair for the Lee Hall home of General Lee, and so I want to present the chair to My Masters Foundation as A tribute to Lee for his Goodness to his colored people. Allways he treated his Colored People good and fine, and After Lee surrendered in 1865, General Lee looked After his Colored People, long as they lived the Lee family Was Instructed to Continue this obligation Long as Any of the Former Slaves lived, and the Lee family has carried out the wishes of the General Lee.

A similar story comes from the home of Alexander H. Stephens, vice president of the Confederate States of America. His home, Liberty Hall, is part of Alexander H. Stephens State Park in Crawfordville, Georgia. The estate offers a guided tour of Liberty Hall and "an impressive Confederate Museum housing uniforms of the men in grey, muskets, swords, documents, letters, diaries, and more than 300 other items related to the war and Alexander H. Stephens," according to the leaflet. Professor Small took both tours in 1996, and Professor Eichstedt did so in 2001. The 1996 tour of the home was led by a white woman in her fifties who focused primarily on the artifacts in the house. During the tour of the house several details of Stephens' ownership of enslaved persons are mentioned. At the same time the tour group was provided with details regarding two specific individuals, Harry and Eliza, who were favorites of Stephens. Eliza was purchased by Stephens when she was twelve, and she worked for him in a "dedicated manner." She met and fell in love with Harry, an enslaved person on a neighboring plantation. Stephens bought Harry so that Eliza could marry him, and they wed in 1850. They lived on the Stephens plantation with their five children in a two-room house specially built for them, whereas most other enslaved persons had one-room houses. The docent said at one point that several of the enslaved individuals owned by Stephens made it clear that "if they were going to be slaves, the would rather be slaves with Mr. Stephens than with anyone else." There are post–Civil War photographs of Harry and Eliza on the wall, and a photo of their daughter and eldest child, Ellen, who had her own one- room house. The pictures and stories of Eliza, Harry, and Ellen work to deflect attention from the fact that they were enslaved and instead suggests that life was good enough for these people that they chose to stay after emancipation.

A final example of this trope was presented at the Houmas House in Louisiana. When we asked if there were slave cabins on the property, the docent, a young white woman dressed in period clothing, replied that they had been located about one and a half miles back from the house and that she didn't know how many there had been. For no apparent reason, she then immediately said, "Burnside was a good owner." She explained that he was Irish and "didn't want to oppress anyone." He reportedly provided the slaves with eight ounces of meat and vegetables daily, as well as an allowance for clothes. This information, presented in answer to a question about slave cabins, was clearly good-owner framing.

Being a good owner, then, is an important claim to be able to make about the whites that are being interpreted at these sites. Claiming that someone was a good owner softens the blow of slavery and in some cases suggests that the enslavers were in fact benevolent. Interestingly, but not surprisingly, there were also contemporary stories of supposed white benevolence told at plantation museums. Perhaps the most striking was told at Beaufort Plantation in relation to the famous African American painter Clementine Hunter. As we toured the plantation home, the docent (a very elderly white woman) pointed out the numerous Hunter paintings on the walls, frequently telling us stories about them. One of them was a painting of the white family that owns Beaufort; it is the "only painting she did of white people." The docent explained that the white family's father had asked Hunter to paint a picture of the family. She responded that she didn't want to, "'cause I don't paint white people." The father then threatened that if she didn't do it, he would shut off her electricity, which he was paying for. When she again refused to paint the picture, he did turn off her electricity. She "came back three weeks later" and said she would do the painting. While the docent was apparently telling this story for humor, for us it was appalling. Here someone who is presented as Hunter's "patron" is described as using economic leverage over her to get her to paint a subject she did not want to paint: whites. Rather than coming across as a story of warmth or humor, it makes clear the ways by which whites continue to exert control over Black lives and resources.

Whites as Hard Workers

Slavery was a system built on the theft of the productive and reproductive capabilities of millions of African-descent people. Clearly the labor of African Americans provided wealth for many great historical figures and lesser-known individuals alike (Oliver and Shapiro 1995; Feagin 2001). However, the idea that the hard work and effort of individual (white) Americans is what made them successful is foundational to American mythology. Individualism demands that individuals create their own destiny from the sweat of their own brow; if we openly discuss or challenge this notion by pointing out that most of America's great white heroes in fact made their wealth from the theft of land from Native Americans and the forced labor of African Americans, then the mythological status of individualism is seriously undermined. What we find at most plantation museum sites is that the story of individualism is left largely intact—in fact, it is warmly and eagerly embraced. These sites present white Americans, especially men, as particularly hardworking and industrious. Such a framing is quite in keeping with the notion that the presentation of the past is often framed to meet contemporary ideological needs—in this case, the need to maintain the fiction of individualism.

We have found that sites across the South frame whites as hardworking primarily through two devices. First, at many sites there is simple mention made of how hard the enslavers, both male and female, worked. At some sites, the images of workers used are of whites laboring in the fields and doing other tasks. In a few cases it is suggested that whites worked harder than those they enslaved. This is suggested by referencing that the master of the plantation had the "hardest job"—that of "overseeing the whole of plantation operations."

An example of framing that emphasizes the efforts of enslavers comes from Stratford Hall Plantation in Virginia. All of the images in the 1998 exhibit "A Self-Sustaining Plantation" are of white people working and playing. There are absolutely no images of slaves. The text reads: "The plantation is a symbol of America in its youth . . . reaching full development in the 18th century, the plantation became a distinct economic, social, and cultural institution. Today, it is the symbol of the elusive thing called the Southern way of life. It will remain the key to understanding the complex culture of the South." A little further down it says, "It was a self-sustaining village." Again, there is absolutely no mention of the role slave labor played in sustaining it.

Another placard in this exhibit says:

> The story of the colonial planter is the story of a great occupational versatility and unremitting toil. The planter was relieved of some of his physical toil by the widespread use of slave labor, but he assumed complete supervisory control of this agricultural and mercantile enterprise.

It goes on to detail all of the planter's responsibilities. It also details the work of his wife, and how her work led to the generosity and graciousness of southern hospitality. The point seems to be that while these people owned slaves, they worked really hard nonetheless, and it was their efforts and sacrifices that made the whole enterprise work.

The labor of white women is noted specifically in 60 percent of the sites. In some cases this may reflect the fact that most of the members of the organizations that restored or operate these homes are women, and so the sites discuss events and issues that are of interest to them. For some docents, though, we believe it also reflects a desire to counter the idea that most white southern women were like Scarlett O'Hara of *Gone with the Wind*. As a woman docent at Belle Grove in Virginia said after explaining how the white mistress of the house was in charge of overseeing all the making of candles and soap for the plantation, "She was no Scarlett O'Hara!" We were told that "women's hands were never idle" and that they "always had work of some sort in their hands." We learned that these women sewed, oversaw the pressing of the linen, developed the menus for meals, and tended to the sick on the plantation (including the enslaved). Like the work of white men, the work of white women is an important part of the story that is told across the South.

The labor of male enslavers was described differently. In many cases, male enslavers were engaged in political work carried out in the larger white political context. Visitors are always told if the enslaver was a judge, ambassador, or politician at the local, regional, or national level. At various sites, docents explained how exhausting politics were to the person under consideration. We learned that Patrick Henry, Thomas Jefferson, and Robert E. Lee all found their public work draining and that they returned to, or longed to return to, their plantation in order to rest and be rejuvenated. We are told about the ways in which Alexander H. Stephens of Georgia loved quiet moments alone at his home. In other cases we learn that even though an individual person was a politician or general, he was at heart a farmer, someone who loved to work with the earth and design new ways of doing things. For instance, Edward Ruffin, who owned Evelynton in Virginia (and who fired the first shot of the Civil War), was discussed extensively in relation to the concept of crop rotation, which he is said to have discovered and wrote about. Thomas Jefferson is framed not just as a president but in light of his inventions at Monticello. The general ingenuity of the (white) people who lived at that time was directly commented upon at eight sites. Docents referred to the "cleverness," "ingenuity," and "smarts" of the people who lived during that period and had to "make do" with much less than we have today. Among the inventions docents tell us they came up with are ingenious fly catchers, special seats to allow a man to sit down with his sword still attached to his belt, and screens to keep "the makeup from melting" off both men's and women's faces as they sat near the fire. These elites, we learned, were no slackers—they were smart and hardworking, just as most white Americans today believe themselves to be.

In addition to the focus on the work of elite whites, there are a few sites that focus on working-class or middle-class whites. These sites stress their difference from the larger or grand plantations and instead focus on the toil of those of much more meager means. Some of these sites are composites or reconstructions. At these locations the class differences between the inhabitants and elite white planters are stressed; the argument is generally made that it is the white working class, particularly males, that provided the "real foundation" of the South. Such framing is provided at the Rural Life Museum in Louisiana, Alabama Old Town in Alabama, and Chippokes Plantation in Virginia, in language indicating that poor whites were distinctly different from elite whites and that they, unlike their wealthy neighbors, tore progress from the earth with their own effort. Instead of glamorizing wealth, these sites emphasize self-sufficiency, hard work, and dedication. Very little attention, if any, is paid to social functions; instead, the focus is on the labor the white inhabitants performed and the tools they crafted to assist their efforts. Such framing is consistent with the larger white narrative of hard work and self-sufficiency that underpins popular contemporary conceptions of the self-made man. These sites rely on this connection with the larger narrative to overcome the fact that they don't offer grand mansions for tourists to visit.

Contemporary Whites as "Slaves"

The final way that white docents and visitors at plantation museums frame themselves in ways that deflect attention from slavery and minimize its meaning is by describing themselves as "slaves." The idea seems to be to make a connection between contemporary working conditions and enslavement.

In Louisiana, whites referenced themselves as "slaves" to Professor Small as he explored The Cabins Restaurant in 1999. As he approached the buildings, he was not sure whether the first building he saw was The Cabins or whether there was another building at the back. He entered the reception area, where he saw two white women. He said that he was looking for The Cabins and asked, "Is this where the slaves were?" One of the women answered with a smile, "We're the only slaves here!"

Similar phrasing was used by docents at Glen Burnie, a Virginia site, when Professor Eichstedt, after the tour was over, inquired about the number of people who had been enslaved on the property. She was told that while there had been a study done at some point, neither of the two people she was talking to could remember how many had been there. The white woman then looked at the elderly white man and said, "Of course, the slaves are still here—we're still here!" At this point both staff members began to laugh.

At Ash-Lawn Highland in Virginia, the framing of contemporary whites as "slaves" was again a source of amusement, this time for guests. At the end of the house tour the white woman guide said that we could tour the slave quarters and overseer's house if we wanted to. At this point, a white male guest asked a white woman, who was apparently his wife, "Do you want to be in a picture with the slave quarters?" She answered with a laugh, "I feel like I should be in there!" He then said with a laugh, " I want a picture of the girls in the slave quarters—it's only appropriate," and they rounded up their daughters to take their pictures.

In all of these cases, contemporary whites are presumably equating the particular hardships they might be experiencing as individuals at that time— as paid employees, or as the providers of unpaid labor within the family—to the systemic and endemically oppressive system of enslavement experienced by the vast majority of African Americans in the United States from the 1770s through the 1860s. In this way they demean the experience of slavery.

Conclusions

Trivialization and deflection work because they are consistent with the larger contemporary framing of African Americans and public discussions of the institution of slavery. Indeed, we would argue that the public does not even consider that the ways of talking we have identified here are trivializing and demeaning to African Americans who were enslaved and those who came after them. The very fit of these types of comments with the larger frames operating in U.S. social discourse masks their presence, weight, and effect for many people attached to the plantation museum industry. That the weight of these constructs is not glaringly obvious to those who either consume or employ them does not obviate their effect. Rather, these practices become that much more pernicious in reaffirming the existing stereotypes.

What should alert us to the power of these images and framings is that they appear, as we'll show, across all types of sites. That is, they are present at sites that are segregated in their presentation (discussed in the next chapter), in those that fall between categories, and in those that practice relative incorporation. Their ubiquity suggests their power and the profoundly degrading ways that the dominant culture portrays African-descent people.

6 ‖ Segregated Knowledge

Among the sites we explored there is a relatively small number that have incorporated information about the presence and contributions of African Americans and the institution of slavery into their sites at more than a minimal level. These are sites where you can find out not just the number of people enslaved there but who they were and how they lived.

There are two general levels at which these sites incorporate this information. On one, knowledge of slavery and those enslaved is segregated into special tours or separate places within the site. On the second, discussion of these issues has been incorporated throughout the whole of the site and all of its tours. In this chapter we will attend to the first of these levels—sites that incorporate information about slavery and African Americans through methods that segregate knowledge of these topics from discussion of the more traditional (that is, white-centric) site information.

Except in the case of places such as Colonial Williamsburg and Carter's Grove (which is part of Colonial Williamsburg, though separated by several miles), the special tours, often called slave life tours, are generally not offered on a daily basis—perhaps once a month, or during certain months of the year. This limits the exposure the public has to this knowledge and reinforces the importance and normalcy of learning only a white-centric view of history.

While a step in the right direction, in that slavery is actually discussed, sites that follow the segregation-of-knowledge strategy don't necessarily increase the likelihood that visitors will learn about slavery, since visitors self-select to attend the special tours. At these sites it is easy to escape any real contemplation of or education about slavery. However, it is impossible to escape being informed about the magnificent architecture, the well-respected owner of the plantation, or period pieces of furniture or china. In these sites, we argue, whiteness is primarily constructed as something untouched by the slavery that is discussed elsewhere at the site.

In this chapter we demonstrate the disjuncture between what staff present as the regular tour and what is presented on separate tours or through segregated displays. We argue that the main sites are still white-centric and employ the discursive formations and strategic rhetorics found at the sites discussed in previous chapters, continuing a racialized regime of representation that valorizes whiteness. While commendable to the extent that they do include discussion of enslavement, which most of their counterparts largely ignore, these sites work to separate knowledge into segregated realms.

There are several sites that offer separate tours, variously called slave life tours, Black history tours, or African American history tours. We employ these terms as they are applied to tours by the sites themselves. These sites are primarily located in the state of Virginia (Mount Vernon, Montpelier, and Carter's Grove). The River Road African American Museum is located on the grounds of Tezcuco Plantation in Louisiana and so could be considered a segregated site; however, because this site was organized by African Americans and not by Tezcuco staff, and attendance is not necessarily related to attendance at Tezcuco, we discuss it in chapter 8. In the present chapter we include Bulloch Hall in Roswell, Georgia, even though it does not have a separate tour focusing on enslaved life, because it has recently built a cabin with extensive text and voice narration about the experience of enslavement in Georgia and at Bulloch Hall. Given that this information is still presented separately from the main tour, we have included it here. Other sites, such as Colonial Williamsburg, Gunston Hall, and Monticello, also offer separate tours about the lives of enslaved peoples but have recently worked to move the content covered in these tours into the experience of those taking the regular tour as well. These sites, then, exist in a liminal state between the segregated-knowledge category and the category of those that have fully incorporated it into their site.

Before going further, however, we need to attend to the language of normalcy. When we visited sites that advertised a special tour, we were told what time (or on what day) these tours occurred and then were encouraged to go on the site's "regular" or "normal" tour. These terms are used for the tours that are about white people and in which the whiteness of the master-enslavers (indeed, the fact that they *were* master-enslavers) was left unarticulated. "Normal" or "regular" tours, then, are those that are largely racially unmarked and which reference people who are supposedly racially unmarked: whites. While this seems an obvious point, it is one worth making. As we've noted before, whiteness continues to be the assumed status of everyone (as is the status of being wealthy) unless we are told otherwise. And while being wealthy is discussed with much gusto, the fact of whiteness is left obscured.

The tours on the sites that incorporated information about slavery and African Americans generally continued the theme of symbolic annihilation or minimization discussed in the previous two chapters. That is, these sites continued to be focused almost exclusively on family life, famous people, architecture, furnishings, and wealth. Examples of this will be provided as we move through the different segregated tour sites.

Slave Life or Black History Tours

Some sites have created tours focused on the experience of African Americans. At most sites that have such tours, they are not given every day that the site is open. For example, at Gunston Hall, Black history tours are offered on the second Sunday of the month; at Mount Vernon, tours are given during the months of April through October. What is presented at different sites also varies. Some sites, such as Colonial Williamsburg, use the slave life tour as an avenue to discuss the institution and experience of slavery more generally, while others, such as Mount Vernon, focus their tour on what they know about the practice of enslavement at that specific site.

Mount Vernon: Glorifying Washington and the Specifics of Slavery

Mount Vernon defines itself as dedicated to the interpretation and celebration of the life of George Washington. The site, which is quite extensive, is open 365 days a year and hosts over a million visitors per year. House tours run continuously, though given the high volume, many visitors have to wait to begin the tour. The tours are highly structured, and due to the very busy schedule, there is not much time for prolonged question-and-answer sessions with the docents during the tour. Visitors begin at the front porch, and in each room a different docent provides information about that area of the house.

Exterior of the west front of the Mount Vernon mansion in Virginia. Photo
courtesy of the Mount Vernon Ladies' Association.

The primary tour at Mount Vernon was taken three times by the researchers; our experience was that the tours changed very little over time.
It was clear that docents were operating from a fairly standard script, and
their presentation varied little. This tour, true to the mission of the site, provides a celebration of George Washington; we were told as we moved
through various rooms that certain architectural features reflected "how
practical and resourceful a man he was." For instance, he did not use a standard dining table, but instead used a large plank of wood on two sawhorses.
In addition to learning about the architecture and the purpose of various
rooms, we also learned of Washington's social life. Mount Vernon was so
frequently visited by friends and travelers, we are told, that Washington referred to it as a "well-appointed tavern" and commented, not surprisingly,
that "here hospitality reigned supreme; no one was turned away." In the
bedroom the height and width of the bed (to accommodate Washington's
large frame) was noted, as was the fact that here "Martha supervised the servants changing the linen." The white women on staff in the kitchen used a
significant amount of passive voice to describe the duties of the enslaved
people who worked there. For instance, we were told that "meat was prepared here" and that "fruits and vegetables were grown." Docents also re-
placed the word *slave* with vague or inaccurate pronouns to describe who

carried out specific labor. For instance, "they would have several fires, and would regulate the temperature" by raising or lowering the cooking pots," or "you can make brick-oven pizza" in the wall oven. On one tour the word *slave* was used two times; on the two other tours no mention of slavery was made at all. There were, however, numerous passive-voice references to the labor that the enslaved performed.

Overall, the main house tour is designed both to teach visitors about the daily life of the Washingtons via furniture and tools and to emphasize the contributions that George Washington made to the development of the country. This is in keeping with the charter of the Mount Vernon Ladies' Association, which runs Mount Vernon. In the regular tour, then, little is communicated about the Washingtons as enslavers; this pattern is continued in the small museum on the property, where the discussion of them as enslavers is couched in terms of the good-owner story. A text plaque in the small museum reproduces part of a letter from Washington's nephew that describes a trip that the master- and mistress-enslaver took: "The servants of the House, and a number of the field negroes made their appearance— to take leave of their mistress—numbers of these poor wretches seemed much affected—my aunt equally so." Here the emotions of the enslaved, as well as of Martha Washington, are emphasized as indicating great fondness and dedication. That this should be the framing at a site dedicated to the celebration of a great national leader is not particularly surprising. Only if one takes the slave life tour at Mount Vernon is this framing even slightly disturbed.

The slave life tours at Mount Vernon are offered four times a day between April 1 and October 31. Visitors are told to gather at a particular location and wait for the tour guide to arrive. When these tours at Mount Vernon were taken by the researchers, the docent, a white woman in her mid-forties, noted that the tour would not discuss slavery in general, instead focusing only on what was known of slavery at Mount Vernon based on the documentation that they had.

We began the tour by walking from the meeting spot toward buildings that were identified as slave quarters. As we walked, the docent told us that "because wheat [which was grown at Mount Vernon] was less labor-intensive than tobacco, there were a surplus of slaves on the plantation." As we moved into one of the buildings she said that we were "fortunate" because these are "some of the most architecturally complete slave quarters," though this particular building has been reconstructed from research. This

These slave quarters at Mount Vernon were described by a white docent as "superior" to others since they were constructed of brick and had windows. Photo courtesy of the Mount Vernon Ladies' Association.

building was "superior" to the other slave quarters that would have existed because it was made of brick and had windows. As we stood in the barracks-like building, the docent explained that "George Washington was born into a society that accepted slavery" and that he owned ten slaves by the time he was eleven years old. Washington, she told us, changed his feelings about slavery over time; he "really believed that the system would end, that it would die on its own." When the cotton gin was developed in 1793 it "escalated an already bad situation," in his opinion.

The docent asked the visitors on the tour to note the differences between the slave quarters and the main house. She explained that the slaves in these quarters were given cornmeal and five ounces of protein daily. A "non-working slave would only get half of the normal rations." Many slaves "grew their own vegetables to supplement the food provided for them." They also were allowed to hunt, fish, and trap. At this point she noted that enslaved people had a "six days a week" work schedule, and they "got time off on Sundays and holidays."

The docent described how two-thirds of the slaves were married, but only some were able to live together, as spouses were often located on other farms and plantations. Here she noted that the law in Virginia was that the condition of the mother determined the condition of the children—if the mother was a slave, so were the children. The term *night-walking*, she told us, referred to walking to other plantations to see one's spouse and other family. George Washington didn't forbid the practice, but he "did complain that slaves spent too much time walking." Also, while the marriages of slaves weren't legal, Washington recognized their unions. At this point the docent said that "slaves were, unfortunately, considered property" and that Washington "felt strongly about keeping together families, though not necessarily physically" in the same cabin, but on the larger plantation in general.

When we walked out of the quarters and toward the museum annex, a white tourist asked if Washington was a "typical slave owner." The docent stopped and said, "The answer is yes. We can only quote from the words of a former slave, who said that 'George Washington was no different a man than any other.' In other words he was the same as any other man." She then added, "When we think of slavery, we tend to think of the nineteenth century, which was harsher. The eighteenth century was different; there were more resident owners, more personal relationships with the slaves. George Washington was demanding, but he was humane." She told us that he was very demanding "of himself as well," and "concerned about the slaves' well-being." She pointed to a building and said that what is now the gardener's house used to be a slave hospital. "He also referred to the slaves as 'his people.'"

The docent pointed out the area where the "house for [enslaved] families" once stood; it was a two-story brick structure that was taken down in 1793 when an additional part of the main house was completed. The museum annex that we entered next contains a variety of artifacts that have been found in archeological digs related to the slave quarters. She told us, while pointing out the display cases, that archaeologists have found bones of wild animals and pottery. "This pottery may have been things that were handed down to them; possibly they were things that were stolen." Stealing, she informed us, "was one form of rebellion." In this location we talked more about the working conditions and various rebellions in which enslaved people engaged.

The typical workday of the slave was from sunup to nightfall. "They kept fifteen-to-sixteen-hour days. It was very demanding, and slaves did rebel." Rebellion, we learned, came in different forms. Washington "complained of the slow work of the slaves, and they pretended illness." Slaves, she told us, also ran away, though not very frequently. At this point she related two stories about enslaved people.

The first was the story of Christopher Shields, who was at Mount Vernon as a young boy. He was bitten by a dog that they thought was rabid; Washington gave Christopher "a lot of money to go be treated by a special doctor in Pennsylvania." Christopher came back from Pennsylvania and returned the remaining money to Washington. When he grew up he married a slave on another plantation. They were planning to run away, but the note that was to be delivered to one was dropped and found (apparently by whites). The docent said, "I don't really know what happened here, but Christopher was at his bedside when George Washington died." Further, Washington "asked Christopher to sit down [at his side when he was dying], so it seems that they mended their differences."

The second story the docent told was that of Hercules, who, we were told, was a "slave cook." When George Washington went to Philadelphia, Hercules went with him. Hercules sold leftover meals from their house and made a bit of money. "He was a bit of a dandy," the docent explained. After the Revolution, when they returned to Mount Vernon, Hercules ran away. (Here the docent adds that after the Revolution, Washington said he wouldn't buy or sell another slave.) After he ran away, a "visitor to Mount Vernon said to Hercules' daughter that she must be sad not to see her father. She said, 'Oh, no, sir, because now he's free.'" The docent said, "So, though George Washington wasn't cruel, they [the slaves] weren't free." She followed this by noting that in 1983 a slave memorial was built at Mount Vernon; it is the "only one of its kind in the country or the state."

George Washington, she explained, "freed slaves when he died—they were to be freed after Martha's death." But then she said that Martha "couldn't free her slaves," though why she couldn't wasn't explained to the tour participants. The docent followed this by saying that a slave named "Sambo Anderson married Agnes, a dowry slave of Martha Washington's. Sambo returned to help build George Washington's tomb when he died." This story apparently was meant to show that those enslaved by Washington had respect (and perhaps no hard feelings) toward the man who enslaved them. The tour guide then said that she was very fortunate to be able to work with a descendant of George Washington's slaves who gave tours on Tuesdays.

Once outside, she reported that Washington never took a public position against slavery, but personal correspondence revealed his distaste. Again, he thought it would die out on its own and that it was a financial drain for slave owners. She repeated that "he did free slaves" and that he owned a total of

316 slaves, but not all were his—presumably Martha owned some. She told us that there were 90 at Mount Vernon. "In 1799, there were second- and third-generation families here. Forty-two percent of them were unable to work, as they were elderly, infirm, or too young." She asserted that "he was supporting them" and that "he provided for them."

We walked the short distance to the overseer's house, where the docent said, "We tell the story of the punishment of Charlotte, a seamstress." Anthony Whiting, who was the white overseer, punished her. (She added as an aside that "Davie was a Black overseer—a slave—at Riverview, and George Washington thought highly of his abilities.") Whiting, she explained, punished Charlotte for her "insolence." They have his letter to Washington detailing her behavior and punishment and Washington's response saying "to punish her if she needed it." Charlotte, the docent said, threatened to tell Martha, which "she obviously does because when Whiting dies six months later, they go to replace him" but said that they wanted someone different because Whiting "set a bad example." "They said that he drank a lot, entertained inappropriately, and was debauched," which, the docent explained, "suggests that Charlotte got to tell her side of the story." The docent noted that Martha tended to intervene more on behalf of enslaved people and to perhaps be "softer" than George.

Outside the overseer's cabin the tour ended with the usual "Are there any questions?" Since there weren't any more questions, the group disbanded, and the researchers took notes on the text in the slave cabins. The text includes the following, from an interview with a former Mount Vernon slave in 1838: "The sun never caught him [George Washington] in bed, and he was unwilling it should find any of his people sleeping." Also noted was that "about half of the slave population worked at the Mansion House Farm and lived in the wings of the greenhouse, in cabins across the lane, and in nearby outbuildings. They included mostly families, some single and widowed adults, and skilled workers whose families lived on outlying farms." It also elaborated the details of one family, made up of "Isaac, a carpenter; his wife, Kitty, a dairy maid; and their nine daughters." As Eichstedt was sitting in the slave quarters, a white couple in their late fifties came in and took pictures. While chatting, the man said, "They didn't live too bad, better than a lot of them do today." The male member of another white couple who entered the site a few minutes later repeated that statement almost verbatim

Overall, this slave life tour provides specific information regarding the experience of enslaved people at Mount Vernon. It is done within the framework of presenting George Washington as an iconic hero and trying simultaneously to humanize him. The tour, to some extent, suffers from this very dynamic. For instance, we were told that while Washington was very demanding of those who were enslaved to him, he was also equally demanding of himself. There is, however, a fundamental difference between being demanding of oneself and having the ability to compel through physical force (carried out by working-class whites in Washington's employ) more than three hundred people to work as hard as oneself. It is noteworthy that the staff here does talk about some of those enslaved people who at least attempted to run away, and notes that though Washington wasn't a particularly bad enslaver, African Americans rebelled in response to their captivity.

Race and Class: Carter's Grove and Colonial Williamsburg

Colonial Williamsburg is an enormous entertainment complex dedicated to informing visitors about life in the capital of Virginia during the Revolutionary period. Colonial Williamsburg is a huge heritage attraction and is composed of both a nonprofit wing and a for-profit corporation. The complex consists of five hundred original and reconstructed buildings on 173 acres. Visitors pay $33 to attend the park for one day, or $39 to $59 to purchase a Patriot Pass valid for one year. Since there have been such excellent descriptions of Colonial Williamsburg provided elsewhere (see, for example, Handler and Gable 1997), we will not provide a deep exploration of the site. However, we will note that in 1998 and 2000 the tour we took of the governor's mansion and the introductory tour that orients visitors to Colonial Williamsburg contained very little information about enslavement. These tours followed the traditional focus on architecture, famous white men and their family lives, and politics. Rather than describing these, we will focus on the "Other Half" tours given at Colonial Williamsburg proper and the tours provided at the slave quarters at the complex's secondary location, Carter's Grove. We will briefly discuss the tour of the mansion at Carter's Grove since it has been less extensively covered in the extant literature. The "Other Half" and slave life tours at these two sites are given daily throughout the year and are designed to teach the visiting public about the experience of enslaved African Americans in the early colonies.

The "Other Half" Tour

The "Other Half" tour at Colonial Williamsburg meets at the Lumber House, which is located at the far end of the Palace Green from the Governor's House. There an African American guide dressed in period garb joined Professor Eichstedt, twenty-two other whites, and seven African Americans. She explained her accent by saying that she was from the West Indies and hoped that no one would have a hard time understanding her speech. She told us that we would be exploring Africa, the Middle Passage, slavery, preparation for sale, urban versus rural enslavement, and the contributions that African Americans made to society. She also told us that there was no such thing as a too private, too personal, or embarrassing question, so that we should feel free to ask whatever we wished.

She began the tour by explaining the history of civilization and slavery in Africa and how slavery within Africa differed from that in Europe and Americas. She also traced the differences between indentured servants and enslaved people and explained the changes in laws over the years. For instance, she began by telling us how the law originally said that people who came from a country that wasn't Christian would be slaves. Later she noted that the laws changed so that even if someone had become a Christian or had been baptized, that person could still be enslaved. She told the story of Alfonso Johnson, one of the original twenty Africans brought to Jamestown in 1619, and how he went on to be free, owning 250 acres of land and sponsoring five indentured servants from England. She stated, however, that it was never an "equal playing field," that things were "based on racism and prejudice." At this point a white visitor asked if Blacks owned slaves, to which she responded yes and gave an example. She then returned to describing the evolution of slave laws over time by telling the story of John Punch, an African-descent servant who ran away with two white indentured friends. The court said that they should all be whipped thirty times, that his white friends, Victor and James, should serve an additional two years of servitude past their original term of indenture, but that Punch would serve for the "rest of his natural life." Throughout the tour she continued this chronology of the changes in slavery.

This tour and the one given at the slave quarters at Carter's Grove are strongly informed by a class and race analysis. Both tours stress the class differences within the white population. For instance, on the "Other Half" tour at Colonial Williamsburg the guide told us that slavery was based on "the class system plus racism plus prejudice." At a building presented as occupied by a free Black shoemaker, the guide told us that "we [the visitors] would be commoners" in the past. She continued by pointing to the street that runs in front of the Governor's House and saying, "If you think this is where your family comes from, you're wrong. No, you were poor. Poor whites had more in common with free Blacks and slaves than with the wealthy." She continued, "The wealthy named poor whites 'crackers'" and felt that "one African Negro was equal to three white trash." She explained that England was dumping convicts in the colony and that those who came this way were far too poor to "afford a slave, because you can't get a slave on credit." "The two percent who make the rules want no competition" from anyone else.

This explicit discussion of class differences among whites prompted nervous laughter from the group; several whites wrinkled their brows and appeared taken aback. She continued by saying that 80 percent of whites were poor and lived similarly to free Blacks and slaves, in a twelve-by-fifteen-foot dirt-floor shack. Such circumstances, she said, led to things such as Bacon's Rebellion, which she described, and then she explained how the wealthy used the law to divide poor whites from free and enslaved Blacks. She also made a reference to the possible parentage by George Wythe of a "mulatto boy who was taught Greek, Latin, and astronomy."

How enslaved people got to the Americas was the next topic of discussion. Here she used our bodies to demonstrate how those brought from Africa were packed either "loose or tight" in slave ships. We were told to stand side by side and then to turn so we faced our neighbor's back and then to pack ourselves tightly together. She told us that twenty-five to thirty percent of those on tightly packed ships died in the crossing, and that the stench was unbelievable. "These things we know," she said, "based on diaries kept by captains of the ships and the ship logs." We then learned of the beginning of Dutch and Portuguese slave trading, the food enslaved people were fed in transport, what killed them (most often diarrhea), and how "two weeks before reaching their destination, slaves were made to dance" in order to try to strengthen them. According to the tour guide, when slave ships arrived, announcements would be made in churches, at the courthouse, and by the town crier about the impending slave auction. Slaves, she told us, worked on plantations of different sizes. Small plantations had five to fourteen slaves. A medium plantation consisted of fifteen to fifty slaves, while a large plantation held over fifty people enslaved.

At this point she said that "slaves were smart people" and used singing to teach work rhythms, to control the pace of labor, and to communicate about the whites on the plantation without them knowing it. In Barbados, she explained, the authorities outlawed drums because they saw that enslaved people were using them to communicate and the whites were afraid of slave uprisings. She continued by explaining how enslaved people "were taken to the West Indies for seasoning" and how brutal that process was. Most slaves brought there "only lived five to seven years." She finished the tour by explaining the general life spans of both whites and Blacks in what became the United States. At the end of the tour, she noted that she had provided us with a great deal of information and asked if there were any questions. Several people stayed to talk with her after the tour ended.

Carter's Grove

The tour at the slave quarters at Carter's Grove was very similar to the one at Colonial Williamsburg in its emphasis on class similarities between poor whites and enslaved African Americans. There was, however, a primary difference: The Carter's Grove tour was set within the slave quarters itself, while the tour at Colonial Williamsburg walked us down one of the mercantile streets in Williamsburg. At Carter's Grove they have reconstructed slave quarters, with a couple of pens for animals and small gardens to demonstrate how slaves would have tried to supplement their diets. Visitors must pass the reconstructed buildings as they exit the main visitor center and enter the grounds. Even visitors who are not planning on learning anything about enslaved people must walk past the buildings and the period-dressed interpreters to get to the mansion or the rest of the site. Based on our limited observations, we suggest that this physical organization sets up an interesting dynamic; the white visitors we observed either studiously avoided looking at the slave quarters as they passed or acknowledged their presence and often stopped and took a tour or spoke with the interpreter. The Black visitors we observed at this site always stopped there when they encountered it.

In addition to the tours at the slave quarters, Carter's Grove also has first-person interpretations occurring away from the site that deal with slavery and its aftermath. When Professor Eichstedt was there in 1999, there was a powerful first-person interpretation called "The Soul of a Sharecropper" being performed. In the visitor center there was a placard noting the time this program would start and telling visitors who were interested in attending where to wait. The group specifically waiting for the start of the program consisted of about ten people; however, by the time the program was over there were approximately thirty-five people in attendance. The interpretation was of Jenny Joseph, a Black woman who told the story of her emancipation and her search for her daughter, who was sold away from her. The interpreter walked slowly up to the group, wearing period clothing and carrying a load of laundry, and began talking to the audience about who she was and what she had been through. She told of the desire slaves felt to name themselves "when freedom comes," and of her friend (their relationship is not made clear) James Henry, his strength and skills in the kitchen and the field, and how "he could be telling good stories." James Henry said that they had been part of an "experiment in freedom." They were part of a group of enslaved people who had fled to a fort occupied by Union soldiers very early in the war. She said that hundred of slaves were there, and "those Yankee boys looked on freed slaves as a nuisance and contraband of war. Yankees didn't treat slaves any better than Southerners did." The commander of the fort wrote to Lincoln and asked what to do with this "contraband"; four months before the Emancipation Proclamation, Lincoln wrote back and said that these people were officially freed. The commander's name was Mitchell, and when the freed people left the stockade they "finds property and starts a village that they called Mitchellville" where "they had their own food, built their own houses and own stores, filled those stores with goods like fabric, pans, and such." The interpreter then looked at the group and asked about the spectacles on a woman's head, and next asked the children if they liked school. She said that it was important that "little Negro children gots to go to school and now are real happy to go to school because they weren't allowed to read and write before." She explained how northern missionaries came to Mitchellville and built churches; there were two Baptist churches and a Methodist church. She said that "these Negroes working on the forts were making four to twelve dollars a month, but others go back to the plantation they from and were working on the farm, but now for a fee." Some freed people "formed things called collectives; they joined money and buy land, and if they can't afford it they rent land." She said they decided in Washington that white southerners who had lost land during and immediately after the war would be allowed to have their land back, and that "now land is taken back by the government" and "that's not right."

The interpreter looked wistful and said that she "likes that story about

At Carter's Grove in Virginia, first-person interpretations give visitors an understanding of the experience of enslavement and newfound freedom. Here, "Jenny Jones" tells listeners how her four-year-old daughter was sold away from her and how she struggled to reunite with her after being freed.

Mitchellville, about people living in freedom. James Henry say they are no longer people in servitude and he's not going to call anyone Massa anymore." She then proclaimed, "I don't want food and land; what I thinks about is my twelve-year-old girl. I can only hope that Mary is still on the same plantation." The interpreter started to look distressed as she recounted how, eight years after her child was sold away from her, she "went to the bottom of the road and pulls what the good Lord gaves to me. I walks up the stairs and knocks on the door." She said, "I was shaking so hard, and a little girl comes to the door and tells me to go around to where the kitchen

First-person interpreter at Carter's Grove, Virginia.

is." Crying, the interpreter said, "I hears a sound, it's Mary, and someone is screaming and pushing me away and then she's pushing me away and saying, 'I don't know you!'" Indicating when her daughter Mary, was sold away from her, she asked, "What can a four-year-old do to help a woman who's just give birth to two babies?" The white woman of the plantation, she told us, started yelling, "Get off my porch." The interpreter said, "I'm not ashamed to say I got on my knees and begs, 'Don't do this to me.' I then feels someone picks me up and I find myself at the bottom of the road without my girl." At this point, at least ten women in the audience, both white and Black, were obviously crying; other people looked distressed.

After this very intense sequence the interpreter broke character and introduced herself. She said she developed this program because she wanted to look at freedom, the prospect of freedom, and what it might mean. She explained that in 1862 "Sea Island folks" ran away to the Union fort and received their freedom before the Emancipation Proclamation. But for this woman, "freedom wasn't freedom if she didn't have her daughter." Her daughter had been sold away from her when she was four; eight years later, the girl was scared because she didn't remember her mother and knew only the house she now worked in. The interpreter explained that she wanted to show how fear affected everyone. The mistress "was feeling fear because her world is changing and she spread her fear to her own daughter and to other people's children as well." This mistress had taught the young Black girl to be afraid if her mother came looking for her. The interpreter said, "Fear was affecting people with Black faces, as well as also affecting people with white faces; so the system of slavery was still in effect." Mitchellville, she told us as an aside, is now Hilton Head, a fancy resort destination.

We were encouraged by the interpreter to stop at the slave quarters, that it would be a "good thing to do." She said that if "my boss told me seven years ago that I'd be out here dressed like this, I would say no, I wouldn't do it. But I've learned that I shouldn't be ashamed to tell my grandmother's story—well, I wasn't ashamed, but I had a lot of anger. I've found telling the story to be very cathartic." The experience, she says, is "very healing." She's seen "white and Black faces there, and knows that a lot of healing happens." She reiterates the times when her interpretation is given and then ends the program by answering questions from the group and speaking with individuals as they slowly disperse.

The tour at the slave quarters begins beneath a spreading tree, where an African American man dressed in clothing that would have been typical for a field slave waited on a bench. He began by telling us there were four buildings set up as living quarters, that the rooms held four to six people each, and that the fences we saw set apart areas for small gardens. He told us that there were sixteen house slaves and twenty-four field slaves at this location.

Drawing on the theme present at Colonial Williamsburg, he made parallels between poor whites and enslaved African Americans; he said that prior to the arrival of slaves, whites on the property had been doing the same work. "There were more poor folks than wealthy, and that both [poor whites and slaves] worked hard." Along with enslaved families there were also white tenant farmers here. The master-enslaver was Nathaniel Burnell, whose grandfather was Robert "King" Carter, who at "one point was wealthier than the king of England." The guide asked everyone in the group to put a hand in the air, and then to put down our hand if we weren't white and male and didn't own acreage. Only one person on the tour was left with his hand up. The interpreter then asked the rest of us, "Who do you think you had the most in common with? Those who have their hand in the air and could make decisions, or all the other people with their hands down?"

The interpreter then shifted from this topic of the similarity of poor whites with enslaved people and free Blacks to the type of lives that enslaved people had on the plantation. He told us that only field laborers took off on

Interior of slave cabin at Carter's Grove, Virginia. The furnishings contrast starkly with those of the main house.

Sundays. Neither the cooks nor the house staff had time off, because they still had to serve those who lived there. He then said that slave marriages weren't legal because "they wanted the right to be able to sell people off." Owners, he said, could be fined ten thousand pounds of tobacco for allowing enslaved people to marry. He asked the group if we had heard about slaves "jumping the broom," to which several people answered affirmatively. He said that when a man and woman were on one side of the broom, they were individuals, but when they crossed it, they were a couple. He told us that most people don't know that jumping the broom can be traced back not only to Africa but to Scotland and Ireland as well—"it wasn't just an African custom."

At this point we entered what he identified as "the gang house." This place served as a sleeping place for unmarried folk; here, he told us, "whites and Blacks slept together" in the same bunkhouse. Children of six and seven were working in the fields on this property. They also spent significant amounts of time with their elders, who were "seen as being important" because they were a source of information, "they have survival skills important then and now." Later he returned to the topic of the elders and said that most people didn't live long in that time; forty to forty-five was the average age at which Black men died, and white men only lived to about fifty. "Here we know of one slave, Paris, who in 1775 was seventy-one years old, and that he died around eighty, which was very old in those days." The interpreter said that enslaved people didn't run away much because their families were there, and that the owner had allowed four generations of slaves to remain on the property without selling them off.

We exited the building into a garden area and were told that chickens were the only domesticated animals enslaved people were allowed to raise for themselves. They were allowed to sell the surplus of their gardens, and while the owners were required to provide food, clothing, and shelter to enslaved people, if they allowed the slaves to produce a little, "they [the owners] had less to do for them." He asserted that the "housing here is common to the way that poor folks were housed then."

Shifting the topic, he said that "slaves were a lot more intelligent that the wealthy gave them credit for," and that he was going to "prove it to you now." He noted that singing was a part of slave life that was very important—it was a way of "communicating, feeling better, and setting the pace." He sang a line—"See old buzzard flying high"—and said, "Now Massa is singing along, clapping hands," and the slaves were smiling because they were "outwitting him. He was the buzzard they were talking about and he didn't even know it!" The guide said that slaves were "passively resisting against the master" and using "slave wit."

He turned back toward the cabins and looked at the crowd, which by this time was made up of thirty-eight whites and two African Americans, and said to the whites, "You folks can't trace your wealth back to Jefferson, George Washington, or Wythe. So I'd like to welcome you home," again referencing the class similarities between poor whites and Blacks. He ended the tour by saying, "Folks, there is nothing we can do about the past; slavery was here and was a bad thing. But we can make sure it doesn't happen again."

The presentation at the main house at Carter's Grove is quite distinct from what is found in the first-person interpretations and the tour of the slave quarters. The story that is told is a very brief story of the building of the house in the 1750s, when the home was "clear evidence of the wealth and status of the planters who ruled the Virginia colony." The home was built by Carter Burrell, who inherited the land upon which it was built from his grandfather, Robert "King" Carter. The introductory video, pamphlets, and tour guides all note that this house has been called the "most beautiful house in America." While the tour provides some interpretation of the earlier inhabitants, its primary focus is on the lives of Archibald and Mollie McCrea, who bought the house in 1928 and who had "the means and the motivation to set things right" with restoration. The McCreas engaged in a variety of restorations and improvements on the property, and therefore much of the interpretation is of life in the 1930s. This was an interesting choice given that the rest of Colonial Williamsburg and Carter's Grove focuses so heavily on the colonial period. Professor Eichstedt did ask one of the white women at the house, an interpreter in her forties or fifties, if there was any interpretation of the earlier history of the house; she indicated that there was some of that. Eichstedt then asked if she knew how many slaves were held on the plantation. The docent answered, "I'm not really sure, I don't answer that question enough, or very often, so I'm always afraid I'll forget, but you can always ask in the slave quarters, because they'll know," and she said, "I think it's something like eleven to fifteen house servants and eighty or sixty field slaves."

Bulloch Hall: A Building Apart

Bulloch Hall in Roswell, Georgia, has a separate display that addresses the lives of enslaved African Americans but does not actually have a separate

Make Sure You
Visit the
ave Quarters
ring Your Tour.

African American dolls on sale at the Carter's Grove gift shop.

guided tour. Like sites that have segregated tours, Bulloch Hall's main tour
focuses almost exclusively on the white enslaver and his family. Visitors have
to enter a different space, without the presence of a guide, to learn about
those who were enslaved.

This site is organized to show off the home of Mittie Bulloch, the mother
of President Theodore Roosevelt and the grandmother of Eleanor Roosevelt. The home tour is organized along the lines of a traditional white-
centric tour and incorporates symbolic annihilation and trivialization. We
toured the site two times, once in 1997 and once in 2001; the tour described
here is the one Professor Eichstedt went on in the winter of 2001, but the
earlier one was substantially the same.

The tour of the main house provides a quite detailed discussion of the
history of the building and its architecture, a more limited discussion of furniture, and extensive exploration of the history of the families that lived at
Bulloch Hall and in the surrounding town. This is one of the few sites, along
with the Archibald Smith Plantation House, that mentioned that the
Cherokee were driven from the land so that whites could confiscate it.
There were four uses of the term *slave* on the tour, which lasted over an
hour; two were in reference to a slave cabin, one provided the number of
people enslaved (forty-three slaves for sixteen acres), and the final mention

Bulloch Hall, in Roswell, Georgia, provides an example of segregated representation and knowledge.

was that slaves had made the bricks used to reconstruct the house after it initially burned down. Euphemism and passive voice were used to refer to other labor performed by enslaved people. For instance, when discussing the floor plan the docent noted that anyone "caring for the house" would go in through the back, and that "food goes up the back stairway and into a holding pattern." While the tour did not include any specific examples of trivialization, faithful slaves are mentioned in detail in the book sold at the plantation, *A Glimpse of the Past* by Clarece Martin (1996). Early in the book, as Martin describes Mittie's childhood, she describes the slaves that were brought with the family from coastal Georgia:

> The slaves were, "Daddy" Luke Mounar, the butler and handyman, a husky Nubian whom Martha Bulloch taught to read and write; his wife "Maum" Charlotte, the housekeeper, a slender and handsome mulatto; "Daddy" Stephen, the coachman-groomsman, gentle and beloved; and his wife, "Maum" Rose, the rotund cook and ruler of her domain. (1996: 9)

Later, as they settle into the home at Bulloch Hall:

> As was customary, Major Bulloch gave a young slave to each of his children, to be his "little black shadow." He gave the slave girl, Lavania, to Mittie, and to Anna

he gave Bess, and the girls slept on straw mats on the floor at the foot of their mistresses' bed at night and followed them everywhere during the day. While Mittie and Anna were attending classes at The Academy, the two-room log schoolhouse for the colonists' children, Lavania and Bess waited on the school steps with the other slave children. They also helped with the household chores. Henry, a mulatto boy, polished the floors of Bulloch Hall by scrubbing them with corn shucks tied to his feet. At mealtime he sat on a stool nearby and shooed the flies away with a feather fan. He often dozed during the meal and the fan would fall into the food on the table, to the children's delight. (Ibid.: 10–11)

Later on in the book, as she describes the wedding of Mittie Bulloch to Theodore Roosevelt Sr. (the future parents of President Theodore Roosevelt), she says, "The servants giggled and chatted as they did last minute chores, and laughter and excitement filled every room" (ibid.: 21). Overall the image is of loving, dedicated slaves, whose activities and idiosyncrasies are also a pleasant source of amusement for the white family and for the reader of this book. On the tour, however, little information is shared about the fact that Mittie belonged to an enslaving family or that she had the personal services of her own "little black shadow."

Bulloch Hall does provide visitors an opportunity to explore slavery through visiting a reconstructed slave cabin near Bulloch Hall mansion itself. This cabin is not on the guided tour; however, we heard two different white women guides tell visitors to make sure they went over to the cabin before leaving. This in some ways is similar to a separate tour in that visitors self-select whether to learn about enslavement.

As Professor Eichstedt approached the slave cabins, she noticed that they did not look like other examples of such cabins she had seen—they appear quite well made and are painted white. However, according to a plaque outside the cabins, they are reconstructions of the "dog-walk" style (a cabin with two separate rooms separated by a covered breezeway) that was known to exist on the plantation in this location. Additionally, "they are painted white because we believe they would have been so painted since they are so close to the main house."

The plaque points out that up to twenty people lived in this building and the other building known to have sat perpendicular to it. The room on the right has been set up as a informational museum of sorts, and the room on the left present material objects that would have been found in slave quarters. The museum exhibit consists of text placards, artifacts, and a voice narration that covers a variety of topics. The written text is organized under a variety of different headings, such as "Telling Their Story," "Economics of Slavery," "Slave Children Growing Up," "Lingers in One's Memory," "Living Day to Day," "Food and Clothing," and "Slave Cabins Inside and Out." The introductory plaque, titled "Slave Life in the Piedmont: The Story of Roswell's Enslaved African Americans," reads:

> Bulloch Hall, Smith Plantation, Barrington Hall, Primrose Cottage, Mimosa Hall, the Presbyterian Church, and other antebellum buildings in Roswell proudly remind us of the wealthy landowners who occupied Roswell before the Civil War. However, little remains to tell us of the enslaved African Americans who built these beautiful homes, tended the gardens, worked in the mills, performed the domestic chores, and minded the children. The small cabins they occupied are absent from the landscape of Roswell except at Smith Plantation. Their names, their lineage, and their lives are forgotten. Here at Bulloch Hall, the reconstruction of this slave cabin, with its living quarters and exhibit, provides opportunities to explore and recognize the role of African-American slaves in the history of Roswell. This exhibit is dedicated to their legacy.

The other text plaques throughout the room contain information gleaned from a variety of sources, including WPA slave narratives (particularly those found in Killion and Waller 1973). Under the heading "Telling Their Story" are a number of different voices and perspectives from those who were enslaved. What is interesting about this display is the relative matching of more positive recollections of enslavement with those that are decidedly negative. For instance, the words of Leah Garrett (interviewed in Augusta) depicted life with a preacher whom she characterized as "one of the meanest men I ever seen":

> Most times he beat his slaves when they hadn't done nothing at all. One Sunday morning his wife told him their cook wouldn't never fix nothing she told her to fix. Time she said it he jumped up from the table went in the kitchen and made the cook go under the porch where he always whipped his slaves. She begged and prayed but he didn't pay no attention to that. He put her up in what us called the swing, and beat her till she couldn't holler. The poor thing already had heart trouble; that's why he put her in the kitchen, but he left her swinging there and went to church, preached and called himself serving God. When he got back home she was dead.

The narrative continues with a story of how an enslaved child fell down a set of high stairs while holding the white child she was watching. While the white baby was not seriously injured, when the preacher came home he "picked up a board and hit this poor little child across the head and killed her right there. Then he told his slaves to take her and throw her in the river. Her Ma begged and prayed, but he didn't pay her no attention; he made them throw the child in." Placed immediately next to this text, which lays out the brutality of enslavement, is a narrative by Neal Upson of Oglethorpe County, who discusses his master's "goodness" in ensuring the safety, education, and well-being of "his slaves." Upson describes how his sister was hired out to a family sixteen miles from his master's farm. However, Anna, his sister, "didn't like it there so she run away" and returned home. Anna tried to get Upton to bring her food without telling anyone she was there; he was so frightened by her thinness, however, that he told "Mammy."

> Her and Marster went and brought Anna to the house and fed her. That poor child was starved most to death. Marster kept her at home for three weeks and fed her up good then he carried her back and told them folks what had hired her that they had better treat Anna good and see that she had plenty of eat. Marster was driving a fast horse that day, but bless your heart, Anna beat him back home. She cried and took on so, begging him not to take her back there no more that he told her she could stay home.
>
> When the war was over they closed the little one-room school what our good Marster had kept in his back yard for his slaves, but our young Miss Ellen learned by sister right on till she got where she could teach school.

In this display, "Telling Their Story," there are three positive remembrances of slavery, two that are clearly negative and highlight brutality, and one that is framed more neutrally. One of the positive remembrances is from Georgia Baker, who was enslaved to "Alexander Stevens [sic], the Vice President of the Confederate States of America." She says she was "born on the plantation of a great man" and that her mother was the cook at the big house and her father was a field hand. She describes the clothes they wore, noting that "winter clothes was good and warm" and that "chillun what was big enough done the spinning and Aunt Betsey and Aunt Tinny, they wove most every night till they rung the bell at ten o'clock for us to go to bed." She goes on to describe the good food they were provided every Christmas day.

The text concludes: "Us sure did have the best master in the world. If ever a man went to Heaven, Marse Alec did. I sure does wish good old Marster was living now." This series of quotes appears to balance the representations of enslavement; the rest of the text takes a similar approach, where both the inhumanity of slavery and efforts of "good owners" are depicted. For instance, under "Slave Children Growing Up" the text indicates that children worked at as young an age as possible. On this placard is also a description of the assignment of slave children at Bulloch Hall as "companion or shadow to each of his [Major Bulloch's] children." After telling how "little black Sarah" and Irvine Bulloch, who were both afraid of the dark, "became inseparable companions" to protect each other from "the imaginary dangers of the house or grounds," the text goes on:

Relationships with these companions were often loving ones; however, this was not a situation of equality. These enslaved companions often waited upon and served their young masters. In *Story of the Roosevelt Family*, A. R. Cowles tells of young Stewart Bulloch shooting and killing his "little shadow" in an attack of temper. Stewart's punishment was to be sent abroad for a year of foreign travel.

Further commentary in this vein follows on another plaque:

Numerous books, articles, and even television documentaries have stated that the King family treated their slaves poorly. In his book *The King Family 1629–1993*, direct descendant Robert N. King says Roswell King "early-on, earned a reputation for his severity of punishment to slaves to produce more and demand less. His attitude toward slaves was revealed by the fact that he was known to have fathered a child by his head-driver's wife. This sort of practice some owners accepted as a right of position."

Malcolm Bell Jr., in *Major Butler's Legacy*, states that King [who ran Butler's rice plantation on the Georgia coast before moving to Roswell] broke up slave families to punish them or to silence quarrels. He also sentenced troublemakers to a penal colony called Five Pound on Little St. Simons Island. . . . Bell's book tells of Roswell King whipping an 18-year-old slave named Chance who refused to work and forcing a captured runaway to walk home on swollen legs all the way from Savannah, more than 60 miles.

In line with the overall approach of the exhibit, however, there is balancing text that focuses on another local owner, Archibald Smith:

On the other hand, Archibald Smith contemplated freeing all of his slaves in the later 1830s. Family documents indicate he tried to prepare them for freedom by teaching them to support and govern themselves. However his attempts failed. Family documents state that Smith believed "they became demoralized." By 1865, Archibald Smith had instituted a sharecropping system. A statement of the crop for that year shows nine slaves raised corn, potatoes, and peas.

In another document dated immediately after the Civil War, Archibald Smith states that he told some his former slaves that "if they choose to stay & work until the crop was got out, I'd not turn them off but would give them their food and clothing. I actually did buy corn for them after their freedom."

Altogether, the various texts present a mixed message about slavery. While there is clear discussion of the labor that enslaved people performed and examples of the brutality of slavery (including sexual exploitation), there are also examples that seem to operate as signifiers of the goodness of at least some master-enslavers. This apparent matching of positives was perhaps most noticeable at this site, but it is also found at others.

The Stonewall Jackson House

The other plantation museum that had a largely segregated display was found in Lexington, Virginia, at the home of Stonewall Jackson. On the tour attended by Professor Eichstedt, the docent was a white woman in her forties, and there were eight other white adults, three white children, and one Asian American child. The tour of the home focused primarily on Jackson's life prior to the war; this included his relationships with his first wife (who died giving birth to a stillborn child) and his second wife, his education at West Point and then his teaching at Virginia Military Institute (VMI), and his everyday life while in Lexington. There was some discussion of furniture and accoutrements, but they were not the focus of the tour. Instead, Stonewall Jackson, the man behind the story of the great military leader, was the primary focus of the tour. For instance, visitors learn of his many idiosyncrasies, such as sleeping in an upright seated position because he thought it was better for his lungs, or his concerns about his eyesight and gastric issues. When asked by a visitor if Jackson was a hypochondriac, the docent said with a smile that they "never use that word around here." We also learned of his devout religiosity; he knelt for prayers every evening and required his "servants" and family to join him in his prayers. That he "started a church and Sunday school for Black children" was also explained, as was the fact that he was "famous for his teaching in this church."

Two other facets of the tour were a consideration of Jackson as a teacher at VMI and a brief discussion of Jackson's role in the Civil War. As a teacher, Jackson was said to "get mixed reviews." Apparently he only taught what he memorized, and "if he was asked to explain a point in class, he would just repeat what he had already said, just louder and slower." The docent said that a former student reported that "he was a good man, considerate, but no teacher."

As for his military career, he was, of course, considered a great military tactician, and the docent noted that he led fighting in several very successful battles—he was thought of as a "dedicated killer of Yankees." The docent went on to say that "as a devout Christian, he held prayer meetings after every battle." She said, on the other hand, when he saw hogs eating dead Yankees after a battle, Jackson is reported to have said, "I knew that hogs didn't have good taste, but didn't think they'd eat Yankees."

The tour itself did include some mention of those who had been enslaved on the property. The docent told us the names of several enslaved people and what work they performed. For instance, "there was the cook slave named Amy, who was purchased before the second marriage." We were also told of Hetty, who "was the laundress," and of "Cyrus and George, who worked outdoors and were a wedding gift from [his wife] Anna's father." A brief mention was also made of "a young girl named Emma, who was bought at five years old to be a companion" to Anna. Finally, we learned of "Albert, who was purchased at his [Albert's] request. He worked in town as a waiter, his wages were sent to Lee and put against his purchase cost, he won freedom that way." Interestingly, when it came to discussing labor performed in the house, the passive voice and euphemisms were primarily used; for instance, we were told that "servants" carried the food upstairs to the dining room. In the slide presentation and narration that guests watch, there was one mention of three enslaved people who "helped grow food" for those who lived in Jackson's house. Overall, the focus was on Jackson as a "devoted family man," a "respected citizen," and "a devout Christian who believed in duty and commitment to the state."

After the tour, the docent said that guests were free to look at the exhibits or explore the kitchen garden or the gift shop. The exhibit that the site had up in 1999 was titled "The African American Experience in Jackson's Lexington." The exhibit, with a variety of artifacts behind glass and on freestanding pedestals, was located in a separate room and was visible through glass walls and a glass door that led into the room. Only one other guest from the tour, a white woman in her thirties, entered the exhibit; she left after approximately ninety seconds. The display worked to share some information regarding the experiences of African Americans, both enslaved and free, who lived in Lexington during Jackson's tenure. The sections had titles such as "Home," "Church," "Slavery in America," "Work," and "Civil War." The first text plaque read:

> By the time that T. J. Jackson moved to Lexington, VA in 1851 to take his position as a professor at VMI, 40% of the city's residents were African American.
>
> Members of the black community, both free and slave, were an important part of the economic, political, and spiritual and social climate that Jackson encountered. . . .
>
> Jackson never clearly stated his views on slavery. The fact that he bought, sold, hired, hired out, and freed slaves suggested that he endorsed the institution. His wife reported that Jackson was a very strict master who required absolute obedience. We do not know his slaves' opinions or how they viewed their experiences with Jackson.

The section titled "Home" was a display in the center of the room that presented a razor and case identified as having belonged to Jackson, a teaspoon, a chamber pot, and a tin drinking cup. The text says, "Whose history is it? Consider objects that Jackson owned and selected, but that his slaves worked with every day. What can they teach us about Jackson, his slaves, their activities?" No answers are provided for the questions that are raised.

The section called "Community" discussed the demographics of Rockbridge County and the situations of both free and enslaved African Americans. The text included the following:

> Between 1850 and 1860 well over 25% of the residents in Rockbridge county were African American. Since it was common in the mid-1800's to list Native Americans as "free black" or "colored" in the census records this figure may include some local Indian residents. The number of slaves in the Shenandoah Valley wasn't as high as it was in the Tidewater region of Virginia, but slavery was just as influential and important to the economy and culture west of the Blue Ridge as it was anywhere in the state.

By 1860 the majority of slaveowners in Rockbridge County only owned several slaves. Fewer than five percent owned 20+ slaves. . . .

Free black residents in the County struggled against restrictive ordinances, economic hardship, and political and social discrimination. Most free black men were identified in records as laborers, domestics or field hands, while nearly all the free black women worked as laundresses and ironers.

As opportunities and profits from slave labor increased in the deep South, Rockbridge area slaves were sought after by traders headed into markets in Tennessee, Georgia and Kentucky. Slave traders advertised in area papers for hundreds of slaves at a time. Local slaves were threatened with the risk of being moved from their homes, families, the region, and the work they knew for hard labor in the fields of the deep South.

In addition to the text provided, there are also objects such as dresses that enslaved women were believed to have worn, and articles produced by enslaved artisans who worked in the iron foundries. Very little is actually said about the enslaved people who lived with Jackson; instead the focus is generally on life in Lexington as a whole.

Conclusions

When visitors attend sites with segregated information they are required to make a choice. From what we've observed, most visitors, the majority of whom are white, choose to attend the white-centric tours and not to visit segregated display spaces (such as at the Stonewall Jackson site). A higher percentage of visitors appears to attend Black history spaces when they are led through them by a tour guide. However, the proportion of visitors attending the slave life or Black history tours out of the total number attending the site is low—we would estimate it to be 10 to 20 percent. These sites are to be commended for developing information about the institution of slavery and those who were enslaved at these locations. This is an improvement over sites that minimally and superficially deal with this issue. These sites offers detailed and insightful examples of the nature and intense emotional effects of slavery, and some provide this from the point of view of those enslaved. To visit and participate in one of these tours, especially Carter's Grove, is to experience a presentation that is diametrically opposed to those found at the sites described in chapters 4 and 5. At the same time, the problem with this organizational strategy is that it creates and maintains segregated knowledge. For example, on the main house tour at Carter's Grove, symbolic annihilation is the organizing strategy.

Should sites that present themselves as historical, as gateways to knowledge about the past, have a responsibility to incorporate information on the enslaved population that lived at that location (at least half and sometimes 90 percent of the total number of people who lived there)? Should everyone who visits a site come away with at least some knowledge of enslavement and how it provided the foundation for the elite lifestyles of the enslavers? Our answer to these questions is yes; the problem with segregated sites is that only those who self-select into learning about slavery take away anything of value about the institution and the people who lived under it. If visitors solely attend the regular tour, they are very likely to learn nothing of any substance about enslavement; they can walk away with their lack of knowledge, understanding, or awareness intact. Worse, a tour experience may distort slavery substantially, actively obliterating its wickedness and oppressive nature or suggesting that the majority of the enslaved were happy, grateful, or loyal to those who enslaved them. All of these notions are totally at odds with the vast majority of research and facts about slavery in the United States.

Segregated tours and displays appear to go to some length to balance the presentation of enslavement; that is, we learn not only of the potential horrors of slavery but of the ways that specific enslavers were good owners. Such balancing is found explicitly at Bulloch Hall and Mount Vernon, for example. At Bulloch Hall, those who organized the display on slavery did include discussion of the brutality of slavery, but matched these portrayals with descriptions of good owners. Additionally, no larger analysis of the slave narratives or Bulloch family history from which these excerpts are taken is provided. For instance, one display presents the fact that one of the Bulloch boys killed his Black attendant in a fit of rage. This would be an excellent opportunity for the absolute power of enslavers to be discussed— that is, the text could provide critical commentary highlighting how enslavers could kill enslaved people with impunity and point out the irony of the boy's "punishment" being world travel. On the other hand, it is unusual that the brutal behavior of enslavers is mentioned at all. Such discussion of the cruelty of prominent leaders of the community is quite rare; it is necessary, however, because it clearly demonstrates the inhumanity of slavery and the absolute power wielded by master-enslavers.

As we've noted, however, representations of brutality are matched with those of benevolence. Such representations make sense when one considers that whites do not wish to represent themselves in ways that make them feel culpable of evil. However, such positive representations must always be framed within the context of lack of freedom. That is, while some owners were better than others, the fact still remains that enslaved people did not have fundamental control over their bodies, their offspring, or any of the arrangements for living.

That at least some white visitors do not understand such facets of enslavement are evidenced by the comments made by several white male visitors to the living quarters of enslaved people at Mount Vernon. When these men said that "they lived better than some of them do now," both pronouns presumably referring to African Americans, it provides evidence that visitors are making links between representations of the past and their racialized understandings of the present moment. The men who made these comments were not on the slave life tours we attended; they were walking the grounds, likely before or after a tour of the main house. The statement that "they [enslaved African Americans] didn't live too bad" suggests a fundamental disregard for the reality of enslavement, and to suggest that the enslaved people lived a lot better than African Americans do today ignores the ways that enslavement and segregation set up the living conditions of contemporary African Americans.

The type of information that is provided at the main house at Mount Vernon does nothing to enable visitors to think critically about the relationships between enslavement and George Washington. As we noted earlier in the chapter, the main house tour contains virtually no inclusion of enslavement; it is the traditional tour about a great white man and his house and furniture. The type of information that is included on the slave life tour could be included in the main house tour, though it would require slowing the tours down. If people do not take the alternative tour, then they are left with little understanding of the largest portion of the population at Mount Vernon.

The "Other Half" tour at Colonial Williamsburg and the slave life tour at Carter's Grove, organized by the same staff, provide something in the world of plantation tourism that is unique: a critical class- and race-based analysis of slavery. The presentations seek to reach visitors by pointing out their own beginnings in a class system that also oppressed poor whites. For white Americans who are not from elite backgrounds, this moves some of the onus for the system of slavery off their shoulders and points out the class dynamics involved. What is interesting is that this is not generally the sort of message that is provided in the rest of Colonial Williamsburg. While there is framing that points out that the Wythes and others who occupied the "main street" were quite wealthy and that there were also "middling" classes who provided services for them, there is little that places visitors in any class position but the elite. As for slavery and the representation of those who were enslaved, Colonial Williamsburg has a mixed past (see Gable 1996 and Handler and Gable 1997 for extended discussions of class and race at this site). During 1998, Colonial Williamsburg had a program called "Enslaving Virginia" that drew much public focus. Perhaps the most dramatic part of the program was an enactment of enslaved people plotting to run away, running away, and being chased by slave hunters. These enactments were designed to interrupt the regular tours; whether or not individuals chose to learn about enslavement, there was a likelihood that knowledge would be thrust upon them. As one journalist reported: "This mini-drama acted out for the tourists evoked raw emotion among the visitors, most of them white. Some gasped in shock. Tears welled up in the eyes of others" (Barisic 1998). However, it did bring more awareness to the topic of slavery in Williamsburg's history and also worked to bring more African American visitors to the complex. This program was interesting because it represented a break with the full segregation of knowledge; however, it lasted for only one season and has not been carried forward into the present time.

In conclusion, these sites represent a plantation museum version of the segregation of knowledge found in education and public holidays. While these sites do break a bit with the racialized regime of representation that erases African Americans, they still do not fundamentally challenge the positioning of African Americans and despicable white behaviors as outside the norm of knowledge and history.

7 || Toward Relative Incorporation
Complicating the Master Narrative

The preceding three chapters detailed strategies that allow for slavery to be erased, trivialized, or segregated from the main body of knowledge presented at plantation museums. In this chapter we explore both sites that are within the bounds of relative incorporation and sites that are moving toward it. We consider two representative sites we have defined as in-between and three sites that ably demonstrate the strategy of relative incorporation.

As we suggested at the beginning of the book, the category of in-between is, in many ways, a residual category. That is, it contains those sites that have moved beyond symbolic annihilation and trivialization as their primary organizational strategies; unlike sites that practice segregation, they attempt to incorporate the discussion of enslavement throughout their tours—or at least some docents do. At the same time they also occasionally lapse back into trivializing practices or, depending on the docent, into symbolic annihilation. This category contains twelve sites (five in Virginia, two in Georgia, and five in Louisiana) and constitutes 9.8 percent of the sites visited.

The category of relative incorporation, which comprises 3.3 percent of all plantation museums, includes the best representational and rhetorical efforts at the sites we have explored. They demonstrate that there has been an obvious effort to incorporate issues regarding slavery and those enslaved throughout the interpretative locations that a visitor might attend at a given site. This moves these sites beyond those plantation museums that present information regarding enslavement in a segregated way Sites that employ relative incorporation are much more likely to raise issues that disturb a positive construction of whiteness and challenge the dominant themes that each state tends to present about its own history.

The sites that we present as engaging in relative incorporation were included because they met, at least on the tours we attended, the following criteria:

1. Throughout the tour, visitors were provided with information about the ways in which the system of slavery operated at that specific site. The information was neither perfunctory nor degrading.
2. The site provided information about those who were enslaved at that site. This demonstrates some investigation into the lives of enslaved people, indicating that such investigation was considered valuable and appropriate.
3. It acknowledged the links between the subjugation of some (enslaved African Americans) and the elevation of others (the enslavers). That is, the site noted that it was the labor of enslaved people that provided the wealth and time for the enslavers to pursue hospitality, political theorizing, and other traits and behaviors that led to the characterization of these men as great.
4. The site complicated the identity of the master-enslaver and the family, so that the fact that they enslaved people is part of their definition. The enslavers are no longer presented as solely romantic, political, hospitable, and so on.

The inclusion of the above information throughout the tour and the complication of the master narrative meant that visitors could not escape being confronted with a discussion of enslavement and those enslaved. Of course, this does not guarantee that visitors will in fact consider such information, but it does mean it has been presented in some sustained fashion. For those sites that fall into the in-between category, the degree to which they meet the criteria we present above varies greatly; we must be attentive to the ways that trivialization is still employed. Additionally, at two sites that fall into the in-between category, we were told by docents themselves that the tour they gave is unlikely to be duplicated by another docent; their coverage of slavery comes from their own conviction that the topic must be covered, and it does not necessarily reflect the efforts of the larger organization.

In the following pages we provide two examples of sites that fall into the in-between category. The first is the Archibald Smith Plantation House, in Georgia, and the second is Destehan Plantation, in Louisiana. Other sites that we do not discuss include Callaway Plantation in Georgia; in Virginia, Pope's Creek (the birthplace of George Washington and a National Park Service site), Monticello, Gunston Hall, Prestwould Plantation, and Piney Grove at Southhall; and the Kent House (which had strong trivialization practices), Longfellow Evangeline (a state site), and Melrose Plantation in Louisiana.

In-Between Sites: Conflicted Stories

The Archibald Smith Plantation House

The Archibald Smith Plantation House demonstrates many of the problems common to sites that fall into the in-between category. As we will see as we move through the site description, incorporation of information on enslavement is often framed through narratives of the grateful slave or the good owner. Additionally, as the docent who led our tour noted, incorporation of information on slavery is not guaranteed; instead, such information was included because of her own knowledge base and not because of any mandate from above.

The Archibald Smith Plantation House, in Roswell, Georgia, is an example of an "in-between" site.

The Archibald Smith Plantation is a publicly owned site located approximately eighteen miles north of Atlanta in Roswell, Georgia. What stood
out on this tour were the numerous mentions of the institution of slavery
and those enslaved—at least twenty-five mentions spread throughout the
tour. The information was provided in a factual manner, and there was no
obvious discomfort evidenced by the tour guide, who maintained eye contact when she discussed slavery with the visitors.

Discussion of slavery began on the porch with the first interpreter to greet
our group of visitors (eight white people, one Asian American woman). This
interpreter was a young white woman dressed in contemporary clothing
who noted that this was a farming plantation and that we would have been
surrounded with fields planted with cotton, which was then processed at the
local cotton mill. She started her discussion by saying that Smith grew up
with slaves, and when his father died he inherited thirty-six slaves. She discussed how the Smiths moved here with Roswell King as part of an effort
to set up a "utopian society for wealthy Presbyterians" and that at one time
Smith was "struck by abolitionist zeal and wanted to educate and free the
slaves." She also noted that it was the removal of Cherokees by the government from the area in 1838 that opened up the land for this "utopian society."

When we went inside, a fortyish white woman interpreter dressed in period costume took over as our tour guide. She began by describing how her
style of dress and hair served to draw viewers' eyes to the shoulder and then
to the waist; the women always sought to "enhance the narrow-waist look."
She said the Archibalds were a relatively isolated agrarian family and that
they lived on a "plantation, which doesn't mean they did everything oneself, it means it was done by slave labor." (This is the only site we visited
that defined the plantation as an agrarian enterprise dependent on slave
labor; the definition was reiterated later in the tour.)

She continued by telling us that Archibald was very conflicted about slavery; he wanted to create a society of slaves and send them back to Liberia.
(At this the crowd giggles.) This, she notes with a wry look, was not a goal
of the slaves themselves. This plan was "a stunning failure" since Archibald
was not able "to teach them to govern themselves." She notes that he tried
to do this all in six months and that "no one can learn to govern themselves
in such a short time." He also "couldn't figure out how to not rely on
slaves." To a visitor's question, "Why not just pay them?" she replied,
"We're not sure; we know it was a financial disaster as well." "He had to
teach them the idea of being ambitious about what you do" and "how to fit

into the already existing social order." They were unable to integrate into that society, which was a slaveholding society. It was, she said, "very common to free slaves in one's will when you died." She continued this by saying that Archibald "couldn't see his great vision happening. He wanted to send them back to their roots, but two hundred years later they didn't have roots. Their roots were here. After the war he presented them with the option of going to a new part of the country, but they refused. They wanted to take property from the plantation, because they said it was their country and land." She said, "This was a problem because you wanted them to leave if they weren't going to farm the land."

This story and its transmittal is intriguing. It is presented because it is factual—that is, Archibald tried this plan, it failed, and we know his thoughts about it because he left writings regarding this event. It also shows that he tried to be good and moral by freeing enslaved people. Finally, it locates a reality that some enslaved people did indeed want land where they were; they did not want to go to Liberia or to leave the kin they had and go elsewhere in America. What is not commented on is that Archibald did have a choice at that point to actually provide the land they asked for, and he apparently chose not to do so. Instead, we are asked through pronoun use to identify with the white owner: "this was a problem because *you* wanted *them* to leave if *they* weren't going to farm the land." What if, instead, we had been asked to identify with the newly freed African Americans? What if we had been told, "Of course, from the perspective of the formerly enslaved it makes perfect sense that you'd want to have land that you, and oftentimes your family, had been farming. That you were expected to move on with nothing was another great injustice that they [the white elite] perpetuated"? This is an example of how changing the viewpoint through which visitors are supposed to identify can have a great impact on the information and how it is framed.

After telling this story, the docent discussed family history, participation in the Civil War, and the fate of the daughters who did not marry but stayed and cared for their father and the plantation. The overall format of the tour was similar to many others; there was much discussion of the personal lives of the enslavers, their activities, clothing, and furniture and accoutrements. The tour also presents a fair amount of gendered information; that is, we learned about the dangers of riding sidesaddle, how women fainted because of the heaviness and restrictiveness of their clothing, and that "while ladies didn't have many freedoms, they could chew tobacco." We also learned that "ladies" were supposed to lift their skirts with only one hand; lifting them with two hands signaled that the woman was a prostitute. Additionally, women "had three seconds to cross a water puddle"—if it took longer than that, then they would drop their skirts into the puddle, since "a lady couldn't show her ankles in public."

Throughout this very typical discussion, however, is information regarding the labor that enslaved people performed. While there is some use of the passive voice, in general the labor of enslaved people was labeled. For instance, we were told that slaves "had to bring in the water and take out the wastewater" for baths and for commodes, and that they brought the food in and served it.

A problematic, and familiar, representation of slavery occurred when we stopped to look at an etching, titled "The Burial of Latane," that hung above the fireplace in one of the rooms. The docent said that General Lee wanted a picture made that would inspire southern people (presumably white people) to continue in the War Between the States, so he approached a painter named Washington. Washington produced an image of white women, white children, and slaves gathered around a soldier who is being buried. The "mistresses served as pastors of the community because they were able to cross the lines of war." The small white girl, she told us, represented innocence. "The slaves on the left also mourn the loss of the young man, because they also saw this as their home and saw the northerners as invaders." After listening to this interpretation, the tour group moved on to another room. Unfortunately, the idea of slaves seeing northerners as invaders and presumably not wanting the South to be "disrupted" was not challenged. Nor was it clear whether the interpretation we were given was the painter's or the tour guide's. She did suggest that the painting was dear to the family because their son Willie got dysentery on the way home from the war and perished in South Carolina. The people who were with him said his last word was "Mother." Upon saying this, the docent put her hand to her chest and said she always found that so hard to say.

After finishing the tour of the interior of the house, we went out to the kitchen, where the tour guide said that work in the kitchen "wasn't easy work" and that "you wouldn't find me in here if I was the lady of the house." She said that for the women who worked here it was "hard, arduous work" and they suffered many burns and injuries. She said that the lady of the house "cared for the injuries." One of the guests asked if the lady of the house never cooked, and she answered, "No, they planned meals, but they didn't do things in here." The guide also talked about the different "levels of slaves" found on a plantation. These included, she said, a higher level of tradesmen, carpenters, and house slaves who would live closer to the main house, while "field hands would live farther out." She noted that although "others in town had slaves, the others weren't plantation homes because this was the only farming place."

One final way that slavery was discussed occurred in the slave cabin. First, the guide noted that the term "slave cabin" does not refer to a specific kind of building; rather, it refers to a cabin that was occupied by enslaved people. She noted that the building on display at Smith Plantation was probably not used to house people because it does not have a chimney in it; however, they use it to demonstrate the dimensions of a typical cabin. The docent indicated, after being asked by a visitor, that she did not know exactly how many people might live in a cabin, but that it could vary tremendously. She then said that "at one time they sold a whole family of slaves, they sold the whole family, nine people to the mill in town [because of debt]. It was the only evidence of the trading of slaves." In reply to a question regarding where children would sleep, the guide engaged in deflection by saying, "On the floor, which is no different from poor whites." She went on to say that "slaves sometimes lived better than poor white families." To back this up, she discussed how the poor whites who worked in the cotton mill were seen as the "lowest of the low," and when Sherman got here, he arrested all of the women and children and put them on the train. At each train stop, another family was put out; "when you read the letters of the [elite] women and children, they say they are better off without them [poor whites] there." She then said that one family walked all the way back after being put off the train in Ohio. It took this woman and her children a full year to walk back, and when she got back, her husband had remarried. She ended up living in the house next door to him and his new wife for the remainder of her life. This is presented as an example of the treatment of poor whites.

This presentation, then, is mixed. Here is a site that incorporates more mentions of the institution of slavery and slaves than most others. However, the framing is at times problematic; included with more factual information and a recognition of the labor of the enslaved are tropes of good owners and loyal slaves, as well as stories of the worse economic position of poor whites. Recall too that the docent herself noted that this "wouldn't necessarily be the typical tour" and that it was her own interest that compelled her to include slavery.

Very, very few Georgia sites incorporated sustained critical discussions of slavery. Perhaps this is related to the dominant *Gone with the Wind* framing that the state as a whole employs. Such framing is inconsistent with anything but loyal slaves, beautiful white southern women, and a noble life. It may be that if white Georgia moves away from this framing, it will be better able to frame a discussion of slavery, those who were enslaved, and their relation to the production of wealth and an elite white lifestyle.

Destrehan Plantation

The presentation found at Destrehan Plantation in Louisiana is similar to that found at the Archibald Smith home. Destrehan's framing, while more incorporative of slavery and the enslaved in terms of sheer numbers of mentions, neither clarifies the economic importance of slavery nor complicates the reading of the white enslavers, but instead leaves intact their construction as hardworking, ingenious, and generally noble. This site should therefore be thought of as representative of the in-between category.

Destrehan Plantation is operated by the River Road Historical Society, which maintains the home and operates tours. At this site, interpreted by white women of varying ages dressed in period clothing, slavery and enslaved people were mentioned five times in the introductory video and seventeen times on the tour.

The video introduced visitors to the history of the plantation and, after a brief introduction, uses the device of having the plantation "speak for itself"—that is, it is given a female voice that talks in the first person. In the introduction we are told that the original owners of the house commissioned a "free mulatto named Charles" to build it and that "Charles was given the use of several slaves to build the house and was paid one hundred piastres, fifty quarts each of rice and corn, a cow and her calf, and a male slave. It took over three years to build the house, nothing considering that everything was hewn and sanded by hand."

When Destrehan "speaks for herself," she tells of her rise to grandeur and her importance in the political life of the early South. Then she tells of different owners and the crops they planted. One of the owners was Zelia Noel and her Scottish-born husband, Stephen Henderson. The narration continues: "Stephen lived until 1838 and his will caused a great deal of controversy. In it, among other things, he wanted to free his slaves and convert the plantation into a manufacturing complex run by them for their passage back

Destrehan Plantation, Louisiana, falls into the "in-between" category because while it included information on the enslaved, the presentation often trivialized their experience.

to Africa. It was contested by the Henderson family and never acted upon." The voice continues by mapping the architectural changes wrought in the 1840s by the next owners. She then addresses the Civil War and the fact that Destrehan Plantation was seized during the Civil War while its owner at the time, Judge Rost, was serving in Europe as a Confederate ambassador. "I was under the control of the Freedman's Bureau, an agency that helped the newly freed slaves. Here families stay while they learned their trades."

The video ends by discussing how the site eventually fell into disrepair— "For the next twelve years I suffered horribly from neglect . . . vandals broke in and built fires on my brick floors to warm their food"—and then was rescued by Amoco's donation of the home to the River Road Historical Society.

After the video ended, the tour began. The tour guide was a white woman in her mid-forties. In addition to Professor Eichstedt, there were six other white people. The tour generally followed the format described throughout this book; however, there was much less discussion of specific pieces of furniture, except when a story could be told that linked the furniture to a specific person in the family, a famous visitor, or the person who made it. Throughout the tour we were told that slaves made the bricks, brought food cooked in the kitchen to the house and to the fields, hauled water to the house for the bathtub and then out when it was dirty, and "would come up [to the dining room] after dinner and move the furniture." The names of the enslaved people who helped build the house were provided, and we were told that "slaves used this to make money to buy their freedom." The docent used the names of slaves several times. We learned of Theodore, the "enslaved coachman who would meet you at the river with a buggy when you arrived," and of Adailade, "a house slave who would have used the windows to see who was here." In one bedroom the "Bayon bed" was said to have been made by "Bayon, a slave" who had bought his freedom. "He in turn had twelve slaves, who carved furniture with him. These pieces are unsigned because it was against the law for slaves to read or write."

Religion is a theme that usually is explored on Louisiana tours, particularly on tours of Creole homes, as most Creoles were Catholic. When we were standing near a slave-carved prie-dieu (a small piece of furniture upon which people knelt to pray), the docent explained how the laws in early Louisiana dictated that everyone who lived there had to be Catholic; if they didn't change their religion, they had to "move on." "Slaves were not given any choice," she said; "religion was forced on them." She also noted that during this time Jews were expelled from the state.

We ended the tour with the docent pointing to the cabins outside and saying that those were "not slave cabins, but sharecropper cabins that had been built later." The slave village she told us was about a quarter of a mile away. The original owner of the home had 59 enslaved people, while the census taken right before the Civil War indicated that there were 251 slaves here. After specifying the number of people enslaved on the plantation, she discussed the "Black Codes" that existed prior to the American takeover of Louisiana. Under those codes, "because they were Catholic, they [the enslaved people] didn't work on Sunday. Also if the owner was too severe, they could approach the Catholic Church for intervention." But, she noted, "we have no records of that happening." When American codes were instituted in the area, owners could be "harsher in treatment, and slaves worked extensive hours." She finished by pointing to the cabins and saying that 210 people lived in twenty-four split cabins (dwellings divided into two halves, with a family living in each end).

This tour, conducted at lightning speed, contained information about the labor of the enslaved, who they were, and the conditions under which they lived. What is lacking here is explicit discussion of the ways that the labor of slaves was used to enrich the white enslavers. Instead, what is noted in the brochure (and also in the tour and the video) is that Jean Noel Destrehan, who acquired the estate from his father-in-law in 1792, "perfected the granulation of sugar, thereby starting an industry that proved to be most profitable to Louisiana planters." Here again, the labor or inventions of the enslavers are noted, not the people whose labor actually made the production of sugar possible. Like all plantation museum homes, this one also suffered from lack of consistency between docents. One of our colleagues who took a different tour was not provided as much information on slavery or those enslaved. Again, this inconsistency weakens the overall quality of the site and explains why it is considered to be in-between.

Relative Incorporation

As we noted at the beginning of the chapter, sites that are examples of relative incorporation demonstrate more commitment and thought to bringing in throughout their tours consideration of slavery and those who were enslaved. Such information is not segregated, nor is it generally belittled by the use of trivializing stories. Instead, it complicates the master narrative by providing information about how slavery operated at a specific site and about those enslaved, acknowledging the link between the enslavement of African Americans and the elevation of white enslavers, and complicating the identity of master-enslavers.

We should note that while we are asserting that these sites have done a better job than the bulk of their cousins, they still have weaknesses in their presentation of this material. One such weakness (which is found in all other sites as well) is that the quality of the tour and the information imparted vary with the docent leading the tour. This is an important point to take note of and one that we encourage sites to address; in some cases certain docents at these sites are not as comfortable discussing slavery or, as one docent noted, slavery is "not their interest." If, then, a visitor had a different docent than we had, he or she might end up with a very different tour, one that either symbolically annihilated or trivialized the experience of enslavement. This is one of the reasons that we cannot unequivocally say that these sites have achieved excellence in their management of the issue of slavery—what is presented is still too variable. At other sites, however, this was not the case; the incorporation of slavery was framed as being important by the organization as a whole.

The first two, and strongest, examples of relative incorporation come from Virginia. (A third Virginia site that practices relative incorporation is Sully Plantation, a public site in northern Virginia.) This state, as a whole, had more sites that were closer to being truly inclusive than the other two states. For the purposes of this chapter we focus on two particular sites—Montpelier, a site owned by the National Trust for Historic Preservation, and the Carlyle House, an urban site owned and operated by the Fairfax County Regional Park Authority in northern Virginia. The two sites explore slavery in very different formats, but both push beyond prior strategies of containment.

Montpelier

Montpelier uses a tour format that is different from the format at virtually all of the other sites we visited. Their tour, which up until fall 2000 included some portions led by a tour guide, is now a self-guided tour in which visitors use an audio guide, shaped like a cellular phone with a numeric pad and earphone, that provides information as they move from room to room inside the house and location to location outside. There are usually four different narrations visitors may listen to at any location; each narration has a number (such as 201) attached to it, and as visitors enter a room, they punch in the number on their audio guide and then listen to the provided information. When Professor Eichstedt first visited the site in June 1999, the audio guide was used for part of the tour, though visitors were provided with some traditional commentary by a docent. By the spring of 2001, docents no longer gave any portion of the tour; instead, visitors managed it all via the audio guide narration.

The four different narrations at each site generally fall into the following categories: "Overview," "History," "A Different Take" (which seems to have been developed specifically with children in mind), and "Story," where actors often give first-person interpretations of different characters that relate to the topic at hand (for instance, James or Dolley Madison, or a relative or other guest). In some cases, such as under "Hospitality," there are additional narrations, in this case eight, which include: the house, Dolley as White House hostess, Dolley Madison and Montpelier's menus, Montpelier after Madison, the Madisons' responsibilities toward their guests, the role of house slaves, Montpelier's furnishings, and art at Montpelier. While not every individual narration mentions slavery or the enslaved, each topic does include information on slavery. For instance, under the "Hospitality" narration on the role of house slaves, the narrator, after explaining how Dolley "supervised servants" who cleaned, took care of children, looked after visitors, and also "planned menus and table settings," says:

> But her success as a hostess depended on the labor of dozens of slaves. For the Madisons' larger parties, slaves were often brought in from their work in the fields. They would change into their finest clothes and help serve dinner. Cooks prepared the meals, and younger slave children hauled water and firewood. Only men served at the dining table; women may have helped bring food from the kitchen, and carried lunch or a snack to guests in their rooms.

This narration, interestingly, goes on to discuss how those enslaved by the Madisons might have felt about them:

> It is difficult to know with accuracy how Montpelier's slaves felt toward their masters. Visitor Margaret Bayard Smith noted of a maid who was helping her: "Nany, you have a good mistress." And Nany replied, "Yes, the best I believe in the world. I am sure I would not change her for any mistress in the whole country."
> It is not possible to know whether this statement reflected Nany's true feelings.

This final statement works against Nany's comment about Dolley's status as a mistress—it rightly calls attention to the fact that an enslaved Nany could not have spoken her "true feelings" to any white woman who was a guest of her enslavers.

Throughout the audio-guided tour are descriptions of the labor performed by enslaved African Americans. As is common at most plantations where slavery is discussed, the kitchen provided much focused discussion of slavery. Under "A Different Take" the narrator explains:

> The kitchen that once stood on this site was mostly staffed by women, slaves trained by other slaves in the fine art of cooking for James and Dolley Madison and their distinguished guests.
> A woman working here would start teaching her own daughters, or other apprentices, from the age of twelve. First came chores such as toting water from the well or firewood needed to keep the big cook fires burning. Later, the young helpers might assist in preparing the French-style dishes served at the main house: fancy roasts, fricassees, ragouts.

Following a discussion of the various foods that might be prepared, the narration continues:

> When mother and daughter were done cooking for the main house, they went home to the family cabin in the nearby slave quarters, where their own meal, a simple stew left simmering all day on a low fire, was waiting for them.

Additional commentary regarding the labor of the enslaved is made on the narrative tour. Enslaved people are recognizing as performing the labor to construct buildings, maintain the roads, plant and harvest crops, be blacksmiths, cooks, caretakers of white people, and so on. Under the topic "Plantation Life," the narration on the economic importance of slavery says in part:

> Tobacco and slaves shaped the landscape of Piedmont Virginia in the early eighteenth century. One hundred years earlier, Virginians learned how to cultivate tobacco, an Indian crop, successfully. At first, white indentured servants provided the labor. But by 1700 they had been replaced by African slaves, who provided lifetime labor, as did their children. Tobacco farms became large plantations and created central Virginia's gentry class.

Under "Plantation Life" there is also a narration on the subtopic "Culture and Traditions" that focuses on the work and social life of those enslaved. It begins with an actor playing John Finch, a guest at the Madisons'. He explains that James Madison explained after dinner on Sunday that since "it was Sunday, he could not have the servants to wait upon them, as they made it a holiday." The narrator continues:

> At most plantations, house servants were on call twenty-four hours a day, seven days a week. Field hands—and house servants when their services were not required—had Sundays off. This was a customary right, honored by many masters but only at their convenience. Some masters who required work on Sunday gave slaves extra food or a little cash in compensation. . . .
>
> During their own time slaves traded surplus food they raised and items such as baked goods among themselves, as well as to itinerant peddlers, workers from other plantations, and even to white masters and mistresses.

The final subtopic under "Plantation Life" is "Resistance and Surviving—The Quest for Freedom."

In 1829 the Marquis de Lafayette urged James Madison to take the lead in eradicating slavery from Virginia. Madison refused, assuring his friend that even to raise the subject among his countrymen would be like "a spark to gunpowder." Blacks outnumbered whites in Piedmont Virginia, and slave owners had reason to fear a slave rebellion. In 1831 Nat Turner led an uprising in Virginia's Southampton County in which almost sixty whites and more than a hundred blacks lost their lives.

Short of armed rebellion, resistance took many forms—feigning illness, breaking tools, work slowdowns, petty theft, even poisoning. Slaves also ran away, sometimes for a few days, sometimes in a real effort to win freedom.

The text goes on to explain that "successful escapes were rare" and then to describe the repeated, and finally successful, efforts of an enslaved person named Anthony to run away. The narration here ends by saying, "Anthony was probably the son of a mother of African descent and a Caucasian father. Perhaps his lighter skin made it easier for him to find refuge among Virginia's growing free black population."

While it is not consistent throughout the narration, often the racial categorization of "white" is explicitly noted when speaking of children, guests, and so on; instead of assuming that everyone is white, people are specified. For instance, under "The Portico: A Different Take" the text notes:

The plantation's children played together until about age ten. Then the white boys went off to school, the white girls continued their education and added domestic lessons—sewing, cooking, table setting—and the children of slaves took up chores, fetching water and firewood, helping in the kitchen.

Finally, narration does note the contradiction of Madison, who is referred to in the narration itself as the "Father of the Constitution," being a proponent of freedom and simultaneously an enslaver of others. The text included as "Story" for the African American cemetery is worth quoting at length.

The first slaves survived a yearlong ordeal that began in the interior of Africa. After the dreaded Middle Passage across the Atlantic and a stop in the West Indies, slave ships worked their way along the coast to rivers that gave access to the interior of Virginia. . . .

Slaves bought in Virginia were mostly women and children, some as young as ten. They were cheaper than men and presumably more docile, yet able to clear fields and plant crops in this mild climate. . . .

It's hard today to put ourselves in the mind of a man like Madison. He condemned what he called "the original sin of slavery." A few of his friends and family members, acting on similar beliefs, freed their slaves. Madison, whose comfortable existence at Montpelier depended on slave labor, did not. By all accounts, he was a humane master. But the philosopher-statesman who fought to create a government of free men remained a slave owner his whole life.

This quote, as well as others on the audio tour, complicates the narrative of Madison. He is not only presented as a statesman, generous host, and so on, but recognized as someone who enslaved other people. Further, his "comfortable existence" is credited to the labor of enslaved people. Not surprisingly, given what we've seen so far, this statement is followed up with one that frames him as a good owner, but the fact that he was a enslaver is not erased. This stands in contradistinction to most of the other representations of good owners or representations of whites in general. Overall, the representation of the Madisons is more complicated than the representation of master-enslavers at most other sites. While clearly Montpelier is set up to celebrate the Madisons, it is also working to present the whole community that resided on the property.

The Carlyle House

Located in Old Town Alexandria, the Carlyle home provides a glimpse into urban slavery. In 1994 the Carlyle House, which is owned and managed by the Regional Park Authority of Northern Virginia, developed an exhibit that focused on urban slavery. After the run of that specific exhibit, they incorporated slavery into the regular tours given every day. In addition, like some other sites, they also provide a tour specifically on slavery for schoolchildren.

If visitors come with time to spare before a tour begins, they are seated in a small auditorium adjacent to the gift shop and the downstairs kitchen and shown a striking film that begins with images of white people sitting, visiting, and eating with other white gentry. The video then provides images of pots, pans, and various other instruments flying through the air, seemingly moving on their own. The voice-over tells us that the Carlyles were not the only inhabitants of the house and that the work required to make the Carlyles' lifestyle possible was performed by enslaved African

The Carlyle House, Virginia. This urban site incorporates numerous stories told from the point of view of enslaved residents.

Americans. At this point Black people dressed in period garb materialize holding the various instruments that had been flying through the air. We are told that we can't understand life at the Carlyles' house if we don't understand the lives of those who lived there as enslaved people. We are then introduced to the various enslaved members of the household and the work they performed to make the Carlyles' lives what they were.

In addition to the film, another thing that makes the site unique is the presence in four rooms of mannequins that represent enslaved African Americans. They have varying skin colors and are dressed in period attire; in each case their dress is used to partly indicate what their tasks were. The mannequins provide the opportunity for the docents to explain whom they represent and the task they are performing. They also are a visual reminder that people other than the Carlyles inhabited the home.

The ongoing program for schoolchildren allows students to learn about slavery, the contributions of those enslaved, and the experience of being enslaved. On the tour we observed, approximately thirty to forty children, all white except for one African American boy and the African American teacher in her fifties, listened to a brief introduction in which the white woman tour guide asked the class who else might have lived in the house

Mannequin figures at Carlyle House, Virginia, positioned to portray the roles played by enslaved servants in the kitchen.

besides the Carlyles. After a white boy answered, "Slaves," she congratulated him on being correct and said, "Today you're going to be learning about people behind the scenes, the people who made that life possible." The group then watched the video described above. After the video the boys and girls were divided into separate tours (the rooms are not large enough to accommodate all of the children at once), and Professor Eichstedt accompanied the boys on their tour.

We started the tour by going up the "servants' stairs" and moving into a room where the walls have been opened up to show the construction and the materials used to build the home. The male docent told the boys that the house was built by slaves and asked what skills a slave would have to have to build a house. Several white boys put up their hands and called out "carpenter" and "bricklayer." The docent added, "Everything that was made of metal in this house, including the nails"—at this point he passed around samples of eighteenth-century nails—"were made on a forge by a blacksmith." This became the introduction to the figure used to represent Joe, the blacksmith. The docent started the taped narration that represents Joe's voice and asked the children to listen for the various tasks that Joe performs. Through the narration Joe tells how he makes horseshoes, shovels, nails, and engines. He also indicates that a good blacksmith can work anywhere, and that it's a job that takes skill; most blacksmiths can read, write, and add. He points out the difference between him and some of the domestic workers: He assists Mr. Carlyle with something very valuable—Mr. Carlyle's business. The narration continues, "I ain't saying Blacksmith Joe's got it made. No, I'm just saying that I know what having a skill can do making a slave's life better. Might get better food or clothes, might get me a family. I might even save a shilling or two to buy my free—well, might save a little." He then says he has to go run an errand and get back to the forge.

The guide asked the boys what things Joe did, and they responded appropriately. The docent went on to elaborate the various things Joe fixed or made; he asked, "Do you think everybody in Alexandria owned their own blacksmith?" Telling the children that this was not the case, he added that this was important to a slave such as Joe, because during the eighteenth century most slaves were allowed part of Sunday off (except for the cook or somebody who was engaged in fixing meals). When he wasn't working for Mr. Carlyle he was allowed to work for other people in town, and the master-enslaver allowed him to keep part of what he was paid.

In the second room we met Moses, John Carlyle's "manservant," who the docent explained did many things, including acting as a butler. The children were told that Moses dressed in clothing like that Carlyle and his friends would have worn. The docent went on, "Moses is the one slave you would have seen. He would have been the guy who opened the front door and greeted you and also would have been the guy who waited on you." The docent took an explicitly critical stance when he said, "Now, when John Carlyle died, he even left Moses a suit of clothing. He probably thought he was doing him a favor, but I'm sure that even though Moses probably had a better life than most other slaves in this house, that he was not happy with his life." He then explained that Moses was the most important slave not only for the running of the house but also to the other slaves. The fact that the slaves in the household were all born on Virginia plantations and were apprenticed to learn a skill at the age of twelve meant that children would be separated from their families at that age and likely would never see them again; since Moses traveled with Carlyle, he could carry valuable information between enslaved people in the city and their families on the outlying farms. "He is your conduit with your family and your friends that you will never get to see again," the docent said, adding, "As you saw in the film, some of the slaves ran away." Since they had lived their whole life either on the plantation or in the city house, "if you want to run away you have to know where to go and who you can see that can help you. Moses is the guy who knows because he's the guy who travels to all these places and knows what's going on, and most importantly, he knows all the slaves . . . so if you want to run away you go to see Moses and he can tell you where to go, he can tell you what's down the road, he can tell you what's around the next bend, and most importantly he can tell you who to see that can help you." After this discussion we went down one flight of stairs, using the main staircase; the docent used this opportunity to point out the difference between the front stairs and stairs slaves had to use.

On the floor below we entered a room that was used for dining. In this room was the figure of an older African American woman, whose name, we were told, is Cook. The docent again pointed out the clothing and noted that it represents the normal way that women, slave or free, would be dressed; he said that "the wife of a tavern owner would likely be dressed the same way." After saying that Cook was responsible for all the meals in the house, he asked the boys where she would do the cooking. He and the children discussed how the kitchen was detached because of smoke, odor, heat, and the "number one reason—fire." He added, "Of course, the distance from the house was an added burden to the slaves, right? Because they had to carry all the food back and forth from the house for every meal." He then began Cook's narration and asked the boys to pay attention to when the Carlyles ate their food, what they ate, and what the slaves had to eat.

Cook describes her chores and what she cooks for the Carlyles and for the other slaves. She also says that the other slaves "expect her and Moses have Mr. Carlyle's respect and trust—'Would you ask Mr. Carlyle this,' 'Would you ask Mr. Carlyle that'—thinking that I can help them get a good word in with Mr. Carlyle or the housekeeper. But I guess that's all right—we looks out for each other that way."

After Cook's narration the docent discussed a typical dinner that the Carlyles ate and explicitly identified the slaves as bringing in the food that Cook prepared and clearing the table. He asked the boys what they thought the slaves ate and then discussed this with the children. He elaborated by saying that what slaves didn't get to eat was sweets, "because sugar was very expensive and had to be imported into the colony. And no one would give sugar to their slaves because they didn't think that slaves were important enough to waste that kind of money on." He also explained how slaves ate hominy because the planters grew corn just to feed to their slaves. He compared that to South Carolina, where they might grow rice on their plantations, and therefore at those places rice would be served to the slaves. "So when times were hard and there weren't a lot of leftovers, the slaves ate a lot of this mush, and they probably weren't real thrilled about that, and you wouldn't be either. So their diet wasn't as good as it could have been most of the time."

The next-to-last room we visited was a parlor where the Carlyles entertained visitors. There we were introduced to a twelve-year-old boy named Jamie who had just come from the plantation to apprentice as a manservant with Moses. We were asked to listen to Jamie's description of life on the plantation and how it was different from living in town.

Jamie describes how, since coming to the house, he stays inside almost all the time and misses going outside the way he did on the plantation. There he gathered firewood, hauled water, and did other chores, but at least he was able to be outside and to see family and friends. In town "we're always expected to be somewhere at all times; there ain't no privacy for yourself; you're always on call for your next assignment . . . people around town are always in a hurry, to say nothing of having time for even a few words to say to you." What he does like is being able to see all kinds of people: "Yesterday I saw a free Black man come riding down Fairfax Street on his horse as slow as you please; I've done seen Negroes dressed finer than even some of the white people walking the street." The narration ends with Jamie saying, "You know, I might miss the plantation from time to time, but better clothing, food, and a few tips can fit into my life."

After the narration ended, the docent started a discussion of how the age of twelve was important for most boys, including free ones. He pointed out a portrait of John Carlyle above the fireplace and said, "Even he, at the age of twelve, became an apprentice; he apprenticed to a merchant in England, and that's how he came to have this job." He then asked the boys to talk about what Jamie didn't like about being in the house, such as having to be always available. In response to the docent's question, a white boy said that he liked seeing a free Black person. The docent then explained the importance of Jamie seeing for the first time in his life a Black man who was free, "because on the plantation where Jamie was from every Black man he saw was a slave." He explained that there were free Black people living in Alexandria and "that gave a slave like Jamie a little bit of hope; he actually had very little hope of ever being free because of the laws in Virginia, but he did know that there were free Black people and he did know that there was a chance that one day he might be free." He then shifted to saying that Jamie also said he liked "tips"; he explained that if enslaved people lived in town, receiving tips was fairly common. He explained that tipping is known to have occurred here because, for example, the diary of George Washington told about tipping the slaves at the Carlyles'. This tip money, the docent said, enabled the slaves to buy a bit better quality of clothing than they might be provided by Carlyle, and to buy better food.

We ended the tour by returning downstairs to the "servants' hall." In this room are two African American figures and a narration visitors can hear by pressing a button on a display. The docent explained the inventory list that is presented in the display and referred the children back to the video, where they "showed you that the slaves were listed on the inventory and that's because, just like the tables and chairs, the people who owned them considered them property. And so when the owner died and they did an inventory of his property, they did a list of the slaves and their values. The slaves were the most valuable thing in this house. They accounted for over one-third of the value of the inventory." He then moved on to explaining the servants' hall, noting that in the 1700s there had been no windows, so it would have been very hot, dim, and smoky—not a very pleasant place to be. He directed the students to look at the hearth and said it was used to heat water for baths and for cleaning dishes. "And so as you saw in the film, one of the slaves, Kate, probably spent most of her day hauling buckets of water upstairs for one thing or another. And you've been up and down those stairs, so you know that probably wasn't a pleasant task." He then encouraged the boys to lift buckets in the room that are filled with a plasticine material that represents the weight of a bucket filled with water. The boys all experimented with picking up the bucket and moaned about how they couldn't carry that up the stairs. This was the end of the tour, and the boys and girls soon regrouped out on the front lawn.

This tour shows how and what students may learn at the homes, urban or rural, of those who were enslavers. The students were provided demographic information and knowledge regarding the labor of enslaved people, their conditions of life, and the restrictions placed upon them. Enslaved people were not treated as if they were a homogeneous group; instead they were given faces, names, and identities. Additionally, the wealth and lifestyle of the Carlyles are attributed to slave labor.

Sites in Virginia were more likely to be either doing a better job of incorporating discussions of enslavement or moving in that direction. One possible reason for this is that Virginia sites, particularly the largest ones, are very much in the public eye. Mount Vernon, the home of George Washington, draws over a million visitors a year. Monticello, the home of Thomas Jefferson, while it does not receive as many visitors, has been the subject of much public scrutiny because of the debate over Jefferson's parentage of children by Sally Hemings, an enslaved woman who worked in his house. A 1997 *Washington Post* article also publicized the general pattern of sites excluding any discussion of slavery. This article describes how two men, one an early-childhood educator and the other a loan counselor for the ACORN Housing Corporation, toured eight plantation homes in Virginia and Maryland and concluded that "it was the rule rather than the exception that they [tour guides] wanted to discuss the founding fathers and the wonderful business aspects of the plantation, but they did not want to discuss the fact that it was a system based on chattel slavery." They called on the sites they visited (including Mount Vernon, Gunston Hall, and Woodlawn Plantation) to do a more complete job of discussing slavery, and they approached lawmakers to request that they begin "legislative action requiring that more information on slavery be included in tours or programs as part of the condition for plantations' receiving taxpayer money" (Melillo 1997). This article reportedly created some stir in the Virginia plantation museum world and may account for some of the increased coverage of enslavement in that state.

Another reason may be that the presence of Mount Vernon, Monticello, and Colonial Williamsburg (which have been presenting information on the enslavement of African Americans, albeit on separate tours) as well as of a relatively greater number of publicly funded sites and sites affiliated with the National Trust for Historic Preservation has increased the consideration of enslavement and those who were enslaved. Further research that explores the decision-making process of curatorial staff (including the pressures they are subject to from boards of directors and from visitors) will help us develop a stronger understanding of the process of transformation.

Laura Plantation

White Louisiana, like white Georgia, tends to frame itself in terms of wealth and grandeur; both have difficulty incorporating the history of slavery. However, Laura Plantation, a large plantation situated on the banks of the Mississippi, practices relative incorporation. It is advertised as being the

Laura Plantation, Louisiana, is a site that succeeds in relative incorporation of issues of enslavement.

"American home" of the Br'er Rabbit stories, which the sign outside the plantation and guides tell us originated in West Africa and traveled here with enslaved people. Laura, like some of the other Louisiana plantations, belonged to Creole French and German families and was therefore not an Anglo plantation. This difference in Louisiana is culturally and politically important. The architecture, bright-colored paint, and social practices represent differences between Creole and Anglo lives and sensibilities. For instance, we learned that according to the last Creole residents of the home, only "animals and Americans come in through the front door," that "Creoles thought the display of wealth was tacky," and that at one point "if you didn't speak French you couldn't come in the house." Politically, being under French or Spanish (versus English) rule was important because women were allowed to inherit property and own it independently of their husbands; under French law, enslaved people were allowed to petition the Church to intervene if their masters were being harsh or depriving them of needed care. At this site, the fact that women were allowed to own property is important—we quickly learned that this plantation was run by women for eighty-four years.

This tour follows the familiar format of walking visitors throughout the

Cutout figure of enslaved worker, Laura Plantation,
Louisiana.

home and discussing furniture, social activities, and so on. However, our
guide, a young white woman in her twenties, also told stories from Laura
Locoul's published memoirs that indicated the cruelty and horror of slavery. Additionally, throughout the tour the labor of enslaved Africans and
African Americans was named as theirs, not appropriated as the labor of the
enslavers. Instead of being told that the enslavers built the house or produced the sugar, we were told that slaves built the house and produced the
sugar. The word *slave* was mentioned a total of fifteen times throughout the
tour, but of course it is not the sheer number of mentions that indicates
whether a site is included in this section; instead, it is the information given
and the context that is provided.

When we toured the plantation (Professor Eichstedt and two graduate students in January 2001, Professor Small in 1997), we were told a story of the building of the plantation while we were in the cellar. In each case the docents said that in order to build the house, the owners hired a slave who was a master builder. This slave was contracted out to build a "house of thirty," which referred to the number of vertical posts that went from eight feet in the ground up through the building. In 1804 a crew of slaves went into the swamp and chopped down and prepped the trees, and in eleven days the superstructure of the house was completed (using pegs, not nails). The tour guide who led Professor Eichstedt's tour also said that the man who was given the commission to build the house was from Senegal, as men from Senegal "were the only ones with knowledge of the construction trades, and this was true until after the Civil War." Later in the tour the guide said that brickmaking and bricklaying were also the province of enslaved people from Senegal and that this was a skill they brought with them. In addition to discussing the number of slaves and various work they performed and skills they had, Professor Eichstedt's tour guide also related two stories regarding slavery that were formative for Laura's impressions of slavery. These stories, which are taken from Laura's published diaries, are noteworthy because of their rarity on tours and because they provide a very different tone than do stories that solely focus on grandeur, wealth, and hospitality.

The first story positioned Laura's grandmother, Elizabeth, as a very bad owner and her father, Emile, as a good owner, shedding light on the tensions that surrounded Laura as she grew up. It is introduced as a way to explain why Emile did not want his mother to pass the running of the plantation on to his daughter when she was old enough; the docent said that he "doesn't want Laura to become the president of the plantation because he had seen what it had done to his mother." She recounted that Elizabeth saw her son Emile as a "Negro spoiler" who was too lenient on slaves. To cure him of this leniency, she sent him abroad to a military school. He stayed abroad for twenty years and didn't appear willing to return home until his mother threatened to disinherit him. At that threat he promptly came home and got married. One day when his daughter was five months old he heard screaming outside and rushed to see what was happening. He found his mother counting money in the yard while two carts, each carrying an enslaved person, headed off in different directions. Anna, a thirty-year-old enslaved woman, was in one cart, and her three-year-old daughter, Toussaint, was in the other—Elizabeth had just sold them apart. Emile "sees the horror of separating the mother and child" and begged his mother not to do this. She refused to change her mind, so he ended up buying the two back from those who had just purchased them. On Professor Eichstedt's tour the docent said Emile bought them back at twice the price that Elizabeth sold them for; on one of the tours taken by a graduate student, the male docent said that Elizabeth "never spoke to him again." Professor Eichstedt's guide said that Anna was so grateful for his action that when Emile went off to fight in the Civil War, she told him that "if God keeps you safe, then I will take care of you for the rest of your life," and she did. When Laura married, long after the end of the Civil War, the newspaper listed Anna as "family who attended the wedding."

Another story of Laura's impression of slavery was told while we were out on the rear balcony. The guide recounted that when Laura was seven years old, she asked Paul Felite, an older enslaved man who had a deep scar on his forehead, how he got the scar, and he said that Elizabeth had branded him with her initials because he'd run away. She didn't want to believe that her grandmother was capable of such action and so ran to her mother, Desiree, and asked her. Desiree wanted to shield the child but told her that indeed her grandmother had done this deed; Laura, in her memoirs, described this as the day she lost her innocence. Finally, the guide told of Laura's disgust with the novel *Gone with the Wind*. She saw her daughters reading it and so began to read it herself but stopped because, she said, she'd never read "such nonsense." The guide told us that in Laura's memoirs she "doesn't mention mint juleps, glory, grandeur of the Old South, but the many horrible and tragic things that occurred here."

Docents on all of the tours also noted that after the Civil War the slaves who had a marketable skill went North. The rest stayed at Laura Plantation for an "option" to get paid $12 per year. Twelve out of thirty-one received no cash at all, but rather a slip of paper saying they owed money to the plantation store. "Nothing much changed in the plantation," said one docent, "but the 'freed' title." Another docent said that Laura felt that "slavery changed in name only." This was the only site that we toured that suggested that the type of sharecropping system put into place after the Civil War amounted to another kind of enslavement and exploitation.

Conclusions

There is a notable difference between those sites that fall into the in-between category and those that engage in relative incorporation. The in-between sites continue to hold to many of the practices of trivialization that undercut serious consideration of the experience of enslavement for those enslaved. The relative incorporation sites, on the other hand, were less likely to use such stories; if they did, they also cast doubt on their truth. Sites that fall under the rubric of relative incorporation, as we suggested earlier, were chosen because they, at least at some levels, disrupt the master narrative that is found at most sites. However, they do not turn over the master narrative; still present are framings of whites as good, just people and of the places they lived as memorable because they demonstrate the enviable lifestyles of the whites who inhabited them. This is why we consider these places as sites of *relative* incorporation. Relative to other sites they have done a better job and should be applauded; they also could go farther in exploring the questions that enslavement poses for how we are to understand the lifestyles, the codes of conduct, and the notion of honor in the pre-emancipation South as well as the lives of the individual white people who inhabited these places. The sites included in this chapter have clearly gone beyond those we describe at the beginning of the book. However, they also have a ways to go. Remember that they are really just the best of the bunch; none of them has reached some pinnacle of inclusion. For instance, these sites are still overwhelmingly about the enslavers who lived there and the feelings, activities, and so on that filled their lives. There is not equal treatment provided to the activities of the enslaved; given that the enslaved usually accounted for at least 50 percent of the resident population and sometimes as much as 90 percent, such inclusion would not be unwarranted. In fact, it would give visitors a truer picture of the life lived at the sites and would strengthen these sites immeasurably.

PART THREE

Alternatives and Conclusions

8 | Counternarratives of Black-Run and Black-Organized Sites

In our work we have outlined a wide range of plantation museum sites, detailed the range and variety of forms they take, and discussed the factors that shape these forms. We have suggested that the material that they present with regard to slavery and enslaved Blacks in plantation tours, in leaflets and brochures, and in videos can best be understood through a common discursive framework, distinctive rhetorical strategies, and diverse representational narratives. We have called these sites white-centric because they present the history of slavery and of the South as one that presumes a dominant white narrative and because they are organized by, and largely for, white people. However, while they are the predominant sites in the South, they are not the only sites that address these questions. A smaller but significant number of sites are organized and staffed largely by African Americans to present history to African Americans. While white-centric sites generally valorize white ways of organizing the world and erase any significant contribution of African Americans, Black-run sites contest the dominant narrative and are organized around a different set of valorizations—of struggle and resistance against brutality, of resilience in the face of injustice, and of dignity in the face of inhumanity. Such sites talk primarily about African Americans and their contributions to southern society, economy, politics, and culture. Many of them came into existence only after a long struggle that involved tremendous efforts to find funds, identify appropriate buildings and locations, and find staff who are knowledgeable, experienced, and available, especially as volunteers.

"For I had much rather starve in England, a free woman, than be a slave for the best man that ever breathed upon the American continent."

Ellen Craft
1826–1897

Images at Black-centric museum sites convey fundamentally different messages about enslaved African Americans than white-centric sites do.

In this chapter we describe the organizational strategies and counternarratives of slavery, southern history and African Americans found at the twenty sites we toured that are organized by, and often for, African Americans. We describe the ways these sites organize their discussion of southern history and enslavement and how they locate those who were enslaved. Many of these sites are about African American history in general, rather than slavery in particular. These are not plantation museum sites in the same way as sites described in the previous chapters—they are not based on plantation mansions or elite white lifestyles. Also, the majority of them do not occupy buildings originating in the era of slavery, though many have artifacts from that period.

When we developed our project on plantation museum sites we were keenly aware that there were many sites organized by and for African Americans that presented this history of slavery from a different perspective. We made the presumption that the information and artifacts in such sites would be organized around a different set of priorities and concerns and that they might begin and end at different points in time. We also had the impression that many—perhaps the majority—of these sites would be far less well funded than the white-centric plantation museum sites, that there would be far fewer of them across the South, and that they would attract far fewer visitors. We did not set out to do a systematic comparison of white-centric and Black-centric sites. That would require a set of questions and priorities different from the ones that we have pursued in this book. However, we feel it is important to include these sites in this book, essentially because they provide an antidote to the white sites. That is to say, they demonstrate in an immediate, palpable, and practical way an alternative perspective on slavery, southern history, and African Americans. They highlight how very similar issues, events, experiences, and people can be presented in fundamentally different ways. In fact, sometimes they cover exactly the same events and experiences as those found at the mainstream sites, but present them in a different way.

The majority of Black sites receive substantial funds from public sources. However, some of the sites we discuss do not fit easily into this category. For example, the Booker T. Washington site in Virginia, the Civil Rights Memorial Center in Atlanta, Georgia, and the Civil Rights Memorial in Montgomery, Alabama, are clearly what might be called multiracial initiatives in that they involve contributions from people besides Blacks and usually came about and are supported with contributions from the state. They meet some of the criteria we have just outlined but did not originate as sites by and for African Americans. Rather, they were developed to portray the multiracial history of the United States and to meet the needs of governments (state and federal) with their own racialized agendas. For instance, the Booker T. Washington site in Virginia was developed, some argue, to lend state support to segregation and the idea that Blacks should "raise themselves" via education and hard work, not through political agitation. On the other hand, the use of public money to support civil rights museums in the present moment can be read as an attempt by states to assert their support for civil rights and integration. But rather than focusing on these sites, we will primarily discuss those originated by African Americans.

A Summary of Black Sites

Black sites are far more varied in organization, structure, resources, and format than are the white-centric plantation sites discussed in this book. Some of the sites focus exclusively on slavery as an institution, persons born into slavery (who may have escaped), or those legally freed from slavery by the Emancipation Proclamation and the ending of the Civil War. A sense of the general motivation underlying the restoration of places of African American historical significance is clearly suggested in the opening sentence to a book produced by the National Park Service on African American historical places: "African Americans have made profound contributions to American history, many of which have been previously overlooked. The story of African Americans in this country is at the very heart of our heritage. . . . All Americans can benefit from the documentation and preservation of the places where we can learn firsthand what the African American experience means to our nation" (Savage 1996: 9). The book lists more than eight hundred sites "recognized in the National Register of Historical Places."

In addition to the sites listed in the register, there are myriad other sites that present a range of topics and periods, including the Black History Tour of Fredericksburg, Virginia; the Negro Heritage Trail in Savannah, Georgia; the Gullah Tour in St. Helena, South Carolina; the Booker T. Washington birthplace in Virginia; and the Booker T. Washington Homestead in Tuskegee, Alabama. Some sites focus on periods after slavery (though slavery might be mentioned), particularly the civil rights period—for example, the King Center for Non-Violent Social Change, which is next to the Martin Luther King Jr. National Historic Site in the Sweet Auburn Historic District in Atlanta, Georgia. Others place greater emphasis on narrowly defined periods such as Reconstruction (for example, Madam John's Legacy in New Orleans, Louisiana) or the Harlem Renaissance. Some cover particular individuals from periods after slavery, as does the Arna Bontemps home in Alexandria, Louisiana. And there are some that cover many general topics—for example, the Tubman African American Museum in Macon, Georgia, and the Chattanooga African American Museum in Tennessee.

In Atlanta, for example, the Sweet Auburn Historic District includes the King Center for Non-Violent Social Change (founded in 1968); the Ebenezer Baptist Church, where King preached; King's birthplace; and his grave, located next door to the birthplace. This district, which from the 1890s through the 1940s was a thriving center of Black enterprise, includes a series of other buildings as well. The focus on King is supported by a series of events over the course of the year, especially in January—the month in which the Martin Luther King Jr. national holiday falls (on the fifteenth) as well as King Week. The National March of Celebration, which emulates the original civil rights marches of three decades ago, according to the Atlanta Heritage Brochure from 1995–96, takes place during King Week. In

February Atlanta is home to the nation's largest set of Black History Month events. There are activities at other times as well—in late June there is an African American street festival, including an "authentic" African village, displays about Black inventors, and other events. Close by is the African American Panoramic Experience (APEX), on Auburn Avenue, which offers large exhibits on African art and local Black history and documents the life of Mores Amos, the first Black registered pharmacist in the nation, through a replica of the drugstore where he worked.

Other sites include the George Washington Carver School in Bryan County, Georgia; the Ralph Johnson Bunch High School in Mississippi; a state historical marker in Bluff Park in Natchez, Mississippi, to honor the author Richard Wright; a statue of Medgar Evers in Jackson, Mississippi; the Fannie Lou Hamer Grave Site in Ruthville, Mississippi (Hamer's famous saying "I'm sick and tired of being sick and tired" is presented there); and the Margaret Walker Alexander National Art Center in Jackson, Mississippi.

Such sites offer a necessary corrective to the partiality and distortion of the larger plantation museum sites. As different as they are, they all tend to operate under far more severe financial and institutional constraints. They are usually smaller in size, have more limited funds, are not as well staffed, are often open shorter hours, are not as well advertised or as easy to locate, and receive fewer visitors than the white-centric sites. The vast majority are public. Their common motivation is to tell a far more inclusive story of southern history and slavery, one that has African Americans at the center of the narrative. They offer a challenge to the dominant stories told in other museum sites, particularly plantation museum sites, and in the American educational system generally. While we discuss different types of sites, our primary concern in this chapter is with sites that focus exclusively or largely on enslavement or on individuals from the period of slavery. We also discuss more inclusive sites that have a large section devoted to slavery-related issues.

A number of these sites are located in the former homes of African Americans, some of whom lived during the era of slavery; none of them is a plantation home of the kind that one is likely to find in the mainstream sites. (Melrose Plantation, which celebrates the life of Marie Thérèse Coincoin, is the home of a person of color who owned enslaved persons. However, we do not regard it as a site organized by and for Black people.

Instead, we regard it as a white-centric site because it is organized around the same values and fits within the celebration of the genteel South with its focus on architecture, grandeur, and elite codes of honor.) Some of them are organized around buildings that existed during the period of slavery, such as the Booker T. Washington Homestead in Tuskegee, Alabama, and the Lucy Craft Laney Museum in Savannah, Georgia. But most of them are organized around or located in buildings that were constructed after slavery ended. In some cases this is because they address periods after slavery, such as the Jim Crow era, the Harlem Renaissance, or the civil rights period. Another reason for this is that very few African Americans were master-enslavers; a third is that so few African Americans owned homes of these kind. Mainly, however, it is because the raison d'être of these Black sites flies in the face of the celebration of plantation slavery and of the grandeur and codes of honor that is the sine qua non of the mainstream sites.

These sites do tend to be smaller than the mainstream white sites. For example, the River Road African American Museum in Louisiana is dwarfed by the big house at Tezcuco Plantation, on whose grounds it is located, and occupies what looks like a barn. The Arna Bontemps home in Alexandria is tiny as well. But the Sweet Auburn district is quite extensive and includes massive buildings. The African American Museum in Chattanooga, Tennessee is large, as are the Tubman African American Museum in Macon, Georgia, and several of the sites on the Negro Heritage Trail in Savannah, Georgia—for example, the First African Baptist Church and the Beach Institute.

Black-centric sites tend not to be as well staffed as many of their white-centric counterparts, which means they are often not open as long each day or on holidays, or they cannot provide docents to cover all aspects of the tour or even to lead any tours. Visitors are more likely to find themselves touring the premises on their own. These sites also tend to have fewer resources—meaning they are less likely to have videos or extensive text plaques describing items and individuals, and may not be able to provide access to documents that are fragile or rare.

For example, in the Arna Bontemps house, a couple of part-time workers were there to answer questions, but we were left on our own to look around the house. Several of the sites that Professor Small visited in Savannah, Georgia, were not open at times that they were advertised to be open—for example, the Beach Institute and the Lucy Craft Laney Museum—with no explanation provided. Taking part in the minibus tour provided access to these sites, as the driver of the minibus had keys to the buildings. Similarly, when Professor Small visited the home of William Johnson, a nineteenth-century legally free person of color, in Natchez, Mississippi, it was difficult to locate, and when he got there, it was closed and locked, even though the leaflet indicated that it should have been open. When he returned to the visitor's center he was told that the house was undergoing some renovations and that it was not known when it would reopen. Professor Eichstedt had similar experiences in both Georgia and Virginia; sites she was attempting to visit were closed even though the posted hours suggested they should be open. We infer from our general experiences at these sites across the South that staffing issues are the most likely reason sites are not open as scheduled.

In addition to the difficulty of identifying and locating these sites and of gaining access to them, there is also the strange case of sites that do not exist other than as a mention in the tourist literature. A prime example of this kind of site is the Amanda America Dickson House, in Augusta, Georgia. Amanda America Dickson was born to a master-enslaver in Hancock County, Georgia, in the middle of the nineteenth century. (Her story is briefly described in chapter 2; see also Leslie 1995.) Her father provided substantial privilege, sheltering her from fieldwork and building a separate, hidden entranceway and rooms for her and her mother in his palatial house. When he died in the 1880s, he left her over half a million dollars, which she had to fight for in court after her father's white family sued to disinherit her. She won the court case, collected the money, and moved to Augusta, Georgia, where she bought a house and retired. Having previously studied the case of Amanda America Dickson, Professor Small was surprised and excited to see in one of the tourist guides that he obtained from the visitor's center that her house still existed and had been turned into a tourist site. He made several attempts to locate the house, returning to the visitor's center several times to get clarification and better directions. It eventually became clear that the building existed but had no marker, no signs, and no information whatsoever available there, having been converted into an office building; the occupants had no idea who Amanda America Dickson was. While this may be an extreme case, we suspect there are many other sites in similar circumstances.

A similar story applies to the William Johnson House in Natchez, Mississippi. Johnson wrote and published an original diary of his experiences as a legally free person of color during slavery. When Professor Small visited Natchez in 1997, he did not see any mention of the house advertised in the

Natchez tourist leaflets. However, when he was walking through town he stumbled upon the house, which was signposted. The sign provided brief details of Johnson—he was born in 1809, legally freed in 1820, and killed by a white man in 1851 in a dispute over cards. It also states that the white man was not prosecuted because Blacks were not allowed to offer testimony in court. But the sign offered no opening times or contact number. Professor Small returned to the visitor's center and inquired about the house. A white woman in her early thirties thought about it a moment, then, realizing what the house was, said, "That is the National Park Service, and we don't handle that here." A Black woman working there overheard the conversation and said that the house was not open. Then a second white woman, who also worked there, said that the house was not open at this time but would be open at some point in the future. They directed Professor Small to a National Park Service office in town, which had a leaflet about the house. A Park Service staff member said that there were plans to open the house, probably within five years; the house is currently slated to open in spring 2003.

Content of Black Sites

These sites tell a story different from the one that dominates the mainstream white-centric sites. These sites are far more likely to mention slavery and those who were enslaved, explicitly and often in detail. They offer a tone of defiance against the sanitized history offered at the mainstream sites. For example, at least 90 percent of the Black-centric sites that we visited make some mention of slavery. When they talk about slavery they are far more likely to be explicit in their description of its brutality, inhumanity, indignity, suffering, and exploitation. It's clear that some of the docents on these tours have consciously organized the tours in this way and do so in opposition to what they know is going on in the white-centric sites. They often make explicit mention of this fact. For example, Professor Small took part in a tour of the Negro Heritage Trail in Savannah, Georgia. The African American man in his thirties who was both bus driver and tour guide said that the tour would take visitors to all the places neglected on the plantation tours and would show them the real contributions of African Americans to the southern plantation economy and how African Americans lived, worked, survived, and entertained themselves. Another example of this is the Gullah Tour in South Carolina. The Black female tour guide made it clear that this would not be like the plantation tours—it would not focus on furniture, architecture, or the lifestyles of rich white people. Rather, it would tell the "real" history of African Americans and their contributions to American society.

Slavery is presented at these sites, not surprisingly, as an experience of cruelty, degradation, inhumanity, and grief. Tour guides mention many experiences of African Americans during enslavement that are studiously avoided in the mainstream tours. They are likely to talk about the drudgery and tedium involved in cooking, cleaning, serving, and working long hours in the homes and fields of master-enslavers and about the fatigue, exhaustion, injury, and death that resulted from such labors. The accounts include stories of whippings, punishment, and torture; also discussed are sexual abuse and rape. Docents and tour guides explicitly mention the underbelly of plantation society, which is what enabled the great houses to be built, the gardens to be laid out and tended, and the rich master-enslavers and their families to live a genteel lifestyle.

The framing in Black-centric sites of the institution of slavery and the experience of enslavement is far more likely to encompass the tropes of survival, resistance, resilience, and dignity. Unlike at white-centric sites, there is no discussion of happy, grateful, or loyal slaves, nor of the benevolence of the institution. Nor do you hear discussions of good owners (in contrast, this occurs at about 50 percent of all white-centric sites that mention slavery or those enslaved), though there are occasionally mentions of the ways in which individual whites assisted African Americans in their quest for freedom and advancement.

These sites humanize the enslaved by personalizing them (giving them names, identities, and histories) and by talking about their individual emotions and attitudes (including their hopes, fears, frustrations, pain, and suffering). Examples include Ellen Craft and William Craft at the Tubman African American Museum in Macon, Georgia, and images and histories of other enslaved people at the River Road African American Museum in Louisiana. In humanizing, personalizing, and centering African Americans, these sites challenge the whole moral universe of slavery and the tenor of the mainstream plantation sites. What master-enslavers describe as theft, they describe as survival; what master-enslavers describe as laziness or indolence, they describe as tactics to evade exhaustion or being overworked. These sites demonstrate the hard work, pain, and exhaustion that went into the creation of a genteel lifestyle. And they often tell stories that show (as others have argued for minstrelsy and for African American humor) that while whites thought Blacks were inferior or stupid, this was largely a performance on the part of the enslaved—an act that demonstrated that the real fools were the master-enslavers and white society. In elaborating such stories, the sites introduce key characters in the pantheon of African American history and centralize the indispensable role of enslaved people in the creation of economic prosperity and wealth for individual master-enslavers, for particular cities and regions, and for the South as a whole.

These sites are far more likely to articulate the link between past and present than are any of the white-centric sites that we visited. And they are more likely to mention the links between Africa and the United States. For example, at the majority of white-centric sites there is no mention of the fact that the origins of enslaved persons were in Africa and no attempt to describe what life was like in West Africa prior to European invasion and colonization. If Africa is mentioned at all, it is in passing—for example, that the enslaved Africans brought skills and knowledge (rice cultivation, medicine, crafts, or building construction) that they had learned in their own societies. In contrast, numerous Black-centric sites incorporated discussion of African traditions, music and art, and religious beliefs. They seek to locate Africa in its proper place in the history of the world and to debunk notions of savagery expressed about Africans in the United States. A striking example of this approach is the African American museum in Chattanooga, which features a huge exhibit on life in Africa prior to European arrival.

While the white-centric sites generally relegate African Americans to positions of support and loyalty to whites, and do so to aggrandize the master-enslaver elites, Black-centric sites position African Americans as human agents, documenting the nature and extent of their real contributions—African knowledge of agriculture (particularly rice cultivation), skills in making tools, and skills in medicine (especially herbal medicine, which benefited both Blacks and whites). The sites also celebrate Blacks' contributions to music, dance, and sport. The African Americans who designed and constructed many of the magnificent buildings or gardens that grace the mainstream sites are represented in these sites as well. Given this focus on accomplishment, apparently meant to counter the white-centric dismissal of African American contributions and achievements, these sites often are organized through a great-man or great-woman framing. This is reflected in the names of some sites—the King Center for Non-Violent Social Change, the Tubman African American Museum, and so on. This framing is similar in some ways to that employed at white-centric sites in that a great individual is used as the draw to the location; however, it should be noted that the larger social context in which such framing exists is one of symbolic annihilation and trivialization of the African American experience.

The Alexander Black History Center

The Alexander Black History Center is located at the outskirts of the Old Town section of Alexandria, Virginia, and was easily locatable. The center is housed in what used to be a segregated library for African Americans, and its brick building still retains a very institutional feel. Some of the exhibits at the center when Professor Eichstedt visited it in 1999 had to do with a general history of Blacks in the area, and others reflected specific research projects of the staff. One of these was titled "Roots of Remembrance: Alexander's Freedman's Cemetery, May 31, 1999–Sept. 12, 1999." This exhibit included both text and images, including pictures of the Freedman's Village in Arlington, Virginia, 1864–1867, and the Freedmans' Barracks in Alexandria, Virginia, 1863–1867. There were also pictures of enslaved persons at a farm called Volusia in the 1860s. The accompanying text notes that the farm was located near Duke Street and Holmes Run. In another project, "Contrabands," images (from the Library of Congress) include two views of the Price and Birch Slave Pen in Alexandria, Virginia, as it looked in the 1800s. Text in the display explains that the term *contrabands* referred to Blacks seized as "contraband of war" by Union soldiers. Such persons were then held in various camps and forts until their fate was determined.

In the center's room dedicated to rotating exhibits, the display was "African Americans in Business in Alexandria." There was a variety of text in the display; some of it detailed specific entrepreneurs who established businesses in Alexandria, and others noted the context of slavery and post-emancipation oppression that shaped the form and content of Black businesses. One part of the display described the role that enslaved African-descent people played in the development of Alexandria as a whole. For instance, under the title "Antebellum Alexandria" the following text was presented:

> What was the role of slave labor in the development of the Commonwealth? The Old South's dependence upon generations of enslaved people and the profits gained at the expense of their labor are well recognized today by economic and

social historians. By 1820, there were 5,615 whites and 1,168 free black sailors, ship's carpenters, warehouse workers, blacksmiths, shoemakers, brick molders, masons, barbers, tailors, caterers and domestics who walked Alexandria's busy streets. A full accounting of the city's early black workers would include the names of hundreds of slaves among the 1,435 bonded men, women and children who were purchased, hired out, or apprenticed to work in the city's homes, distilleries, tanneries, sugar refineries, textile mills and brewery.

Another text poster was titled "Progress after Emancipation":

Economic progress for black Alexandrians was not a simple proposition. From owning nothing to acquiring the means and licenses of a profession, to establishing businesses of their own—ingrained customs and discriminatory laws stood in the way. What were the barriers to progress?

- Because few whites were willing to perform the servile jobs of cooling, cleaning, or waiting tables, blacks held these exclusively.
- Outside of work, blacks could not congregate without a minister.
- There were evening curfews for the black population.
- Slaves and free blacks were forbidden to cross the Potomac River on public conveyance without a pass or certificate of freedom.
- Feeble attempts to contain abolitionist sentiment outlawed teaching blacks to read and write in 1830.
- After a revolt of slaves led by Nat Turner in 1831, the Society for the Relief of People Illegally Held in Bondage, an emancipation association founded in Alexandria by Quakers in 1796, quietly dissolved.
- City ordinances required free Negroes to register in the City (with descriptions).

The text continues:

After emancipation in 1863, only barbers retained their firm hold on the traditional occupations open to African Americans. Immigrant workers competed with blacks for skilled jobs. Artisans of color, many of them former slaves, were barred from craft unions. Black Alexandrians accustomed themselves to serving a black clientele in their segregated neighborhoods. Racial solidarity helped capitalism take root.

On the Negro Heritage Trail tour, visitors learn about African American contributions to the history of Savannah, Georgia.

In addition to these plaques, others provided information on where businesses were located and how membership in a variety of benevolent societies (for example, Masons, Odd Fellows, or Elks) "provided security and status for African Americans, whose actions were often under scrutiny."

A discussion of George Seaton, the son of formerly enslaved parents belonging to the family of George Washington, was provided in the "Antebellum Alexandria" exhibit. It was noted that he "was a master carpenter, built many houses and the first two public schools for African American children—the Snowden School for Boys, Hollowell School for girls." Seaton, visitors learn, was also very active in city government and a representative at the Republican convention in August 1867. We are told that "Seaton was highly respected in the eyes of the African American and White communities."

In addition to discussion of specific leaders within the African American community there is also discussion, as the above text demonstrates, of the overall contribution of African Americans to the development of Alexandria. Throughout the exhibits are numerous pictures that show various movers and shakers within the Black Alexandria community. As is common at most Black history sites, too, included are images and some text describing the struggle for civil rights in Alexandria. This final framing is consistent with a focus on great men or women; however, it is not the sole focus of the display. Instead, the framing is one of community struggle and the successes of individuals within a community effort.

The Negro Heritage Trail

Professor Small took part in a tour of the Negro Heritage Trail in April 1997. The tour lasted about two and a half hours and entailed visits to a range of African American historical sites around Savannah, Georgia. It began downtown, near the visitor's center, and drove visitors out into a number of Black neighborhoods. The tour took place in a minibus with about twelve seats, and besides Professor Small, two other persons took the tour—an African American woman and her young daughter. The bus driver was an African American male in his early thirties. The sites visited on the tour included the First African Baptist Church, the Civil Rights Museum, the Beach Institute, and the King-Tisdell Cottage. As the tour proceeded, the driver provided a running commentary, which included mention of various markers of African American historical sites, key individuals, and key events in African American history, including events during slavery and during the civil rights movement. At some of the sites we descended from the bus and spent a short while walking around the site, accompanied sometimes by the minibus driver, at other times by a tour guide from the site, and in some places on our own.

One of the first things that we were told was that this tour would take us to places that the other tours did not visit and that it would provide us with the "real" history of African Americans in Savannah. When we crossed some railroad tracks, we were told that this section of the Georgia railroad was "built by slaves—three hundred slaves—and they used handmade bricks, Hermitage bricks" (Hermitage was a plantation, though this was not mentioned here). The driver said that we would never know many of the things that happened to the slaves "because the secrets died with the slaves." We were told that "there were no slaves at the start of Georgia's history" but then "slaves were brought in through the back door" from South Carolina. The driver added, "Forty percent of our people came through Charleston . . . they washed us with vinegar." The driver told us that there are many historically important buildings in the city, which people from around the country and world come to visit, and added: "Our people built eighty percent of the buildings in Savannah" by hand. He continued, telling us that West Africans were a skilled group of people and brought many of those skills with them. These skills were then used for the benefit of America. For example, "Oglethorpe [the founder of Georgia; see Bartley 1983 and Coleman 1977] got credit for the squares in Savannah, but it was Black workers who really built them."

We visited the First African Baptist Church, which dates to 1859 and took four years to build. The tour included the first floor, the downstairs area, and the upstairs area. The driver said that at the time, "whites let us worship [by] ourselves." One of the preachers was Reverend George Leile; he had the freedom to preach and went to Jamaica in 1782 with the British. The church has survived several hurricanes, and it still has its original floor, made of Georgia pine. The driver pointed to a number of holes in the floor, which, we were told, were "a hiding place for slaves." He added that there are fourteen tunnels outside the church that were part of the Underground Railroad. In the church a number of songs were used by the slaves as a means of communication; for example, "Steal Away Sweet Jesus," "Swing Low Sweet Chariot," "Wade in the Water," and "Michael Row the Boat Ashore" all had double meanings. We were told that the church has an archives section and that it contains numerous church records dating back to the last century. Nearby, Professor Small saw portraits of seventeen ministers who had preached in the church. Upstairs, the driver described the glass windows and the organ, which we were told was built in 1834 and was the oldest pipe organ in Georgia. The pews dated to 1901. The church seats sixteen hundred people. At this point the driver then told us that during the days of slavery the "whites mixed us up"—they took different Africans speaking the same language and separated them so that they could not speak their own language. Out of this a new language developed—"Gullah, which is a language just like English" Gullah is also associated with a particular belief system, and the driver pointed to some "tribal markings" on the side of the pews. He said that the "whites put metal bits in our mouths to stop us communicating, but we found other ways to communicate." He continued, "Africans were a highly skilled people," and, pointing upward, said that only one beam supports the entire ceiling.

We left the church and headed to Franklin Square, where the driver pointed to a red building and said that it used to be a slave market belonging to J. Bryan, who owned Brampton Plantation and who enslaved Andrew Bryan, one of the early preachers at the African Baptist Church. We drove down Martin Luther King Jr. Boulevard and heard several other stories about individuals and events in Georgia history, including mention of several white master-enslavers "who had Black children," including W. E. Stiles of the Stiles Rice Plantation—"his Black family is now a major contractor" in Savannah, said the driver. We drove through a number of old streets and were told that this was Frogtown, where in the past most Blacks lived.

Next we stopped at the Civil Rights Museum, housed in a 1914 building, and it was mentioned that in 1927 the largest Black bank in the nation was here in Savannah. An African American man named W. W. Law, who was president of the Savannah NAACP branch, raised $2 million to open the museum. The museum is only about the civil rights movement in Savannah, not in the larger United States.

We watched a video that lasted approximately eighteen minutes and described key aspects of the civil rights movement in Savannah—the first sit-ins in Savannah in the 1960s, a key boycott that lasted fifteen months, efforts to integrate the beach at Tybee Island. It mentioned Levy's Department Store, which was segregated, but not by law—segregation here, the video said, was simply local custom. A number of the laws in Georgia were mentioned, including a law passed in 1866 that stipulated that anyone who was "one-eighth Black was Black" and one in 1927 that stipulated that any person with "any ascertainable trace of Negro, African, West Indian, or Asian Indian blood" was to be regarded as Black. A series of other issues and events was described, including the fact that free Blacks were not allowed on the west side of Bull Street, the location of General Sherman's headquarters in Madison Square, and details of "Field Order 15" concerning "forty acres and a mule," which originated in Savannah.

Following this we visited the King-Tisdell Cottage, an 1896 Victorian building that was relocated to this location from its original site in 1979. The King family owned a dry cleaning store, and when Mr. King died, his widow remarried and became Mrs. Tisdell. The house has furniture from the 1890s. There were originals of five bills of sale for slaves, framed on the wall. Close by was a drawing of a slave auction and mention of a person named Ben Ali, with a meditation in Arabic. Other items in the house included a poem regarding the slave quarters on St. Catharine Island and a number of baskets woven by African Americans that indicate the contributions of African skills. In the basement were a number of artifacts, including a model of the ship *Wanderer*, which illegally brought enslaved Africans to the coast of Georgia in 1859. There was also a replica of a dugout canoe, a sewing machine, fishnet, more baskets in glass cases, and a stove, pot, and music box from the early 1900s.

We visited the Beach Institute, an art school and museum with numerous paintings and portraits from both past and present artists. The institute is located in a huge building built in 1867; we were told that it is the oldest extant school in Georgia. One of the pieces of art located in it has images of many U.S. presidents altered to show "Negro features and color." In one of the rooms was a number of glass cases: one with examples of African art, another with an exhibit on Frederick Douglass, and other artworks such as "Garden of Eden" and "Hands of Freedom." Upstairs, where classrooms are located, was a detailed map of African American history and a drawing of John Brown. When we returned to the minibus the driver played a tape explaining the development of Gullah and then a number of songs from the region.

In addition to the detailed attention given to African American history, we were also told a number of things that were not primarily about African Americans—for example, the driver identified buildings belonging to the Savannah College of Art and Design, which happens to be the largest such school in the country; informed us that Savannah used to build over 90 percent of U.S. ships; and told us that the Savannah Bridge, built in 1991, is 2,394 meters long. We were told some of the history of the various Native American groups that inhabited the region prior to the arrival of Europeans—the area in what is now north Georgia was Cherokee, that of south Georgia was Creek, and Yamacraws lived in the area around Savannah. The driver mentioned that Governor Talmadge (in office 1933–42) had promised white Georgians that he would ban Blacks from the state. We were told that the city hall has a gold dome that cost a quarter of a million dollars. Some of the streets still have eighteenth-century English cobblestones—we could feel them under the wheels as we rode down the street. A large bell was pointed out, and the driver mentioned that it was last rung in the 1860s. He also pointed out a number of guns and told us that George Washington gave the guns to the city in 1791. We were told the story of how General Sherman arrived in Savannah and how, to prevent him from burning the city to the ground, the mayor got on his knees and begged him. That is why so many of the buildings from that period still remain in the city, whereas in other parts of Georgia and in other states, hundreds of buildings were destroyed. We were then told that "in Savannah white soldiers did not rape Black women " and "there were no mulatto children walking around our communities."

The driver mentioned a number of Black inventors—we were told that a Black engineer had the idea for the cotton gin, and that Georgia was the world's largest producer of cotton at first. We passed some cotton warehouses circa 1850 and were told that cotton was shipped from Savannah to Liverpool and then Manchester. The driver explained that Father Divine, an African American preacher who had a large multiracial congregation on Long Island, New York, in the 1920s and 1930s, began his career in Georgia.

While visitors were presented with some information that was more generically about Savannah, this tour was organized as a salute to African American resilience and as a tribute to key individuals and organizations that represent the struggles and successes of African Americans historically. The tour covered a wide range of time periods and historical events. During the tour there was no hesitation about challenging the more conventional white-centric stories of the contributions of the South and of its great men to the nation, and indicating that many achievements claimed by rich whites were really the work of African Americans, especially those enslaved. Nor was there any hesitation in describing the brutality of the treatment handed out to Blacks by whites—including explicit mention of rape—along with the measures taken by African Americans to prevent and minimize this treatment and to organize their lives in the ways that they deemed best met their needs. It was clear that the driver sought to reveal the hidden, less well known, or less frequently told aspects of American history and to highlight the real, sustained, and important contributions made to American history by African Americans.

The River Road African American Museum

The River Road African American Museum is located on the same site as the Tezcuco Plantation in Louisiana. It is a large, high-roofed wooden building with several dividers that create roomlike spaces within its single large interior area. Its huge collection covers a wide range of periods and topics and is organized as sections and subsections throughout the room. The leaflet handed out at the museum spells out its mission clearly and links past experience to present needs:

The River Road African American Museum & Gallery is dedicated to collecting, preserving and interpreting artifacts that provide positive information about the history and culture of African-Americans. The museum pays tribute to the hundreds of slaves who were "purchased" and brought to Burnside, Louisiana in 1858. Many of their descendants continue to live in the rural communities along the Mississippi River, and visitors to the museum can research African-American ancestry in the extensive records housed here.

It continues, "You will experience a part of history that cannot be found in history books," and "The enslaved Africans who worked on the plantation coped with slavery through a strong sense of family, church, and cultural traditions." As you walk into the museum several things greet you: a sign from the Jim Crow era that says Colored Served in the Rear, another sign that says You Are Making History Each Day That You Live, and a card that says that the museum is dedicated to "grandmother & grandfather." Also close to the front door is a bust (about three feet tall) of Pierre Landry, the first African American mayor of Donaldsville, elected in 1868. A poster at the side has details of Landry and his family, including the fact that he was "enslaved at Houmas Plantation." There is also a portrait of Abe Hawkes, a jockey.

Also at the entrance to the room is a small television and VCR on which is played *River Parish Requiem*, a video that lasts about twenty minutes. The video is narrated by Kathy Harbrick, an African American woman who was instrumental in setting up the River Road African American Museum; she also appears in the video. Harbrick comments that when she visited some of the existing plantation homes in the River Road district, "chills went through me"—she could feel the presence of Africans, and their spirituality was evident. She adds poignantly, "I started to cry for fifteen minutes uncontrollably." She then relates that she went on every tour of plantations that she could locate, and found that every tour was consistent—there was "no mention of slavery" on any of them. Surprised, dismayed, and saddened, Harbrick dedicated herself to doing research that would allow the story of Africans and African Americans during slavery to be told. She spent two and a half years doing research and trying to raise funds, and in March 1994 the River Road African American Museum was opened. Harbrick set out to demonstrate that African Americans are proud of the part that people of African descent have played in the history of Louisiana and of this area. She was determined to make African and African Americans lives real and personal; in particular, she tried to find a way to enable people to know the names of their ancestors and not to leave Black people as unidentified, impersonal beings. In the video, Harbrick begins to name some individuals—for example, Leonard Julien, from Donalsonville, Louisiana, who was an inventor. As Harbrick was doing the research, she met a number of African Americans in the district who told her that they wanted her to help them find their ancestors. She went out into rural areas to try to locate people and construct genealogies. For example, she located an African American woman, Mrs. Roburn, who she was horrified to discover was still living in what had been a slave cabin. The interior walls of the cabin were made of cardboard, and there was no inside toilet.

She also discovered many facets of African American history and presence in the region and was concerned about how she would be able to preserve it all. She initiated a number of discussions with museum organizations and began to contact various government agencies. Then she established the Louisiana African American Museums Association. One of the goals of the association is to get professional and experienced people to provide workshops to help the association preserve many of the artifacts that have been located and unearthed. Harbrick stressed that she wants the River Road African American Museum to be "a healing place" for all. In particular, she emphasizes that African Americans "have nothing to be ashamed of if our ancestors were slaves" and should be "proud to be a descendant of the survivors."

Professor Small visited the museum in the summer of 1999. When he entered, he was met by an African American woman in her sixties who told him that her name was Gwendolyn Smith and informed him that the museum was organized around a self-guided tour and that he should start with the video, which provides an overview. She said that efforts were being made to develop a new museum with funds from Texaco. As Professor Small continued throughout the room, she would occasionally call out a comment to explain a particular item, highlight a specific artifact or photograph, or briefly describe what one of the sections was about.

The museum has several sections, covering artifacts, music, inventing, slavery, River Road doctors, and modern art. One of the first artifacts sections included items such as barrels and pots, an oven, an iron, a spittoon, and a kettle. A placard provided some details of African food and of the linguistic connections between African languages and dialects of English spoken by African Americans. We are told that the word *yam* came from the

African word *njam*, and that words such as *jambalaya*, *gumbo*, and *bongo* all have African origins.

There was a section devoted to music, with a huge color poster titled *Evolution of the Blues*. There was a black-and-white photo of Mahalia Jackson close by, one of a New Orleans singing group, and another of a local gospel group. A section on inventors named Louisiana-born Leonard Julien (mentioned briefly above) as the inventor of the sugarcane-planting machine. There was also a poster featuring a number of Black inventors (this poster has been available for decades, and Professor Small had seen it previously not only in other museums in the United States but in the offices and homes of African Americans as well as in some Black community organizations in England).

Another section is devoted to the slave era. It begins with a huge portrait of L. L. Fernandez, a legally free man of color. Close by are a time line of slavery listing key dates and important events, a large black-and-white photo of human captives, newspaper clippings related to slavery, and a horrifying photograph of an enslaved person with his back ripped apart from the whip. A black-and-white photograph presents another intense image of Wilson Chin, an enslaved person from Louisiana who had been branded. There are also many images of instruments of torture, used to punish enslaved persons. An 1858 list of John Burnside's slaves includes some names and ages. One entry indicates that John S. Preston of Columbia, South Carolina, was sold to John Burnside of New Orleans. After all these images from the period of slavery, the visitor is then confronted with a text plaque carrying the statement "Could these be your ancestors?" While one can presume that this is primarily intended for an African American audience, it will not escape the reflective visitor that these could also be the ancestors of many white people.

This section includes quite a number of portraits of well-known African Americans from this period, such as Frederick Douglass and Harriet Tubman. Close by are several African drums on the floor and a huge copy of the Emancipation Proclamation. To the side of them is a large black-and-white poster of Madam C. S. Walker. There is a section on Black doctors, with mention of numerous individuals—for example, John H. Lowery, Ulysses Grant Daily, E. N. Ezidore, and Feaster Dean. There is also information on a number of prominent Black Republican leaders in the 1920s.

This museum, then, provides a stark contrast with the tenor, content, and motivation of white-centric museum sites. The exhibit begins with a video that expresses pain, sadness, and determination, and highlights the efforts made to ensure that African American struggles, suffering, and contributions are brought into the foreground of collective memory and that the other half of the story gets told. It is no accident that the section on slavery begins with a free man of color to challenge the stereotypes and upset the normative way of thinking. This exhibit is about pride and dignity, about the quest for recognition for contributions made, and about the linkages between past and present. It does not shy away from the brutalities and cruelty of the institution, nor from the shame and discomfort that might be felt by today's great-great-grandchildren of those who were enslaved.

Commonalities across Black-centric and White-centric Sites

Black-centric and white-centric sites, despite some of the more obvious and striking differences, actually have a number of things in common. Both kinds of sites use evocative language, expressions of emotion, and imagery to present their story, but they do it in fundamentally different ways and with different foci. The white-centric sites focus on the elegance and beauty of houses and gardens and on the codes of honor, decency, gentility, and romance of elite whites. They do so to show that the era of slavery was a beautiful period that we should remember fondly and with honor and appreciation. In contrast, Black-centric sites focus on pride, dignity, and respect in the face of humiliation; courage and perseverance in the face of pain, brutality, and adversity; dedication and perseverance in the face of overwhelming odds; commitment to and love of family; and forgiveness in the face of revenge and extreme brutality. Overall, they portray resilience.

Second, both mainstream and Black-centric sites are shaped a great deal by contemporary values and needs. Both frame the people they represent as victims and as descendants of peoples who should be remembered with honor, glory, and nostalgia. The white South wants to remember an aristocratic civilization, a society that is the backbone of American society and economy, decent people who were full of honor and courtesy, and honorable men who fought for a cause that they believed in. Blacks want an acknowledgment of the pain and suffering of the enslaved, the injustices heaped upon them, the contributions they made to the economy and culture of America, and how they suffered so that elite whites might enjoy wonderful lives; they also want to show up the contradictions of the American dream, denied to African Americans.

The two types of sites embrace similar discursive strategies, but for different purposes. First, both highlight great men, great women, great events, great structures. But white-centric sites' strategies serve to aggrandize the elites, to valorize whiteness, to support gender relations, to assuage guilt, and to make present inequalities seem just. Black-centric sites use these strategies to highlight resistance and resilience, to humanize Blacks, and to challenge contemporary inequalities by showing how they were achieved through past inequities. Second, both predicate the stories they tell about the past on values that prevail in the present. For mainstream sites, American history is the realization of the American dream—escape from oppressive aristocracies in Europe, the ability to lift oneself through hard work, and freedom for all (whites). Today's society is seen as just and fair, and history indicates how it became that way. For Black-centric sites, what shapes historical narrative is contemporary needs and feelings around racialized injustice, discrimination, and the failure to provide an accurate and complete history of African Americans lives, experiences, and successes.

Conclusions

Black-centric sites offer a stark contrast to the narratives of the white-centric sites, and visits to the former offer a glaring illustration of the partiality of the latter. On these tours the stories are more likely to begin in Africa, rather than in slavery; to be explicit on the suffering and exploitation of people of African origin; to highlight African American resistance, especially through narratives of famous Blacks, both under and since slavery; to offer personal details of individual African Americans; and to highlight the contributions made by the African Americans who built the great houses, polished the furniture, grew the food, and cooked and served the meals, as well as by those who produced artwork or weaving and music. They are also far more likely to use language that evokes the pain and suffering experienced during slavery. Theirs is not a story of admiration for the buildings that were built by the enslaved, of celebration of a genteel and decent way of life, or of sorrow for days gone by. Rather, they present a critique of an inherently abusive institution and praise for the spirit of resilience so common among African Americans in the face of systematic and sustained oppression.

At sites that present a counternarrative, there is more of a focus on periods after slavery, and in particular on the civil rights era and on the heroes and events that are part of the grand narrative of that time. This should not be surprising; African Americans do not wish to be understood or defined as a people by their experience of enslavement. By way of concrete example, at one relative incorporation site in Virginia, staff reported that following a school tour they were contacted by one African American parent who was outraged that the children had been taken on a tour of a site in Virginia that provided extensive details of slavery. It is clear that there are some African Americans who would prefer, for various reasons, to avoid exposing their children (or themselves) to these issues, and we recognize that there are many whites, perhaps a majority, who would also like to avoid such exposure. However, given the contours of racialized inequality, the central role that discrimination plays in sustaining such inequality, and the kinds of racialized hostility that continues to create immense costs for contemporary Black people, we would suggest that the burden of these representations of history impacts in far greater measure on Blacks than whites. It also leads white Americans to continue to place lies and half-truths at the center of the story they tell about themselves and others. However, the Black sites we've visited, which grew out of the civil rights and Black power movements, will continue to press for a more accurate retelling of U.S. history.

9 ||| Conclusions

In a country that has been and continues to be organized around racialized oppression, business as usual means that oppressive behaviors, institutions, and representational strategies will continue. This is as true in the museum world as it is anywhere else, and it is perhaps particularly true in the plantation museum world, since such museums' very parameters—the buildings, locations, and actors—were created in and through the institution of slavery, with its exploitation and debasement of human beings. And overwhelmingly, the enslavement of millions of human beings is not discussed. Instead, there is a ringing, terrible silence; where silence doesn't reign, stories of Black loyalty and white benevolence are whispered.

It is legitimate to ask why anyone should care what happens at these sites. Our answer is that to ignore the locations where racialized, and racialist, stories are told over and over—stories that not only are framed around presumed racial difference but work to maintain inequality and oppression based upon such presumed difference—is to continue with business as usual, a disgraceful and inhumane situation that perpetuates lies that corrode the lives of all they touch. These lies include the idea that Black people have been inconsequential to the formation of the United States; that Black people don't really mind subordination; that whites are generally benevolent and well-intentioned, even when acting in direct ways to create and maintain oppression; that class differences among whites are largely inconsequential; and that being white is the "universally human" position.

Lies, for some, is a strong word; it implies malice and intent to deceive by

telling stories that are incomplete, partial, and distorted. We are not arguing that those who staff mainstream plantation museum sites are malicious
or intentionally deceiving the public. Direct intent on the part of many participants is generally not needed once racist systems are in place. While
some people who participate in the plantation museum system may have explicitly racialist beliefs that accept and perpetuate white supremacy, we assume that many do not. Indeed, neither structural nor cultural racism requires for its replication any active intent on the part of most participants.
Instead, following "the path of least resistance" (Johnson 2000)—that is,
going along with the regular, everyday behaviors accepted by members of
the dominant society, whether or not one realizes that these behaviors replicate racism—maintains the production and consumption of racist ideologies, images, strategies of representation, and distribution of resources. Representational styles that present whites as the only important contributors
to the development of the United States are still central to the official and
unofficial culture of this country, even after hundreds of years of resistance
on the part of peoples of color and thirty years of academic demonstrations
that this myopic view is wrong. When sites replicate this view, they are con-
tributing to a way of thinking that is fundamentally racialist and racist.

We have demonstrated that the mainstream plantation museum infrastructure creates and re-creates a discursive framework of the South as genteel, honorable, and romantic. This framing is found across all 122 of the
white-centric sites that we explored and is carried out through representational strategies that "manage" or "contain" the fact of enslavement. These
strategies include symbolic annihilation, trivialization and deflection, segregation, and relative incorporation. Additionally, some sites are best understood as a mix of the various strategies (including relative incorporation)
and hence fall in between the other categories. This larger discursive
framework of the South and the strategies used to contain and organize the
discussion of slavery resonate with larger racial formations, as well as racial
formation projects that elevate whites and whiteness and subjugate African
Americans and other peoples of color.

As we demonstrated in chapter 4, the primary way that a white-centric
view is produced on plantation museums is through the strategy we have
called symbolic annihilation. A total of 55.7 percent of all the white-centric
sites we visited engage only in symbolic annihilation—they completely erase
or significantly minimize the presence, labor, and contributions of African
Americans. Given the vast number of plantation sites that exist across the

South, this constitutes a massive and gross distortion of what transpired during slavery. It means that at sites where Blacks were the numerical majority of the resident population, their presence is simply not mentioned or is mentioned in such a perfunctory way that its significance is minimized. In addition to perfunctory mentions of those enslaved, symbolic annihilation works through the use of euphemisms that refuse to name enslavement; the use of passive voice, which erases the labor that enslaved African Americans performed; and complete silence about the fact that much of the accumulated wealth of white people in the North and South was built on a foundation of stolen labor.

Going hand in hand with the erasure of the presence and contributions of Blacks and their experience of enslavement is the elevation of the status of rich whites. These are the people, we are told, who really made the world. Their lives are the primary focus for all the tours—we are told in detail of their hopes, dreams, frustrations, and fears, how they laughed or cried, worked hard for success or suffered in failure, cared for one another, and dedicated themselves to the nation. These are the only people who are the central, active, human participants in the drama of this nation. This elevation of the wealthy is not, of course, a practice confined to the United States; it flourishes in Europe (Lowenthal 1998). What is seemingly different in the United States is that most plantation museums work to erase the class differences between their middle-class white visitors and their elite white former residents. At many locations white visitors are told that had they been visitors in a past era, they would have stayed in a specific room or eaten certain foods as they took the midday meal with the plantation owners. Note, as we said in chapter 1, that this sort of thing was never said to Professor Small, who is Black British, but Professor Eichstedt, who is European American, was told numerous times where she would have stayed or what she would have eaten if she had come to visit. White wealth is held up as the prize that all hardworking (white) individuals might attain. Such collapsing of class differences among whites is a long-standing strategy, well documented by W. E. B. Dubois and others, designed to ensure that whites believe they share a racialized bond that trumps any class affiliation that poor, working-class, or middle-class whites share with poor, working-class, or middle-class Blacks. This strategy ensured white loyalty first to slavery and then to Jim Crow segregation (Dubois 1989; Saxton 1990; Roediger 1991). In the present day this strategy functions in much the same way, with race used to erase or mask class differences and exploitation. Such practices at plantation museums also work to erase the reality and presence of all but elite whites; the sameness of whites is emphasized at the same moment that wealth is celebrated.

Therefore, the practice of symbolic annihilation, at the same time that it erases the presence of African Americans and elevates white wealth, reinforces the American belief in the work ethic and individualism. At the vast majority of plantation museums whites are the only ones who are presented as hardworking—we are told over and over about the time and toil they invested in building their plantations, growing the crops, constructing impressive buildings, and furnishing their homes elegantly. At the same time, many of the images that we see are of whites working in fields, who are presented as if they toiled there alone. Erased is the labor and presence of enslaved African Americans; instead the sacrifices and hard work of the white elite are emphasized.

We were also told that these elite whites are the people who really suffered when what they had worked so hard to create was taken away or destroyed by northern aggressors. This trope of suffering—and the way it is rewritten and its focus narrowed—is found in other societies that have atrocities in their pasts. As Irwin-Zarecka notes in her work on Polish and German efforts to represent the Holocaust, non-Jewish Poles shifted the frame of suffering onto themselves as victims of German intrusion and then of scorn from outsiders; they became the ones in need of sympathy, and the concern for Jews was sidestepped. The same dynamic operates in the contemporary South. Here, white elite southerners are the victims of northern hostility and aggression, losing everything; they become the "true" victims. Additionally, the Civil War has been successfully reframed in the minds of many people as a war for "states' rights"—as if the right that southern states fought to defend were not the right to enslave other human beings. Acknowledging this does not mean we cannot also acknowledge that economic struggles between the North and South were at play; again, however, the economic struggle was fundamentally wrapped up in the institution of slavery. But victim status is incredibly powerful and seductive—if one is a victim oneself, it seems, one cannot be held accountable for one's own abhorrent behavior. Shifting the talk to the victimization of white southerners apparently means that we don't need to talk about what transpired before or since; white victimization is the ultimate tool of deflection. Presentations of whites as victims is found not only within the plantation museum industry but in the larger dominant culture. David Wellman (1996) calls this a modern minstrel show, where white men position themselves as victims of unjust discrimination to deflect attention from the ways that whites, and particularly white elite men, continue to receive racialized and gendered advantages and privileges. Victimization within the plantation museum industry parallels this larger trend by working in ways that further erase the presence and experience of enslaved African Americans. It is easier to talk about victim status for southern whites if one erases the very presence of African Americans, and certainly if one erases the ways in which southern whites systematically victimized African Americans. Of course, the other way to escape having to think about African Americans' experience of enslavement as brutal or dehumanizing is to present images of docile, happy, loyal, and devoted slaves, and that is the second most common strategy presented at the sites we've visited.

As we stated in chapter 5, we categorized 27.0 percent of sites as locations where trivialization and deflection were the predominant racialized strategy. These sites also met the criteria for the category of symbolic annihilation. Of all the sites in our study, a full 44.6 percent engaged in trivialization. This included almost every site in the in-between category and one from the relative incorporation category. Trivialization and deflection are represented most clearly by the images of enslavement as benevolent, of the enslaved as happy, grateful, and loyal, and of enslaved people as prone to theft and laziness. The flip side of this, of course, is the representation of whites as hardworking, good owners.

Trivialization works because it meshes with long-standing racist constructions of African Americans. Ed Guerrero, who traces the ways that African Americans have been represented in film, argues the following about mainstream Hollywood framings of Blackness:

> Instead of inspiring aesthetic, cultural, and political masterworks aimed at liberating the human potential, Hollywood, for the most part, has tended to focus narrowly its increasingly shallow product on escapism, sentiment, glamour, romance, and more recently, spectacular orgies of violence and sexploitation, all in the service of feeding the dulled cravings and fantasies of the dominant social order. What all this means, specifically, for African Americans (and extrapolated to a wide range of other minorities) is that in almost every instance, the representation of black people on the commercial screen has amounted to one grand, multifaceted

illusion. For blacks have been subordinated, marginalized, positioned and devalued in every possible manner to glorify and relentlessly hold in place the white-dominated symbolic order and racial hierarchy of American society. (1993: 2)

This characterization of Hollywood can be transferred almost wholesale to the plantation museum industry. Here also the racialized symbolic order is reproduced on a daily basis in the emphasis on romance and glory compared with the servile behavior of enslaved African Americans. It is probably the case that most sites represent stories of loyalty and service because those are the stories that the master-enslavers memorialized in letters, diaries, and oral tradition. That is, these may be the only documented stories that sites have access to, and so these are the ones that are retold to visitors. The problem is that in the absence of any other representations, ones that celebrate loyal "servants" and grateful slaves suggest that such loyalty and gratitude were representative of those who were enslaved. It must also be remembered that the representation of loyal slaves and good masters found at these sites do not exist in a vacuum; instead, they are situated within the context of continued imagery of Mammy, servile Uncle Toms, and shiftless "coons" produced from the 1850s through the present moment (Goings 1994; Turner 1994).

When loyalty wasn't discussed, the insubordination of enslaved peoples was suggested. The threat of subordination comes through clearly as we look at the repetition of imagery and stories across sites. For instance, at many of the sites that we visited, docents present the fact that white mistresses kept valuable foods and spices, cutlery, and jewelry under lock and key. At many of these sites visitors are explicitly told that it is because these things were expensive and owners didn't want "servants" taking them. When we heard this story repeatedly, especially in connection with other stories about the need to devise systems that kept enslaved people from shirking their duties (such as having them whistle as they carried food from the kitchen to the dining room), it sounded like an assertion about the untrustworthiness of enslaved people: Blacks will steal unless white people lock things away from their thieving hands. Is this the message that specific plantation museums want to send? We assume, based on Professor Eichstedt's limited interviews conducted with curators of twelve sites, that this is not the case; however, this story does not stand alone. In most plantation museums it is connected to a larger silence about the experience of enslaved people. The fact that the vast bulk of white enslavers' wealth was produced by enslaved people, who were provided with the basic necessities of life (sometimes not even that) and nothing else beyond what they were able to grow, hunt, or make during their "free time," is excluded from consideration.

Stories of possible theft are also connected to contemporary public imagery of Blacks as dangerous, dishonest, and basically problematic. This imagery was begun during the period of enslavement, rose to a fever pitch after legal enslavement ended, and continues to this day (see Anti-Defamation League 1993; Feagin 2000; Entman and Rojecki 2000). When a specific site tells a story, it must be understood as being located in a web of other stories told at other plantation museums as well as at other racialized sites. When a visitor hears the story of possible theft once, it may not have much of an effect. However, when one considers the framing of these stories within the larger context of racialized imagery, the interpretation cannot be assumed to be without effect. Additionally, if plantation museum visitors generally visit more than one site (which is suggested by our experience visiting multiple sites in the same region and seeing the same visitors move from plantation to plantation), this becomes a cumulative message: whites, even then, had to guard against the thieving tendencies of Blacks.

Are we overreading the messages found in museum sites? Perhaps. However, lest readers easily dismiss the connections we are making, consider comments (noted in chapter 6) made by two separate white male visitors in their fifties at Mount Vernon. Both men, who stopped with their white female companions in the reconstructed barracks-style housing provided for "house servants," connected what they saw there with the present moment. One said, "They didn't live too bad, better than a lot of them do today," and the other said something substantially similar. The "they" here clearly refers to Black people, and enslavement is being posited as superior to the life "they" live now. This demonstrates that visitors do indeed make connections between stories or representations of the past and actions in the present, at least sometimes. What we don't know for sure, and what only research with visitors can teach us, is how common this linkage is.

In addition to exploring visitor assessments at places where symbolic annihilation and trivialization predominate, similar research at locations with segregationist and relative incorporation strategies should also be undertaken. These sites, we've argued, are different in some limited ways from those dominated by annihilation and trivialization. The ways they differ, however, are limited.

Sites where segregation and the marginalization of knowledge occurred as the primary organizing strategy accounted for 4.1 percent of all sites. These sites have incorporated discussion of enslavement into their larger sites; however, they have confined this knowledge to a physically distinct space. This allows visitors to take only the white-centric tour if they desire and thus never engage information about slavery and those who were enslaved except in the perfunctory, limited, and trivializing ways these topics are discussed on white-centric tours.

Segregation of knowledge "works," we believe, for three reasons. First, it allows sites to attract visitors who only want to hear the message of the main tour; visitors aren't forced to confront something (enslavement) they may not want to confront. Second, such segregation allows only those docents who wish to present issues of enslavement to be trained in that knowledge; those who are unwilling to talk about these issues aren't required to discuss them. Third, the topic of enslavement can be covered in more depth on its own forty-five-minute tour than if information on enslavement was incorporated into a house tour that is forty-five minutes in and of itself.

These may seem like good reasons, at least on the surface, to segregate information regarding enslavement. Of course, there is a significant cost—visitors (and staff) can choose to continue to be ignorant of a substantial piece of the country's history and continue to believe that whites alone made the country what it is now. This segregation, like segregationist practices that confine the teaching of Black history or the history of any group other than elite white males to the margins, allows the actions of elite white men to still be considered "real history." This seriously undercuts plantation museums' ability to be taken seriously as sites presenting any sort of complete history, even though they characterize themselves as such. These sites should build on the knowledge they have already gathered, incorporating at least a significant amount of this work into their regular tours. This will help teach visitors that learning about issues of enslavement (or about the genocide of American Indians) is fundamental to understanding the history that has led us to the present moment.

Those sites that we've designated as using relative incorporation as their primary strategy have gone the farthest among the sites we visited in incorporating issues related to enslavement throughout their programs. However, they also constitute only 3.3 percent of all sites. Their close brethren, in-between sites, make up 9.8 percent of all sites. Additionally, as our discussion of these sites shows, these sites still often have a long way to go to fully honor the multiple experiences that occurred at their location. One of the primary issues facing these sites is the variation in content and tour quality that occurs when tours are led by different docents. This is an issue that complicates sites' abilities to address problematic representations of slavery, those who were enslaved, and whiteness. If the content of tours is left to the interests and comfort level of specific docents, it is likely that significant change will not occur unless there is a turnover of docents and new docents are not only required to present inclusive information but trained to do so.

The consistency of information provision across docents is one of the markers that moves sites from being in-between in their handling of enslavement to the relative incorporation category. Sites cannot be understood as being substantially more committed to the discussion of enslavement and what it meant to both those enslaved and those who enslaved them if the provision of that information is hit-or-miss. Developing uniformity across docents is a difficult task, not only in the arena of discussing enslavement but also in discussing any aspect of the site's white-centric history, as docents invariably come with different interests of their own. However, this issue must be addressed, and prospective docents need to understand that discussing enslavement will be part of what they are expected to do if sites are to be successful in their inclusion of this topic. This is a particularly significant issue for those sites that we categorized as in-between, where the incorporation and treatment of enslavement varied tremendously across docents, and the content was more likely to trivialize enslavement.

We've also demonstrated that while these different representational strategies are similar in many ways across sites in the same category, there are significant regional inflections (what we have called narrative styles) in the ways in which these stories are told. That is, the particular ways in which the main theme of the genteel South is emphasized and the manner in which slavery is erased, circumvented, segregated, or relatively incorporated is achieved through a focus on differing issues, particularly issues deemed unique to a particular state. In other words, different types of stories prevail in the different states. As we have shown, in Virginia the primary story deployed is that of the state as the "birthplace of democracy." In Virginia we also find a stress on the gentility, civility, and hospitality of the master-enslavers of that state. In Georgia's sites stories are often framed through references to the movie *Gone with the Wind* and to the romance and nostalgia it evokes. Also common in Georgia is an emphasis on the Civil War. Finally, in Louisiana, the financial and human tragedy of the Civil War is the primary trope through which plantation tours are organized. Louisiana plantation sites also place an emphasis on eighteenth-century life and on the differences between Creoles of French origin and culture in the southern part of the state, Cajuns in the southwest, and the English in the parishes immediately below Mississippi. What these regional inflections mean is that a visitor to sites in all of these states can still experience the common features of the portrayal of the romantic, genteel South while enjoying the rich, textured details of individual state histories.

But it is not just white-centric sites that seek to tell the story of what happened during slavery. A number of Black-centric museums and exhibits cover many of the same topics. As we have shown in chapter 8, we believe that many of the essential problems that pervade the white-centric plantation museums sites become glaringly visible—palpable, even—when one visits Black-centric museums and exhibits. As we make clear, these sites are not plantation museum sites in the sense in which we use the term to describe white-centric sites. The twenty Black sites that we visited are not based on plantation big houses or buildings that originate in the slavery era, and they do not focus their attention on the lifestyles of elite whites. Instead, they are mainly based in buildings constructed after slavery, and they are dedicated to describing the lives and struggles of African Americans in general and the lives of important figures in African American history. They seek to acknowledge and highlight the contributions made by African Americans to the economy and society of the South and the nation more generally.

While Black-centric sites discuss slavery and the experiences of the enslaved, they do not restrict themselves to a focus on slavery; instead they also focus on other periods in African American history, in particular the civil rights movement. Their goal is not to celebrate a genteel South nor to glorify the white elites who dominated that region. Instead, they seek to acknowledge, celebrate, and honor the struggles of African Americans and their perseverance, dignity, and resilience in the face of exploitation, hostility, and oppression. At these sites we do not hear about faithful, loyal, happy, or shiftless slaves, but of individual struggle and suffering, collective resistance and identity, and human dignity in the face of oppression. At these sites, African Americans are humanized and individualized—we hear of their struggles as human agents in a nation that promised equality but delivered so little. And these sites themselves persevere despite lacking resources and personnel, despite lacking the glamour and elegance of huge mansions, and despite their marginalization, even segregation, in the overall tourist infrastructure.

When we visited some of these sites it was made clear to us that the docents and organizers were acutely aware of the white-centric sites. Some of these sites were organized in specific opposition to the partiality and silences so manifest in the white-centric sites. Others arose from the partiality and silences so ubiquitous in American education and history more generally. When they focus on slavery, these sites cover many of the same topics as the white-centric sites, raise many of the same issues, and even focus on some of the same people. But, as we have shown in chapter 8, they do it from a fundamentally different premise and with a fundamentally different motivation. We believe that the existence of these sites—the stories they provide, the images that they present, and the struggles that they face—is an indispensable corrective to many of the silences and lies we have identified at the white-centric plantation museum sites. These alternative narratives make transparent the partiality and self-serving interests of the white-centric sites.

As we've asserted throughout the book, and this chapter in particular, the contrasting, conflicting, and often troubling approaches to the topic of enslavement at these sites reflect conflicted, troubled, and problematic approaches in the larger social, economic, and political world to the history of enslavement and, indeed, African Americans' continued presence in the United States. That basic information about enslavement is excluded from tours is based on longer-standing practices in the plantation museum industry that in turn are linked to racialized ideologies that exist in the larger national and regional community. These long-standing racialized ideologies overdetermine the shape that plantation museums have historically taken in the South. These ideologies include national constructions of America as a white land (see Lopez 1996; Feagin 2000; Saxton 1990; Takaki 1990), the "Lost Cause" story (Foster 1987) developed after the Civil War, individualism as the primary trope for understanding the distribution of all good things in life, and fundamentally racist constructions of African Americans. These ideologies are then articulated at the ground level in plantation museums through the tropes and strategies we've discussed throughout this book. The dominant social narrative of race is upheld.

As we have already stated, the master narrative is, not surprisingly, the narrative of master-enslavers. While there are some whites who are presented as breaking with the dominant constructions of whites as moral, generous, democratic, and hardworking, they are really the exceptions that prove the rule. In general, those who lived as enslavers are presented as worthy of our admiration. The sin of enslavement need not be brought up, or if it is, it can be dealt with as though it were inconsequential. This presentation of enslavement as inconsequential is flawed at its foundation. It assumes that enslavement did not profoundly impact all aspects of society both in the past and at present, and that the consequences of enslavement in both the material and psychic worlds have dissolved. However, a range of scholarship has proved that untrue. For instance, many notable scholars demonstrate the continuing impact of enslavement and subsequent discrimination on the material and psychological lives of people of African descent (Oliver and Shapiro 1995; Massey and Denton 1993; Feagin 2000). Others note that important stereotypes that continue to permeate dominant U.S. culture and media were born during slavery as ways for elite whites to justify the enslavement of others (Bogle 1973). No one has summarized it more succinctly or more eloquently than Toni Morrison:

> In what public discourse does the reference to black people not exist? It exists in every one of this nation's mightiest struggles. The presence of black people is not only a major referent in the framing of the Constitution, it is also in the battle over enfranchising unpropertied citizens, women, the illiterate. It is there in the construction of a free and public school system; the balancing of representation in legislative bodies; jurisprudence and legal definitions of justice. It is there in theological discourse; the memoranda of banking houses; the concept of manifest destiny and the preeminent narrative that accompanies (if it does not precede) the initiation of every immigrant into the community of American citizens. The presence of black people is inherent, along with gender and family ties, in the earliest lesson every child is taught regarding his or her distinctiveness. Africanism is inextricable from the definition of Americanness—from its origins on through its integrated or disintegrating twentieth-century self. (1992: 65)

As for whites, the lie that was at the heart of constructing whiteness continues to flourish; it is built upon a separating out of some imagined "white self" from all other human beings. Such lies and exclusions preclude the creation of true democracy. But given the fact that many of these lies and exclusions are taken as commonsense truths by most whites, and that there is no sustained dialogue in the public sphere of the link between historical and contemporary inequalities, it seems that the development of a full and accurate accounting of white-centric sites is unlikely. The fact that most whites we saw during our tours were attending white-centric sites as opposed to Black-centric sites where they could learn alternative histories makes it seem unlikely that this particular infrastructure will soon become one that participates in social change.

As we have demonstrated in this book, the majority of white-centric sites are committed to telling a story that is exclusively about elite whites. Based on their presentations, it appears that they want to maintain their focus on architectural splendor, elite white lifestyles, European ancestry, the southern aristocracy, and all the trimmings of the genteel South. At the same time, our experience with many sites and with many docents indicate that a number of them might respond positively to some of the criticisms that we offer in this book and that they might be open to making more than superficial changes to the nature and content of their tours, the stories they tell, and the images they present. We don't know how many might respond in this way, nor do we naively expect that fundamental changes will come about quickly. But our experience is sufficient to convince us that it is worth trying to engage in a discussion with sites and docents that might lead to this kind of change. We believe that some of these sites have already responded constructively to evaluations and criticisms of the kinds we offer here—particularly some of the sites that we have described in Virginia. These sites have changed from what they were before; for example, only within the last ten years has Gunston Hall begun to incorporate information on enslavement and to take seriously public scrutiny regarding its representation of enslavement. We would like to urge other organizations and individuals involved in the management and funding of these sites to take up some of the many issues that we raise. We believe that public sites have an obligation to the people they serve to make these sites more inclusive. We also believe that ways should be found to encourage private sites to become more inclusive. We believe that such changes would be more beneficial to the sites themselves, as well as to the broader, more general efforts to provide an inclusive history of the South.

We agree, ultimately, with the challenges raised by Gaither in 1992:

First, museums must serve an ever-broader public in ever-bolder ways. And second, museums must honor America's diversity without paternalism and condescension. . . . Museums have obligations as both educational and social institutions to participate in and contribute toward the restoration of wholeness in the communities of our country. . . . They ought to help give substance, correction, and reality to the often incomplete and distorted stories we hear about art and social history. They should not dodge the controversy that often arises from the reappraisal of our common and overlapping pasts. . . . The United States' social health is too important to go unaddressed by any significant sector of its institutions. (1992: 58)

Sites that represent themselves as telling the story of history have a special function, or so they say. Their job is to communicate about the past so that we may understand the present and prepare for the future. If the stories that are told walk in step with the injustices that exist in the larger culture, then these sites work as agents of social injustice; that is, they perpetuate domination and oppression, reinforcing the silences, stereotypes, and erasures in people's minds that legitimate social inequities of the highest order. This is why sites that represent history must be held to the most stringent standards. It is also why the industry we have addressed in our work must look at the ways it legitimates racialized social forgetting.

Creating a racially just society, or developing some of the mechanisms that will allow such a society to develop, is a goal that both authors of this book share. If the statement with which we began the book with is true— that justice cannot be forged if at least one of the parties in a dispute believes that the injury inflicted has not been properly acknowledged—then the many silences about enslavement (and Jim Crow legislation and so on) that continue to this day only exacerbate racialized distance, distrust, and inequality. Some people believe that ignoring the past or whitewashing it (literally) will allow healing to occur; that we can get on with a just world by simply looking forward from today; that there need be no accounting of the past, no dredging up of old skeletons, no probing of old wounds. We fundamentally challenge this assertion. We believe that without a full and open discussion of the past, its relation to contemporary inequalities and oppressions, and considerations of how to respond to these historical and contemporary inequalities, true healing cannot take place. Sites that pride themselves as providing history to the masses have an important role to play in this process—either as maintainers of oppressive patterns or as teachers for a just future.

Appendix
Categories of Plantation Museum Sites

Georgia Plantation Museum Sites	Category
Alexander H. Stephens National Historic Site	Trivialization and deflection
Antebellum Plantation at Stone Mountain	Symbolic annihilation
Archibald Smith Plantation House	In-between
Bellevue Plantation	Symbolic annihilation
Br'er Rabbit Museum	Trivialization and deflection
Bulloch Hall	Segregated
Callaway Plantation	In-between
Cannonball House	Symbolic annihilation
Hampton Plantation (Slave Cabin Ruins) at St. Simons Island	Symbolic annihilation
Hay House (Johnston-Felton-Hay House)	Symbolic annihilation
Heritage Hall	Trivialization and deflection
Hofwyl-Broadfield Plantation	Trivialization and deflection
Inn Scarlett's Footsteps	Symbolic annihilation
Jarrell Plantation	Symbolic annihilation
Meadow Park	Symbolic annihilation
Oak Grove Plantation	Symbolic annihilation
Pemberton House	Symbolic annihilation
Road to Tara Museum, Stone Mountain	Symbolic annihilation
Road to Tara Museum, Jonesboro	Symbolic annihilation
Robert Toombs Plantation	Trivialization and deflection
Rodgers House	Symbolic annihilation
Ruins of Retreat Plantation Hospital on St. Simons Island	Symbolic annihilation
Stately Oaks Plantation	Symbolic annihilation
Tabby Sugar Works of John Houston McIntosh	Symbolic annihilation

Thomas Butler Chimney and Rice Stack	Symbolic annihilation
Tullie Smith Farm	Symbolic annihilation
Walker-Peters Langden House	Symbolic annihilation
Wesville Village	Symbolic annihilation
Wormsloe Historic Site	Symbolic annihilation

Georgia African American Sites

Beach Institute
First African Baptist Church
King Center for Non-Violent Social Change
King-Tisdell Cottage
Lucy Craft Laney Museum
Martin Luther King Jr. Civil Rights Memorial Center
Morgan County African American Museum
Negro Heritage Tour
Ralph Mark Gilbert Civil Rights Museum
Sweet Auburn District
Tubman African American Museum

Louisiana Plantation Museum Sites	**Category**
Acadian Village	Symbolic annihilation
Alexander Moulton House	Symbolic annihilation
Arlington Plantation Home	Symbolic annihilation
Beauforte Plantation	Trivialization and deflection
Butler Greenwood Plantation	Symbolic annihilation
The Cabins Restaurant	Symbolic annihilation
Chretien Point Plantation	Symbolic annihilation
Cottage Plantation	Symbolic annihilation
Destrehan Plantation Home	In-between
1850 House and Bookstore	Symbolic annihilation
Frogmore Plantation	In-between
Gallier House	Symbolic annihilation
Greenwood Plantation	Symbolic annihilation
Grevemburg House	Symbolic annihilation
Houmas House	Trivialization and deflection
Kent House Plantation	In-between
Laura: A Creole Plantation	Relative incorporation
Le Monde Creole	Trivialization and deflection
Longfellow Evangeline	In-between
Loyd Hall Plantation	Trivialization and deflection

Madewood Plantation	Trivialization and deflection
Magnolia Mound Plantation	Symbolic annihilation
Magnolia Ridge	Symbolic annihilation
Melrose Plantation	In-between
Memorial Hall Confederate Museum	Symbolic annihilation
Mount Hope Plantation	Symbolic annihilation
Myrtles Plantation	Symbolic annihilation
Nottoway Plantation	Symbolic annihilation
Oak Alley Plantation	Symbolic annihilation
Oaklawn Plantation	Symbolic annihilation
Oakley Plantation at Audubon State Commemorative Park	Symbolic annihilation
Ormond Plantation	Symbolic annihilation
Rosedown Plantation	Trivialization and deflection
San Francisco Plantation	Symbolic annihilation
Shadows on the Teche	Trivialization and deflection
Southdown Plantation/ Terrebonne Museum	Symbolic annihilation
Tante Huppe House	Symbolic annihilation
Tezcuco	Trivialization and deflection
Venus House (listed in African American History/Tourism Guide as a home built by a free woman of color; however, there was no real discussion of this)	Trivialization and deflection

Louisiana African American Sites

Arna Bontemps African American Cultural Center
Madam Johns Legacy
River Road African American Museum

Virginia Plantation Museum Sites	Category
Appomattox Plantation	Symbolic annihilation
Arlington House	Trivialization and deflection
Ash-Lawn Highland	Trivialization and deflection
Bacon's Castle	Symbolic annihilation
Belle Aire	Trivialization and deflection
Belle Grove Plantation	Trivialization and deflection
Berkeley	Trivialization and deflection
Boyhood Home of Robert E. Lee	Symbolic annihilation
Carlyle House	Relative incorporation
Carter's Grove	Segregated
Chatham Manor	Trivialization and deflection

Chelsea Plantation	Trivialization and deflection
Cherry Hill Farm	Symbolic annihilation
Claude Moore Farm	Symbolic annihilation
Colonial Williamsburg	Segregated
Endview Plantation	Trivialization and deflection
Evelynton	Symbolic annihilation
Ferry Farm	Symbolic annihilation
Flowerdew Hundred	Symbolic annihilation
Glen Burnie	Trivialization and deflection
Gunston Hall	In-between
John Marshall House	Symbolic annihilation
Kenmore Plantation	Trivialization and deflection
Laurel Hill—J. E. B. Stuart	Symbolic annihilation
Lee Hall Mansion	Symbolic annihilation
Lee-Fendall House	Symbolic annihilation
Magnolia Grange	Trivialization and deflection
Mary Washington House	Symbolic annihilation
Meadow Farm Museum	Trivialization and deflection
Montpelier	Relative incorporation
Monticello	In-between
Morven Park	Symbolic annihilation
Mt. Vernon	Segregated
Museum and White House of the Confederacy	Symbolic annihilation
North Bend Plantation	Symbolic annihilation
Oatlands Plantation	Trivialization and deflection
Piney Grove at Southhall	In-between
Pope's Creek	In-between
Poplar Forest	Symbolic annihilation
Prestwould Plantation	In-between
Red Hill	Trivialization and deflection
Scotchtown	Trivialization and deflection
Sherwood Forest	Trivialization and deflection
Shirley Plantation	Symbolic annihilation
Smith's Fort	Symbolic annihilation
Smithfield Plantation	Trivialization and deflection
Stonewall Jackson House	Segregated
Stratford Hall	Trivialization and deflection
Sully Plantation	Relative incorporation
Tuckahoe Plantation	Trivialization and deflection
Weston Manor	Symbolic annihilation
Westover	Symbolic annihilation
Wilton House Museum	Symbolic annihilation
Woodlawn	Symbolic annihilation

Virginia African American Sites

Alexandria Black History Center
Booker T. Washington Monument
Fredericksburg Black History Tour
Harrison African American History
Newsome House Museum and Cultural Center
Richmond Black History Museum

References

Ames, Michael
  1992　*Cannibal Tours and Glass Boxes: The Anthropology of Museums.* Vancouver: University of British Columbia Press.
Anderson, Benedict
  1983　*Imagined Communities: Reflection on the Origin and Spread of Nationalism.* New York: Verso.
Ansell, Amy
  1997　*New Right, New Racism: Race and Reaction in the United States and Britain.* New York: New York University Press.
Auslander, G. K., and Howard Litwin
  1998　Sociability and Patters of Participation: Implications for Social Service Policy. *Journal of Voluntary Action Research* 17, 2: 25–37.
Azoulay, Airella
  1994　"With Open Doors: Museums and Historical Narratives in Israel's Public Space." In Daniel J. Sherman and Irit Rogoff, eds., *Museum Culture: Histories, Discourses, Spectacles.* Minneapolis: University of Minnesota Press.
Bancroft, Frederic
  1959　*Slave Trading in the Old South.* New York: Frederick Unger. (Originally published 1931.)
Banton, Michael
  1987　*Racial Theories.* Cambridge: Cambridge University Press.
Barisic, Sonja
  1999　Williamsburg Now Shows Slavery. *San Diego Union Tribune,* July 28, 1999, A10.

Barthes, Roland
    1972   *Mythologies*. London: Cape.
    1977   *Image-Music-Text*. Glasgow: Fontana.
Bartley, Numan V.
    1983   *The Creation of Modern Georgia*. Athens: University of Georgia Press.
Beauvoir, Simone de
    1953   *The Second Sex*. New York. Knopf.
Bell, Derrick
    1992   *Faces at the Bottom of the Well: The Permanence of Racism*. New York: Basic Books.
Benson, Susan Porter, Stephen Brier, and Roy Rosenzweig, eds.
    1986   *Presenting the Past: Essays on History and the Public*. Philadelphia: Temple
            University Press.
Berlin, Ira
    1974   *Slaves without Masters: The Free Negro in the Antebellum South*. New York:
            Vintage Books.
Bhabha, Homi K.
    1994   *The Location of Culture*. New York: Routledge.
Bishir, C.
    1993   Landmarks of Power: Building a Southern Past. *Southern Cultures* 1, 1: 5–46.
Blassingame, John
    1979   *The Slave Community: Plantation Life in the Antebellum South*. New York:
            Oxford University Press.
Blatti, Jo, ed.
    1987   *Past Meets Present: Essays about Historic Interpretation and Public Audiences*.
            Washington, D.C.: Smithsonian Institution Press.
Bodnar, John
    1992   *Remaking America: Public Memory, Commemoration, and Patriotism in the
            Twentieth Century*. Princeton: Princeton University Press.
Bogle, Donald
    1973   *Toms, Coons, Mulattoes, Mammies, and Bucks: An Interpretive History of Blacks
            in American Film*. New York: Bantam Books.
Boles, John B.
    1983   *Black Southerners, 1619–1869*. Lexington: University Press of Kentucky.
Bond, George C., and Angela Gilliam
    1994   *Social Construction of the Past: Representation as Power*. One World Archeology
            Series. New York: Routledge.
Boskin, Joseph
    1986   *Sambo*. New York: Oxford University Press.
Bourdieu, Pierre
    1984   *Distinction: A Social Critique of the Judgement of Taste*. London: Routledge
            and Kegan Paul.
    1993   *The Field of Cultural Production*. Oxford: Polity Press.

Bragg, William Harris
  1987 *Joe Brown's Army: The Georgia State Line, 1862–1865*. Macon: Mercer University Press.
Brasseaux, Carl A.
  1992 *Acadian to Cajun: Transformation of a People, 1803–1877*. Jackson: University Press of Mississippi.
Briskman, Darin
  1998 Georgia in the Civil War. At www.cherokeerose.com, accessed April 18, 2002.
Brown, Kathleen M.
  1996 *Good Wives, Nasty Wenches, and Anxious Patriarchs: Gender, Race, and Power in Colonial Virginia*. Chapel Hill: University of North Carolina Press.
Brown, Rodger Lyle
  1997 *Ghost Dancing on the Cracker Circuit: The Culture of Festivals in the American South*. Jackson: University Press of Mississippi.
Bryan, Thomas Conn
  1953 *Confederate Georgia*. Athens: University of Georgia Press.
Campbell, Edward D. C., Jr.
  1981 *The Celluloid South*. Knoxville: University of Tennessee Press.
Civil War Sites Advisory Commission
  1997 *Civil War Sites Advisory Commission Report on the Nation's Civil War Battlefields*. 2 vols. Washington, D.C.: National Park Service.
Clifford, James
  1988 *The Predicament of Culture*. Cambridge: Harvard University Press.
  1991 Four Northwest Coast Museums: Travel Reflections. In Ivan Karp and Steven D. Lavine, eds., *Exhibiting Cultures: The Poetics and Politics of Museum Display*. Washington, D.C.: Smithsonian Institution Press.
Clinton, Catherine
  1982 *The Plantation Mistress: Woman's World in the Old South*. New York: Pantheon Books.
  1995 *Tara Revisited: Women, War, and the Plantation Legend*. New York: Abbeville Publishers.
Coleman, Kenneth, ed.
  1977 *A History of Georgia*. Athens: University of Georgia Press.
Collins, Patricia Hill
  1990 *Black Feminist Thought: Knowledge, Consciousness, and the Politics of Empowerment*. New York: Routledge.
Dabney, Virginius
  1971 *Virginia: The New Dominion, A History from 1607 to the Present*. Charlottesville: University Press of Virginia.
De Hart, Jess
  1982 *Plantations of Louisiana*. Gretna, La.: Pelican Publishing Company.

DiMaggio, Paul J., Michael Useem, and Paula Brown
  1978   *Audience Studies in the Performing Arts and Museums: A Critical Review.*
          Washington D.C.: National Endowment for the Arts.
Du Bois, W. E. B.
  1965   *Black Reconstruction.* New York: Russell and Russell. (Originally published
          1935.)
  1989   *The Souls of Black Folk.* New York: Penguin Books. (Originally published
          1903.)
Dusinberre, William
  1996   *Them Dark Days: Slavery in the American Rice Swamps.* New York: Oxford
          University Press.
Dyer, Richard
  1997   *White.* New York: Routledge.
Elkins, Stanley M.
  1976   *Slavery: A Problem in American Institutional and Intellectual Life.* Chicago:
          University of Chicago Press, 1976.
Entman, Robert M., and Andrew Rojecki
  2000   *The Black Image in the White Mind.* Chicago: University of Chicago Press.
Fanon, Frantz
  1967   *Black Skin, White Masks.* New York: Grove Press.
Faust, Drew Gilpin
  1991   Slavery in the American Experience. In Edward D. C. Campbell and Kym
          S. Rice, eds., *Before Freedom Came: African-American Life in the Antebellum
          South.* Richmond and Charlottesville: Museum of the Confederacy and
          University Press of Virginia.
Feagin, Joe R.
  2000   *Racist America: Roots, Current Realities, and Future Reparations.* New York and
          London: Routledge.
Feagin, Joe R., and Hernan Vera
  1995   *White Racism: The Basics.* New York: Routledge.
Ferber, Abby L.
  1998   *White Man Falling: Race, Gender, and White Supremacy.* Boulder and New
          York: Rowman and Littlefield.
Fiske, John
  1993   *Power Works, Power Plays.* London and New York: Verso.
  1994   *Media Matters: Everyday Culture and Political Change.* Minneapolis:
          University of Minnesota Press.
Fogel, Robert William
  1989   *Without Consent or Contract: The Rise and Fall of American Slavery.* New York:
          W. W. Norton.
Fogel, Robert William, and Stanley L. Engerman
  1984   *Time on the Cross: The Economics of American Negro Slavery.* Boston: Little,
          Brown.

Foster, Gaines M.
　1987　*Ghosts of the Confederacy: Defeat, the Lost Cause, and the Emergence of the New South 1865 to 1913*. New York: Oxford University Press.

Foner, Laura
　1970　The Free People of Color in Louisiana and St. Domingue. *Journal of Social History* 3, 4: 406–30.

Fox-Genovese, Elizabeth
　1988　*Within the Plantation Household: Black and White Women of the Old South*. Chapel Hill: University of North Carolina Press.

Frankenberg, Ruth, ed.
　1997　*Displacing Whiteness: Essays in Social and Cultural Criticism*. Durham: Duke University Press.

Franklin, John Hope
　1964　*The Militant South, 1800–1861*. Boston: Beacon Press. (Originally published 1956.)

Franklin, John Hope, and Alfred A. Moss
　1998　*From Slavery to Freedom: A History of African Americans*. 7th ed., vol. 1. New York: Alfred Knopf.

Fredrickson, George
　1981　*White Supremacy: A Comparative Study in American and South African History*. New York: Oxford University Press.

Fyfe, Gordon, and Max Ross
　1996　Decoding the Visitor's Gaze: Rethinking Museum Visiting. In Sharon Macdonald and Gordon Fyfe, eds., *Theorizing Museums: Representing Identity and Diversity in a Changing World*. Cambridge, Mass.: Blackwell Publishers.

Gable, Eric
　1996　Maintaining Boundaries, or "Mainstreaming" Black History in a White Museum. In Sharon Macdonald and Gordon Fyfe, eds., *Theorizing Museums: Representing Identity and Diversity in a Changing World*. Cambridge, Mass.: Blackwell Publishers.

Gable, Eric, Richard Handler, and Anna Lawson
　1992　On the Uses of Relativism: Fact, Conjecture, and Black and White Histories at Colonial Williamsburg. *American Ethnologist* 19, 4: 791–804.

Gabriel, John
　1998　*Whitewashed: Racial Politics and the Media*. London: Routledge.

Gaither, Edmund Barry
　1992　"Hey! That's Mine": Thoughts on Pluralism and American Museums. In Ivan Karp, Christine Mullen Kreamer, and Steven D. Lavine, eds., *Museums and Communities: The Politics of Public Culture*. Washington, D.C.: Smithsonian Institution Press.

Genovese, Eugene D.
　1968　*In Red and Black: Marxian Explorations in Southern and Afro-American History*. New York: Vintage.

Gerbner, George
   1972   Violence in Television Drama: Trends and Symbolic Functions. In George
           Comstock and Eli Rubinstein, eds., *Television and Social Behavior: Media
           Content and Control*, vol. 1. Washington, D.C.: U.S. Government Printing
           Office.
Giddings, Paula
   1984   *Where and When I Enter: The Impact of Black Women on Race and Sex in
           America*. New York: William Morrow.
Gilmartin, Patricia, and Stanely D. Brunn
   1998   The Representation of Women in Political Cartoons of the 1995 World
           Conference on Women. *Women's Studies International Forum* 21, 5: 535–50.
Giroux, Henry A.
   1997   *Channel Surfing: Race Talk and the Destruction of Today's Youth*. New York: St.
           Martin's Press.
   2000   *Impure Acts: The Practical Politics of Cultural Studies*. New York: Routledge.
Goings, Kenneth W.
   1994   *Mammy and Uncle Mose: Black Collectibles and American Stereotyping*.
           Bloomington: Indiana University Press.
Goldberg, David Theo
   1997   *Racial Subjects: Writing on Race in America*. New York: Routledge.
Goldberg, David Theo, ed.
   1990   *Anatomy of Racism*. Minneapolis: University of Minnesota Press.
Gossett, Thomas
   1965   *Race: The History of an Idea in America*. New York: Schocken.
Grantham, Dewey W.
   1994   *The South in Modern America: A Region at Odds*. New York: HarperCollins.
Gray, Herman
   1995   *Watching Race: Television and the Struggle for Blackness*. Minneapolis:
           University of Minnesota Press.
Gray, Ralph, and Betty Wood
   1976   The Transition from Indentured to Involuntary Servitude in Colonial
           Georgia. *Explorations in Economic History* 13: 353–70.
Greenfield, Thomas A.
   1975   Race and Passive Voice at Monticello. *Crisis* 82, 4: 146–47.
Guerrero, Ed
   1993   *Framing Blackness: The African American Image in Film*. Philadelphia:
           Temple University Press.
Gutek, Gerald, and Patricia Gutek
   1996   *Plantations and Outdoor Museums in America's Historic South*. Columbia:
           University of South Carolina Press.
Gutman, H.
   1976   *The Black Family in Slavery and Freedom, 1750–1925*. New York: Pantheon.

Halbwachs, Maurice
  1980   *The Collective Memory*. New York: Harper and Row. (Originally published
          1950.)
Hall, Stuart
  1980   Encoding and Decoding. In S. Hall et al., eds., *Culture, Media, Language*.
          London: Hutchinson.
  1982   The Whites of Their Eyes: Racist Ideologies and the Media. In G. Bridges
          and R. Brunt, eds., *Silver Linings: Some Strategies for the Eighties*. London:
          Lawrence and Wishart.
  1997   The Spectacle of the Other. In Stuart Hall, ed., *Representation: Cultural
          Representations and Signifying Practices*. Thousand Oaks, Calif.: Sage.
Handler, Richard, and Eric Gable
  1997   *The New History in an Old Museum: Creating the Past at Colonial Williams-
          burg*. Durham: Duke University Press.
Haney López, Ian F.
  1996   *White by Law: The Legal Construction of Race*. New York: New York
          University Press.
Harris, Cheryl
  1995   Whiteness as Property. In Kimberle Crenshaw, Neil Gotanda, Gary Peller,
          and Kendall Thomas, eds., *Critical Race Theory*. New York: New Press.
Harris, J. William
  1985   *Plain Folk and Gentry in a Slave Society: White Liberty and Black Slavery in
          Augusta's Hinterlands*. Middletown, Conn.: Wesleyan University Press.
Higginbotham, Leon A., Jr.
  1978   *In the Matter of Color: Race and the American Legal Process: The Colonial Period*.
          New York: Oxford University Press.
Higginbotham, Sylvia
  2000   *Marvelous Old Mansions and Other Southern Treasures*. Winston-Salem:
          John F. Blair.
Hobsbawm, Eric, and Terence Ranger, eds.
  1983   *The Invention of Tradition*. Cambridge: Cambridge University Press.
Hodgkinson, V. A., M. Weitzman, S. M. Noga, and H. A. Gorski
  1992   *Giving and Volunteering in the United States: 1992 Edition*. Washington, D.C.:
          Independent Sector.
Hoffman, Detlef
  1994   The German Art Museum and the History of the Nation. In Daniel J.
          Sherman and Irit Rogoff, eds., *Museum Culture: Histories, Discourses,
          Spectacles*. Minneapolis: University of Minnesota Press.
Honninghausen, L., and V. E. Lerda, eds.
  1993   *Rewriting the South: History and Fiction*. Tübingen: Francke.
hooks, bell
  1984   *Feminist Theory: From Margin to Center*. Boston: South End Press.

1989   *Talking Back*. Boston: South End Press.

1990   *Yearning: Race, Gender, and Cultural Politics*. Boston: South End Press.

1992   *Black Looks: Race and Representation*. Boston: South End Press.

Hooper-Greenhill, E.

1992   *Museums and the Shaping of Knowledge*. London: Routledge.

1995   *Museum, Media, Message*. London: Routledge.

Horton, James Oliver, and Spencer R. Crew

1989   Afro-Americans and Museums: Towards a Policy of Inclusion. In Warren Leon and Roy Rosenzweig, eds., *History Museums in the United States: A Critical Assessment*. Urbana and Chicago: University of Illinois Press.

Horwitz, Tony

1998   *Confederates in the Attic: Dispatches from the Unfinished Civil War*. New York: Vintage.

Hudson, P.

1992   Beyond Moonlight and Magnolias. *Americana* 19, 6: 24–31.

Huggins, Nathan

1979   *Black Odyssey: The Afro-American Ordeal in Slavery*. 2nd ed. New York: Vintage.

Inscoe, John C.

1989   *Mountain Masters, Slavery, and the Sectional Crisis in Western North Carolina*. Knoxville: University of Tennessee Press.

Irwin-Zarecka, Iwona

1994   *Frames of Remembrance: The Dynamics of Collective Memory*. New Brunswick: Transaction Publishers.

Isaac, Rhys

1988   *Transformation of Virginia, 1740–1790*. New York: W. W. Norton.

Johnson, Allan G.

2001   *Privilege, Power, and Difference*. Mountain View, Calif.: Mayfield Publishers.

Johnson, Whittington B.

1980   Free Blacks in Antebellum Savannah: An Economic Profile. *Georgia Historical Quarterly* 64, 4: 418–31.

Jones, Jacqueline

1986   *Labor of Love, Labor of Sorrow: Black Women, Work, and the Family from Slavery to the Present*. New York: Vintage.

Jordan, Winthrop D.

1968   *White over Black: American Attitudes towards the Negro, 1550–1812*. Chapel Hill: University of North Carolina Press.

Karp, Ivan, Christine Mullen Kreamer, and Steven D. Lavine, eds.

1992   *Museums and Communities: The Politics of Public Culture*. Washington, D.C.: Smithsonian Institution Press.

Karp, Ivan, and Steven D. Lavine, eds.

1990   *Exhibiting Cutlures: The Poetics and Politics of Museum Display*. Washington, D.C.: Smithsonian Institution Press.

Katriel, Tamar
   1999   Sites of Memory: Discourses of the Past in Israeli Pioneering Settlement
          Museums. In Dan Ben Amos and Liliane Weissberg, eds., *Cultural Memory
          and the Construction of Identity*. Detroit: Wayne State University Press.
Kemble, Frances Anne
   1961   *Journal of a Residence on a Georgia Plantation in 1838–1839*. Ed. John A.
          Scott. New York: Alfred A. Knopf. (Originally published 1863.)
Kielwasser, Alfred P., and Michelle A. Wolf
   1992   Mainstream Television, Adolescent Homosexuality, and Significant Silence.
          Critical Studies in Mass Communication 9, 4: 350–73.
Killion, Ronald, and Charles Waller, eds.
   1973   *Slavery Time When I Was Chillun down on Marster's Plantation: Interviews with
          Georgia Slaves*. Savannah: Beehive Press.
Kincheloe, Joe L., Shirley R. Steinberg, Nelson M. Rodriguez, and Ronald E. Chennault
   1998   *White Reign: Deploying Whiteness in America*. New York: St. Martin's Press.
King, Richard H., and Helen Taylor, eds.
   1996   *Dixie Debates: Perspectives on Southern Cultures*. New York: New York
          University Press.
Klein, Herbert, S.
   1971   *Slavery in the Americas: A Comparative Study of Virginia and Cuba*. Chicago:
          Quadrangle Paperbacks.
Kolchin, Peter
   1983   Reevaluating the Antebellum Slave Community: A Comparative Perspec-
          tive. *Journal of American History* 70: 579–601.
Kolger, Larry
   1985   *Black Slaveowners: Free Black Slave Masters in South Carolina, 1790–1860*.
          Columbia: University of South Carolina Press.
Leslie, Kent Anderson
   1995   *Woman of Color, Daughter of Privilege: Amanda America Dickson, 1849–1893*.
          Athens: University of Georgia Press.
Levine, Lawrence
   1971   *Black Culture and Black Consciousness*. New York: Oxford University Press.
Lewis, Michael, and Jacqueline Serbu
   1999   Kommemorating the Ku Klux Klan. *Sociological Quarterly* 40, 1: 139–57.
Lipsitz, George
   1998   *The Possessive Investment in Whiteness: How White People Profit from Identity
          Politics*. Philadelphia: Temple University Press.
Lidchi, Henrietta
   1997   The Poetics and the Politics of Exhibiting Other Cultures. In Stuart Hall,
          ed., *Representation: Cultural Representations and Signifying Practices*. Thousand
          Oaks, Calif.: Sage.

Lowenthal, David
  1998   *The Heritage Crusade and the Spoils of History.* Cambridge: Cambridge
          University Press.
Loewen, James W.
  1995   *Lies My Teacher Told Me: Everything Your American History Book Got Wrong.*
          New York: Touchstone.
Macdonald, Sharon
  1996   Theorizing Museums: An Introduction. In Sharon Macdonald and Gordon
          Fyfe, eds., *Theorizing Museums: Representing Identity and Diversity in a
          Changing World.* Cambridge, Mass.: Blackwell.
Malone, Ann Patton
  1992   *Sweet Chariot: Slave Family and Household Structure in Nineteenth-Century
          Louisiana.* Chapel Hill: University of North Carolina Press.
Malone, Lee
  1986   *Louisiana Plantation Homes: A Return to Splendor.* Gretna, La.: Pelican.
Massey, Douglas S., and Nancy A. Denton
  1993   *American Apartheid: Segregation and the Making of the Underclass.* Cambridge:
          Harvard University Press.
McLaren, Peter
  1997   *Revolutionary Multiculturalism: Pedagogies of Dissent for the New Millennium.*
          Boulder: Westview Press.
Melillo, Wendy
  1997   Looking Past the Mansions: Two Men on a Mission to Make Information
          on Slavery a Bigger Part of Plantation Tours. *Washington Post,* September
          25, 1997, V1.
Memmi, Albert
  1965   *The Colonizer and the Colonized.* Boston: Beacon.
Merskin, Debra
  1998   Sending Up Signals: A Survey of Native American Media Use and Repre-
          sentation in the Mass Media. *Howard Journal of Communications* 9, 4:
          333–45.
Miles, Robert
  1989   *Racism.* London and New York: Routledge.
Moon, Dreama
  1999   White Enculturation and Bourgeois Ideology: The Discursive Production of
          Good (White) Girls. In Thomas K. Nakayama and Judith N. Martin, eds.,
          Whiteness: The Communication of Social Identity. Thousand Oaks, Calif.: Sage.
Moorehead, Caroline
  1980   *Hostages to Fortune: A Study of Kidnapping in the World Today.* New York:
          Atheneum.
Morgan, Edmund S.
  1975   *American Slavery, American Freedom: The Ordeal of Colonial Virginia.* New
          York: Norton.

Morris, Richard
  1997   *Sinners, Lovers, and Heroes: An Essay on Memorializing in Three American Cultures.* Albany: State University of New York Press.
Morrison, Toni
  1992   *Playing in the Dark: Whiteness and the Literary Imagination.* New York: Vintage.
Muse, Vance
  1988   *Old New Orleans: Great American Homes.* Birmingham, Ala.: Oxmoor House.
Nash, Gary
  1992   *Red, White, and Black: The Peoples of Early North America.* Upper Saddle River, N.J.: Prentice Hall
Olick, Jeffrey K., and Daniel Levy
  1997   Collective Memory and Cultural Constraint: Holocaust Myth and Rationality in German Politics. *American Sociological Review* 62: 921–36.
Oliver, Melvin L., and Thomas M. Shapiro
  1995   *Black Wealth/White Wealth: A New Perspective on Racial Inequality.* New York: Routledge.
Omi, Michael, and Howard Winant
  1994   *Racial Formations.* 2nd ed. New York: Routledge.
Palsi, B. J., and B. Korn
  1989   National Trends in Voluntary Association Membership: 1974–1984. *Nonprofit and Voluntary Sector Quarterly* 18, 2: 179–90.
Patterson, Orlando
  1982   *Slavery and Social Death: A Comparative Study.* Cambridge, Mass.: Harvard University Press.
Phillips, Ulrich B.
  1968   *Life and Labor in the Old South.* Boston: Little, Brown.
  1966   *American Negro Slavery.* Baton Rouge: Louisiana State University Press. (Originally published 1918.)
Potts, Bobby
  1992   *Historic Houses of the Deep South and Delta Country.* New Orleans: Express Publishing.
Prösler, Martin
  1996   Museums and Globalization. In Sharon Macdonald and Gordon Fyfe, eds., *Theorizing Museums: Representing Identity and Diversity in a Changing World.* Cambridge, Mass.: Blackwell.
Rahier, Jean Muteba, and Michael Hawkins
  1999   "Gone with the Wind" versus the Holocaust Metaphor: Louisiana Plantation Narratives in Black and White. In Thomas Durant Jr. and David J. Knottnerus, eds., *Plantation Society and Race Relations: The Origins of Inequality.* Wesport, Conn.: Praeger.
Rawick, George P.
  1972   *From Sundown to Sunup: The Making of the Black Community.* Westport, Conn.: Greenwood.

Reidy, Joseph
   1992   *From Slavery to Agrarian Capitalism in the Cotton Plantation South: Central Georgia, 1800–1880.* Chapel Hill: University of North Carolina Press.
Roberts, Bruce
   1990   *Plantation Homes of the James River.* Chapel Hill: University of North Carolina Press.
Roediger, David R.
   1991   *The Wages of Whiteness: Race and the Making of the American Working Class.* New York: Verso.
Rogin, Michael
   1996   *Black Skin, White Noise: Jewish Immigrants in the Hollywood Melting Pot.* Berkeley: University of California Press.
Ruffins, Fath Davis
   1992   Mythos, Memory, and History: African American Preservation Efforts, 1820–1990. In Ivan Karp, Christine Mullen Kreamer, and Steven D. Lavine, eds., *Museums and Communities: The Politics of Public Culture.* Washington, D.C.: Smithsonian Institution Press.
Said, Edward
   1978   *Orientalism.* Harmondsworth: Penguin.
St. George, Robert Blair
   1999   Placing Race at Jefferson's Monticello. In Dan Ben Amos and Liliane Weissberg, eds., *Cultural Memory and the Construction of Identity.* Detroit: Wayne State University Press.
Savage, Beth, ed.
   1996   *African American Historic Places.* New York: John Wiley and Sons.
Saxton, Alexander
   1990   *The Rise and the Fall of the White Republic: Class Politics and Mass Culture in Nineteenth-Century America.* New York: Verso.
Schwartz, Barry
   1998   Frame Images: Towards a Semiotics of Collective Memory. *Semiotica* 121, 1–2: 1–40.
Scott, James C.
   1990   *Domination and the Arts of Resistance.* New Haven: Yale University Press.
Sears, John F.
   1989   *Sacred Places: American Tourist Attractions in the Nineteenth Century.* New York: Oxford University Press.
Shavin, Norman, and Robert Peters
   1985   *The Antebellum Plantation at Georgia's Stone Mountain Park.* Atlanta: Capricorn.
Sherman, Daniel J., and Irit Rogoff, eds.
   1994   *Museum Culture: Histories, Discourses, Spectacles.* Minneapolis: University of Minnesota Press.

Shugg, Roger W.

1939   *Origins of Class Struggle in Louisiana: A Social History of White Farmers and Laborers during Slavery and After, 1840–1875.* Baton Rouge: Louisiana State University Press.

Shohat, Ella, and Robert Stam

1994   *Unthinking Eurocentrism.* New York: Routledge.

Small, Stephen

1994   *Racialised Barriers: The Black Experience in the United States and England in the 1980s.* New York: Routledge.

1997   Contextualizing the Black Presence in British Museums: Representations, Resources, and Response. In Eileen Hooper Greenhill, ed., *Museums and Multiculturalism in Britain.* Leicester: Leicester University Press.

Smith, David Horton

1994   Determinants of Voluntary Association Participation and Volunteering: A Literature Review. *Nonprofit and Voluntary Sector Quarterly* 23, 3: 243–63.

Smith, Julia Floyd

1985   *Slavery and Rice Culture in Low Country Georgia, 1750–1860.* Knoxville: University of Tennessee Press.

Sobel, Mechal

1987   *The World They Made Together: Black and White Values in Eighteenth-Century Virginia.* Princeton: Princeton University Press.

Stampp, Kenneth M.

1964   *The Peculiar Institution: Slavery in the Ante-bellum South.* New York: Vintage Books.

Steele, Shelby

1990   *The Content of Our Character: A New Vision of Race in America.* New York: St. Martin's Press.

Sterkx, H. E.

1972   *The Free Negro in Ante-bellum Louisiana.* Rutherford, N.J.: Fairleigh Dickinson University Press.

Sullivan, Buddy

1990   *Early Days on the Georgia Tidewater: The Story of McIntosh County and Sapelo: Being a Documented Narrative Account, with Particular Attention to the County's Waterway and Maritime Heritage; Plantation Culture and Uses of the Land in the 19th Century; and a Detailed Analysis of the History of Sapelo Island.* Darien, Ga.: McIntosh County Board of Commissioners.

Sweat, Edward Forrest

1957   The Free Negro in Antebellum Georgia. Ph.D. dissertation, Indiana University.

Tadman, Michael

1989   *Speculators and Slaves: Masters, Traders, and Slaves in the Old South.* Madison: University of Wisconsin Press.

Takaki, Ronald
  1990   *Iron Cages: Race and Class in Nineteenth-Century America*. New York: Oxford
          University Press.

Tiehen, Laura
  2000   Has Working More Caused Married Women to Volunteer Less? Evidence
          from Time Diary Data, 1965 to 1993. *Nonprofit and Voluntary Sector
          Quarterly* 29, 4: 505–29.

Tuchman, Gaye, Arlene Kaplan Daniels, and James Benét
  1978   *Hearth and Home: Images of Women in the Mass Media*. New York: Oxford
          University Press.

Turner, Patricia A.
  1994   *Ceramic Uncles and Celluloid Mammies: Black Images and Their Influence on
          Culture*. New York: Bantam Doubleday Dell.

Urry, John
  1996   How Societies Remember the Past. In Sharon Macdonald and Gordon
          Fyfe, eds., *Theorizing Museums*. Cambridge, Mass.: Blackwell.

Vlach, John M.
  1991   Plantation Landscapes of the Antebellum South. In Edward D. C. Camp-
          bell and Kym S. Rice, eds., *Before Freedom Came: African-American Life in
          the Antebellum South*. Richmond and Charlottesville: Museum of the Con-
          federacy and University Press of Virginia.

Wallace, Michael
  1987   The Politics of Public History. In Jo Blatti, ed., *Past Meets Present: Essays
          about Historic Interpretation and Public Audiences*. Washington, D.C.:
          Smithsonian Institution Press.

Wallenstein, Peter
  1987   *From Slave South to New South: Public Policy in Nineteenth-Century Georgia*.
          Chapel Hill: University of North Carolina Press.

Ware, Vron
  1992   *Beyond the Pale: White Women, Racism, and History*. London: Verso.

Waters, Mary C.
  1990   *Ethnic Options: Choosing Identities in America*. Berkeley: University of
          California Press.

Wellman, David T.
  1993   *Portraits of White Racism*. 2nd ed. New York: Cambridge University Press.
  1996   From "New Political Linguistics" to Anti-Affirmative-Action Minstrel
          Shows. *Socialist Review* 26, 1–2: 147–54.

West, Cornel
  1993   *Race Matters*. Boston: Beacon Press.

West, Patricia
  1999   *Domesticating History: The Political Origins of America's House Museums*.
          Washington, D.C.: Smithsonian Institution Press.

Wilds, John, Charles L. DuFour, and Walter G. Cowan
   1996   *Louisiana Yesterday and Today: A Historical Guide to the State.* Baton Rouge: Louisiana State University Press.
Wilson, William J.
   1978   *Declining Significance of Race: Blacks and Changing American Institutions.* Chicago: University of Chicago Press.
   1996   *When Work Disappears: The World of the New Urban Poor.* New York: Alfred A. Knopf.
Wood, Betty
   1984   *Slavery in Colonial Georgia, 1730–1775.* Athens: University of Georgia Press.
Zinn, Howard
   1999   *A People's History of the United States: 1492–Present.* 20th anniversary ed. New York: HarperCollins.
Zolberg, Vera L.
   1992   Barrier or Leveler? The Case of the Art Museum. In Michele Lamont and Marcel Fournier, eds., *Cultivating Differences: Symbolic Boundaries and the Making of Inequality.* Chicago: University of Chicago Press.

Index